THE DAILY STUDY BIBLE

(OLD TESTAMENT)

General Editor: John C. L. Gibson

CHRONICLES

CHRONICLES

J. G. McCONVILLE

THE SAINT ANDREW PRESS
EDINBURGH

THE WESTMINSTER PRESS
PHILADELPHIA

Copyright © J. G. McConville 1984

Published by
The Saint Andrew Press
Edinburgh, Scotland
and
The Westminster Press®
Philadelphia, Pennsylvania

Printed and bound in Great Britain
by Thomson Litho Ltd., East Kilbride, Scotland

ISBN (Great Britain) 0 7152 0527 7

GENERAL PREFACE

This series of commentaries on the Old Testament, to which Dr. McConville's volume on *Chronicles* belongs, has been planned as a companion series to the much-acclaimed New Testament series of the late Professor William Barclay. As with that series, each volume is arranged in successive headed portions suitable for daily study. The Biblical text followed is that of the Revised Standard Version or Common Bible. Eleven contributors share the work, each being responsible for from one to three volumes. The series is issued in the hope that it will do for the Old Testament what Professor Barclay's series succeeded so splendidly in doing for the New Testament—make it come alive for the Christian believer in the twentieth century.

Its two-fold aim is the same as his. Firstly, it is intended to introduce the reader to some of the more important results and fascinating insights of modern Old Testament scholarship. Most of the contributors are already established experts in the field with many publications to their credit. Some are younger scholars who have yet to make their names but who in my judgment as General Editor are now ready to be tested. I can assure those who use these commentaries that they are in the hands of competent teachers who know what is of real consequence in their subject and are able to present it in a form that will appeal to the general public.

The primary purpose of the series, however, is *not* an academic one. Professor Barclay summed it up for his New Testament series in the words of Richard of Chichester's prayer—to enable men and women "to know Jesus Christ more clearly, to love Him more dearly, and to follow Him more nearly." In the case of the Old Testament we have to be a little more circumspect than that. The Old Testament was completed long before the time of Our Lord, and it was (as it still is) the sole Bible of the Jews, God's first people, before it became part of the Christian Bible. We must take this fact seriously.

Yet in its strangely compelling way, sometimes dimly and sometimes directly, sometimes charmingly and sometimes embarrassingly, it holds up before us the things of Christ. It should not be forgotten that Jesus Himself was raised on this Book, that He based His whole ministry on what it says, and that He approached His death with its words on His lips. Christian men and women have in this ancient collection of Jewish writings a uniquely illuminating avenue not only into the will and purposes of God the Father, but into the mind and heart of Him who is named God's Son, who was Himself born a Jew but went on through the Cross and Resurrection to become the Saviour of the world. Read reverently and imaginatively the Old Testament can become a living and relevant force in their everyday lives.

It is the prayer of myself and my colleagues that this series may be used by its readers and blessed by God to that end.

New College   JOHN C. L. GIBSON
Edinburgh   General Editor

AUTHOR'S PREFACE

Without wishing to keep the reader much longer from his main task, I would like to express my gratitude to a number of people: to the Rev. Dr. J. C. L. Gibson, the general editor of the series, for inviting this contribution; to Mrs. Vicky Monaghan and Mrs. Norma Richards for prompt and efficient typing of the manuscript; to my wife Helen, for the application of her wisdom to it as it developed, and for too often letting it come first.

Nevertheless I would like to dedicate this volume to my parents, who have waited for it for a long time, in the hope that they will not be disappointed.

CONTENTS

CONTENTS

DATES OF ACCESSION OF THE MONARCHS OF THE UNITED KINGDOM
AND OF JUDAH

Saul	c. 1050 B.C.			
David	1011			
Solomon	971			
Rehoboam	931			
Abijah	913			
Asa	911			
Jehoshaphat	870			
Jehoram	848			
Ahaziah	841			
Athaliah	841			
Joash	835			
Amaziah	796			
Uzziah	767 (co-regent from 791)			
Jotham	740 (	,,	,,	750)
Ahaz	732 (	,,	,,	735)
Hezekiah	716 (	,,	,,	729)
Manasseh	687 (	,,	,,	696)
Amon	642			
Josiah	640			
Jehoahaz	609			
Jehoiakim	609			
Jehoiachin	597			
Zedekiah	597			

INTRODUCTION

DATE AND AUTHOR

The Books of Chronicles (hereafter Chr.), which are actually a single work, only artificially divided in two, are of unknown authorship, and we are therefore obliged to refer to the author merely as "the Chronicler". The date is generally but not precisely known. The final two verses of 2 Chr. show that the perspective of the whole work is that of a time later than the Babylonian exile, i.e. after 539 B.C. This means that it probably belongs in the period between that year and 331 B.C. during which the Persian Empire exercised sovereignty over what was then the rather small and politically emasculated province of Judah, the sole remnant of Israel with its once mighty royal house. Probability places Chr. somewhere in the fourth century B.C. Its position roughly in the middle of our English Old Testament disguises this fact. The Hebrew Bible, however, places it last.

It is widely held that the author of Chr. (the Chronicler) was also responsible for the Books of Ezra and Nehemiah. This is partly because the latter provide a sequel to Chr., as appears from the fact that the last two verses of Chr. are more or less the same as the first three of Ezra. If Chr. takes us up to the point at which we ask what happened to the returned exiles, Ezra and Nehemiah begin to answer that question. While scholarly agreement about the authorship of Chr.-Neh. is not universal, there is a sense in which it does not matter. The importance of the recognition that they belong together *somehow* lies in the stress that this lays upon the post-exilic origin and perspective of Chr. The fact that Chr. was written for the restoration community (as the returned exiles are often called) is an important factor in the interpretation of the book.

CONTENT AND KIND OF LITERATURE

Chr. is sometimes thought of as a kind of alternative to the Books of Samuel and Kings. The Greek Old Testament called it the Book of Things Left Out, thus viewing it merely as a source of additional information to that which was available elsewhere. This is to do it a complete disservice. In the first place, it attempts a far greater coverage of what we might call sacred history than any other book of the Old Testament, standing alongside not Sam.-Kings only, but *Genesis*-Kings, since its genealogies (1 Chr. 1–9) take us from Adam right up to Saul.

Furthermore, far from merely filling in gaps (which would not in any case explain the fact that it *repeats* a substantial amount of material from elsewhere) it offers a wholly individual perspective upon the vistas of history on which it is based. This perspective, as we have said, is conditioned by its setting some time after the exile. While the Books of Kings leave the reader feeling (though the impression is superficial) that the exile has an air of finality about it, Chr. does precisely the opposite (see below on 1 Chr. 1–9 and on 2 Chr. 36). The question "Why does the Old Testament have two histories of Israel?" is misguided because it assumes that biblical history-writing is merely factual and purely objective. There is in reality no such thing, whether in the Bible or not. All history-writing is the fruit of reflection upon and interpretation of reported events. Every writer of history operates within his own understanding of reality. The biblical historians are historians as much as modern historians are. They differ from modern historians by virtue of their different intellectual framework, whose central characteristic is the general belief that the meaning of history is imparted to it by the character and purposes of God. If there are differences between the Chronicler and the authors of Sam.-Kings in their reflection upon Israel's history, it is because the specific question which each must ask, viz. "What is God's purpose for his people here and now?" is spoken from their different historical situations.

The implication of the foregoing, nevertheless, is that "the Chronicler" is no mere chronicler! He is a theologian, sharing with all the biblical writers the burden of interpreting God's ways to human beings. That is why he is worth reading. For the same reason, however, the Chronicler's work seems to stand in stark contrast to Sam.-Kings at many points, in a way that can be unsettling to some readers. Yet it is unproductive to attempt to resolve detailed differences between the two works outside the context of a total interpretation of them. That would be to fall into the trap of thinking that we were dealing with "bare" history. Certain *kinds* of deviation from Sam.-Kings occur regularly in Chr., leading to the inevitable conclusion that they are produced by fundamental interests of the author. This means that it is precisely at the points of divergence from Sam.-Kings that Chr. becomes most interesting and we begin to know the writer's mind. Such divergences occur not merely sporadically, but in a thorough-going and decisive way, making the reading of Chr. a very distinct exercise from the reading of the other books.

The present commentary, because of its scope, will inevitably concentrate on bringing out Chr.'s main thrusts. This will involve evaluating differences from Sam.-Kings where the work of interpretation demands it (which will be frequent), but not for its own sake. This means, for example, that there will be no recurring attempt to explain the large numbers in Chr. Numerical deviations from Sam.-Kings are so frequent that one must look for underlying reasons rather than fresh explanations on each occasion. Sometimes Chr.'s numbers will be taken simply as convenient round figures, and sometimes as symbolical. On occasions textual corruption is responsible for an improbable number. It is possible too that many of the numbers have been misinterpreted, and are not as high as they seem (in this regard the suggestion that the word *'eleph*, "a thousand", should often be taken to refer to a military unit which might actually consist of many fewer than a thousand men is particularly interesting).

For all this, it should not be thought that the Chronicler is an irresponsible historian. Though he has often been held in low esteem, it is now widely believed that he had access to sources which were apparently not available to the authors of Sam.-Kings, and that he used them carefully. These are often mentioned in the text, e.g. at 2 Chr. 33:19. They are not, of course, equivalent to any extant book.

The Chronicler uses the history of the monarchy as the basis for a message of repentance and salvation to his contemporaries. It will be immediately observed that the reigns of David and Solomon occupy a disproportionate amount of space in the whole work (1 Chr. 11—2 Chr. 9). This is because he wishes to set them up as models for imitation by their successors, in contrast to the negative model of Saul (1 Chr. 10). Thus, while faithfulness and obedience to the Lord bring blessing, in the form of security in the land, ascendancy over other nations, and wealth, as typified by David and Solomon, disobedience, like that of Saul, brings their opposites. This thesis is then elaborated throughout the history of Judah, from Solomon's immediate successor Rehoboam, down to the Babylonian exile. (Under Rehoboam the Davidic-Solomonic empire split into the northern kingdom, consisting of ten tribes and often referred to simply as "Israel", and a southern kingdom, known as Judah, though also incorporating Benjamin. The northern kingdom receives no separate treatment from the Chronicler, since he regards it as being "in rebellion against the house of David", 2 Chr. 10:19.) While the Babylonian exile was, historically, uniquely catastrophic for Judah, he views it as no different in kind from a succession of preceding "exiles" that occurred throughout the history of Judah at times of rebellion against the Lord (usually in the form of defection to the gods of the neighbouring peoples). The effect of his preaching is to hold out to his own contemporaries the dual possibility of impoverishment or blessing, depending upon their new response to the Lord in every generation.

Chr.'s doctrine of rewards and punishments is often characterized as one of "immediate retribution". That is, in contrast to the pattern in Sam.-Kings, the successes or failures of kings habitually have the effect of blessing or punishment within their own lifetime. Often, indeed, there will be a dramatic swing in the fortunes of a king. The idea of "immediate retribution" does not quite meet the point, however. The writer's real concern is to show that, however low the people of God sink, their cause is never totally lost, but there is always a way back, through repentance, to God's favour. Similarly, that favour can so easily be squandered by a lapse from faithfulness. The context of his theology in an urgent call to repentance is all-important, and should not lead to the mechanical equation of sin and suffering, blessing and righteousness, which is clearly condemned elsewhere in the Bible (cf. the experience of Job, and John 9:2f.).

A final word needs to be said about the materiality of some aspects of the Chronicler's religion. Right worship in Chr. has much to do with proper attention to the externals of religion. Much of his praise for David and Solomon arises from their planning and building of the Temple, and their organization of worship there under a priesthood legally constituted according to the Mosaic law. Furthermore, there is a strong material dimension to blessing in his view, as witness the great wealth of Solomon. The modern reader will want, rightly, to translate this blessing into the spiritual terms which the New Testament has taught (e.g. Eph. 1:3). It would be wide of the mark, however, to think that the Chronicler's view of religion is unspiritual, for despite his deep concern for the Temple etc., he knows that only a heartfelt "seeking" of the Lord is acceptable in his sight. The words of the Lord to Solomon (2 Chr. 7:14) are as urgent today as they were for the people of the Chronicler's generation:

> If my people who are called by my name humble themselves, and pray and seek my face, and turn from their wicked ways, then I will hear from heaven, and will forgive their sin and heal their land.

THE FIRST BOOK OF CHRONICLES

ORIGINS

1 Chronicles 1:1–9:44

These nine chapters consist almost entirely of genealogies, re-
lieved only very occasionally by a little extra information. It is
hardly necessary to print them, though readers may care to go
through them quickly in their own Bibles so as to catch their
flavour and prepare themselves for the comments which follow;
in these an attempt will be made to explain briefly why, dull as
they are, they find a place in the Bible.

(a) *Endless Genealogies?*

The modern reader, if he approaches biblical genealogies at all,
does so with some bewilderment. If he is accustomed to think of
the Bible as "profitable for teaching" (2 Tim. 3:16), they may
leave him feeling untaught. Despite their formidable character,
however, the genealogies afford important insights into the
character of biblical religion. Their function, broadly speaking, is
to show that the promises and purposes of God continue. Those
of Gen. 5, for example, convey at once the ideas of the filling of
the earth which belongs to the original commission to mankind
(Gen. 1:28), and of the entry of death (in the refrain "and he
died") following the first rebellion against God (Gen. 3). Those
of Matt. 1 place the birth of Jesus in succession to the promise to
Abraham (cf. Gen 12:1–3) and to the Israelite royal line. In these
places, as in Chr., genealogies are much more than a succession
of dry "begats". They affirm a divine plan for creation, within
which mankind enjoys a special place (Gen. 1:26ff.). They show

at once how Israel's present arises out of its past, and how God's initial purposes for mankind are fulfilled in her. They show how God's plans for Israel are ultimately brought to fruition by Jesus Christ.

It follows that genealogies are highly selective. None of them attempts to name every individual who ever lived (though it may seem like that when we read them), nor even to represent every generation within a given line (hence the uselessness of genealogies for attempting to establish the age of humanity). It is possible that Chr. drew the names from official records, including military census lists. The form in which we have the genealogies now has probably been determined partly by the availability of material, and partly by the balance which the Chronicler wished to achieve. Be that as it may, the individuals whose names appear in succession before our eyes have little historical significance. About the great majority of them we know practically nothing. Thus in a curious way the greatness and the littleness of humanity are conveyed together, intimately bound up: the greatness, because each individual belongs to the march of mankind towards a glorious destiny, and the littleness because he is nevertheless but a small link in the huge chain. (Notice in this connection the brief record of the name of Moses, 1 Chr. 6:3—not a case of "How are the mighty fallen!" so much as a putting in perspective of human greatness.) It matters little to the modern reader that the sons of Perez were Hezron and Hamul (1 Chr. 2:5). What does matter is the total picture, whose chief impact is to demonstrate God's care for people, not in any generalized way, but in a distinguishing and comprehensive way. It matters to *God* that the sons of Perez were Hezron and Hamul, even if they are mentioned in a context which draws the reader's attention to goals which transcend the lives of individuals.

(b) *The Line of Promise*

We have noted above that genealogies are highly selective. It will be immediately apparent that much the greater part of 1 Chr. 1–9 is devoted to the ancestry of Israel as opposed to other nations (chs. 2–9). Even within Israel an apparently disproportionate amount of space is devoted to the tribes of Judah (2:3–4:23), Levi (6:1–81) and little Benjamin (7:6–12; 8:1–40). Contrast the few verses allotted to mighty Ephraim (7:20–29). This unevenness can be accounted for largely by the idea of a line of promise. It is present in the first two words of the book, "Adam, Seth, . . .". Chr. is here at its most laconic, assuming the reader's knowledge of the early chapters of Genesis, and in particular the story of Cain's murder of Abel, his own disgrace and God's replacement of Abel by a third son Seth, through whom the line continued of those for whom God appeared to have a special purpose, especially Noah and Abraham (Gen. 4:1–16, 25f.; 6:8; 12:1–3). Chr. goes on to show its interest in such a line in the way in which it deals with groups of sons. Thus while Noah's sons are first mentioned in the order Shem, Ham and Japheth (v. 4), that order is reversed when their separate lines are elaborated, allowing the author to deal with Shem, through whom the line will continue, last of the three, leading naturally into that of Abraham (1:4–27).

Within the tribes of Israel, Judah is given precedence because it was from this tribe that the Davidic royal dynasty later emerged, which was not only to dominate 1 and 2 Chr., but also to become the major focus of messianic hope in Israel (cf. e.g. Isa. 11:1). 1 Chr. 5:1f. explains the dislodging of the first-born Reuben from his natural precedence ("because he polluted his father's couch"; see Gen. 35:22). The line of promise is thus continued from the pre-Israelite generations into those of Israel. One thing that emerges from these general observations is that *natural* precedence counts for little in biblical theology. The principle of divine election makes few concessions to greatness or even merit (cf. Deut. 7:6ff.). Only that greatness which is bestowed by God is true.

It is in place here to notice that the genealogies say something about God's government of the universe not only in terms of the election of Israel but also in terms of moral order. Even a casual perusal reveals that the lists of names are occasionally spiced with a comment about this or that group or individual. Jabez, for

example, of whom we know only that he was handicapped by a
name related to a word meaning "pain"—in a day when names
were felt to have an effect upon the character and experience of
their bearers—prays that he might be delivered from such effects.
(The word "hurt" in 4:10 is closely related to that translated
"pain", v. 9.) His prayer is heard and blessing ensues. In 5:18ff.
Chr. reports a war involving a number of the tribes, in which they
sought God and were granted victory. (About the date of this war
it is impossible to say more than that it must have occurred before
the fall of the northern kingdom, to which the words "the exile",
v. 22, refer.) Conversely, vv. 23ff. show that, on another occasion, idolatry on the part of the Manassites resulted in their
deportation to Assyria by Tiglath-Pileser, a few years before the
final fall of the north.

These themes of expansion as a result of faithfulness to the
Lord and devastation as a consequence of its opposite will play a
major role in the unfolding of the Chronicler's tale. The genealogies serve to prepare the reader for them, and show that the
principles which he wishes to teach have always obtained. If this
seems a simplistic theology it should be noted that a further
theme of Chr., that of the Lord's willingness to start afresh with
his errant people, is also tucked away almost unnoticed in the
genealogies. If the line of promise stretches from the patriarch
Judah to David, 1 Chr. 2:5 makes no attempt to disguise the fact
that it had its beginnings in Judah's illicit relationship with his
daughter-in-law Tamar. (The story is told in Gen. 38.) Fresh
starts like this do not in fact occur without suitable contrition on
the part of the offender, as Chr. will labour to show. Nevertheless
the motif of the readiness of God to forgive and continue with his
people is thus introduced.

CONTEXT

1 Chronicles 1:1–9:44 (*cont'd*)

The point at which the genealogies end is as important for our
interpretation of them as the point at which they begin. While 1

Chr. chapters 2–8 cover generations from the twelve patriarchs into the later monarchy period, ch. 9 rounds off the genealogical introduction to Chr. with lists drawn from the post-exilic period. The exile itself is mentioned briefly in v. 1. It is not recorded for its own sake, however. No stress is laid upon its magnitude as a disaster for Judah. Rather it serves merely as a prelude to the record of those who returned from exile, following the decree of Cyrus (cf. 2 Chr. 36:22f.), to "dwell again in their possessions".

The reason for the Chronicler's interest in this period is that, to all intents and purposes, it is that of the restoration community to which he himself belonged (even if the precise date of his work is obscure; see the Introduction). His vital interest in this period emerges from the fact that not only the genealogies but the Books of Chronicles as a whole end there. Notice also close similarities between 1 Chr. 9:2–17 and Neh. 11:3–19, another book of the restoration community. It is this perspective of Chr. which has determined the form of the genealogies. The restoration community, being the successor of the southern kingdom, consisted, broadly speaking, of the tribes of Judah and Benjamin. There were also a number of priests and Levites, i.e. members of the tribe of Levi, since they had always been scattered throughout the historic territory of Israel (cf. Josh. 21). Some of these will always have been resident in Judah and Benjamin. Others migrated there at the fall of the northern kingdom (2 Chr. 11:13). It is for this reason that so much attention is devoted to these three tribes in the genealogies. Chr. primarily wishes to address them, since for practical purposes they now constitute "Israel".

Having observed that the genealogies are written for the restored community, it remains to ask what Chr. wished to say to it through them. The answer is indicated by 9:1f. The brief record there of the Babylonian exile serves not only to determine the historical period in question, but also to make a theological statement. The exile was not the end of the history of Israel. Rather, with it behind, Israelites came again to "dwell in their cities", to repossess the territory, or part of it at any rate, which the Lord had procured for them centuries before, and of which the exile had seemed to deprive them for ever (cf. Deut.

28:47ff.). In this respect the genealogies make the point which is subsequently made, more elaborately, at the end of 2 Chr. There too the Babylonian exile is recorded as something which is now in the past. The book ends, 2 Chr. 36:22f., with the decree of the Persian Emperor Cyrus that the exiles might return to their homeland. The genealogies stand in parallel with the remainder of the Book of Chronicles in leading the reader through the history of Israel up to this point.

The reason is not far to seek. The post-exilic community of Judah must have looked very little like the Israel of its forefathers. Not much is actually known about the period of Persian rule in Judah which immediately followed the Babylonian exile and lasted for over two hundred years. What *is* clear is that the community merely had the status of a small imperial province. In its early days it suffered because of the jealousies of neighbouring provinces (Neh. 2:19; ch. 4), and this may have become habitual. It is possible, indeed there are indications, that there were periods of repression at the hands of the imperial government itself, which may not always have been cast in the mould of the benevolent Cyrus. These adverse factors, the more intolerable because of the great hopes of a glorious future which the return from exile must have encouraged (in the light of prophecies such as Ezek. chs. 34, 37–39), may have produced despondency from time to time. To such defeatism the Chronicler answers that his small community is in reality the successor of Israel at its greatest, and that all God's commitments to their forefathers still stand, and are now focused on them. The function of ch. 9 is to show that God's plans, which are plans for the whole world (hence the scope of ch. 1), were centred upon Israel throughout its history (chs. 2–8) and are now being taken forward in the unlikely-looking remnant that clustered around Persian Jerusalem. Before that people are set great possibilities. There can yet be a glorious future. This is why David and Solomon, under whom ancient Israel was at its greatest, ranking with the Empires of the day, are held up as the outstanding examples of what faithfulness to God can bring. This is also why Chr., though concentrating on Judah, retains throughout the idea of a whole-Israel, consisting of the full twelve tribes, as something which may in principle be realized again. (This is mainly embodied in the genealogies themselves, but cf. 2 Chr. 28:12ff.; 30:10f., 18.)

Do Chr.'s genealogies speak, therefore, to Christians today? Wherever the Church in the twentieth century feels itself to be of little account in the world, to have a precarious existence, despised and without real hope, its situation is in all essential respects like that of the Chronicler's Judah. And in all essential respects God's word to her is as it was then. There is yet a glorious future for the people of God. An abundance of blessing, strength and influence (properly and spiritually understood) is available to them, to the extent that they truly seek their God. And at the end stands the heavenly kingdom of Jesus Christ, an end which the Chronicler in his day could only dimly intuit through the special grandeur which he saw in David, and the Davidic shape which he gave to the hope he offered to his contemporaries. We in our day, with an advantage even over the angels (1 Pet. 1:12), have seen that end more clearly, and it will obtain a greater clarity yet (1 Cor. 13:12).

SAUL—A GREAT FAILURE

1 Chronicles 10:1–14

¹Now the Philistines fought against Israel; and the men of Israel fled before the Philistines, and fell slain on Mount Gilboa. ²And the Philistines overtook Saul and his sons; and the Philistines slew Jonathan and Abinadab and Malchishua, the sons of Saul. ³The battle pressed hard upon Saul, and the archers found him; and he was wounded by the archers. ⁴Then Saul said to his armour-bearer, "Draw your sword, and thrust me through with it, lest these uncircumcised come and make sport of me." But his armour-bearer would not; for he feared greatly. Therefore Saul took his own sword, and fell upon it. ⁵And when his armour-bearer saw that Saul was dead, he also fell upon his sword, and died. ⁶Thus Saul died; he and his three sons and all his house died together. ⁷And when all the men of Israel who were in the valley saw that the army had fled and that Saul and his sons were dead, they forsook their cities and fled; and the Philistines came and dwelt in them.

⁸On the morrow, when the Philistines came to strip the slain, they found Saul and his sons fallen on Mount Gilboa. ⁹And they stripped him and took his head and his armour, and sent messengers throughout the land of the Philistines, to carry the good news to their idols and to the people. ¹⁰And they put his armour in the temple of their gods, and fastened his head in the temple of Dagon. ¹¹But when all Jabesh-gilead heard all that the Philistines had done to Saul, ¹²all the valiant men arose, and took away the body of Saul and the bodies of his sons, and brought them to Jabesh. And they buried their bones under the oak in Jabesh, and fasted seven days.

¹³So Saul died for his unfaithfulness; he was unfaithful to the Lord in that he did not keep the command of the Lord, and also consulted a medium, seeking guidance, ¹⁴and did not seek guidance from the Lord. Therefore the Lord slew him, and turned the kingdom over to David the son of Jesse.

The Chronicler now abandons his method of compressing long eras into genealogies, and resorts to narrative. He has arrived at the beginning of the monarchy, and here is the focus of his particular interest. Despite the new expansiveness, however, he is still leaning on earlier parts of the OT, namely 1 Samuel. And as in the genealogies we must be as much aware of what he has omitted as of what he has said.

1 Samuel lingers for twenty-three chapters (1 Sam. 9–31) over the story of Saul—and even then it is not quite finished. Chr. allows him only one. The tortured question as to the rightness of having a king in Israel at all (1 Sam. 8–12) is not even aired here. Nor do we read of the choice of Saul (1 Sam. 9), nor of his jealous pursuit of David, which occupied the greater part of his reign and absorbed so much of the energy which should have been directed against the Philistines.

These things are passed over because, whereas the authors of Sam.-Kings harked back to the days of the judges, and perhaps compared their monarchical system with them, the Chronicler looks no further than the monarchy itself for a model, which he then uses to reflect on his own post-restoration (and non-monarchical) community. He accepts kingship as an institution. It has for him an admitted *potential* for the good of God's people. The issue is not "whether kingship", but rather *how* kings discharge their duties. (cf. Solomon's prayer for wisdom to do it well, 2 Chr. 1:8ff.) Through the judgments that are made on the various kings, he aims to point his own community along the path of God's will.

Saul is the first, and perhaps saddest, "exhibit". As to potential, he was well ahead of the field. Chr.'s readers would know of the ready acclaim which met his choice (by lot) as king (1 Sam. 10:24). Yet here he has become the very image of failure and disobedience. Chr. does not feel it necessary to marshal the sordid details of Saul's wasted life. Rather it presents him starkly as an example of what could happen to a great man as a consequence of self-orientation as opposed to God-orientation; and not simply to a great man as such, but to a leader in the household of God, whose fate was bound up with his.

The totality of Saul's failure is enshrined even in the way in which the Chronicler tells his story. Great things are at stake here. The land which God had promised (Exod. 23:27–33)—and therefore life itself (Deut. 8:1)—was threatened by the Philistines. Indeed he presents a picture of a total conquest by them. Mt. Gilboa, the site of Saul's "last stand", was strategic for the defence and possession of the land. Already well within Israel—its heartland, in contrast to the Philistines' own coastal territory—possession of the Gilboa range affords access to the great Vale of Jezreel (the "valley" of v. 7), and therefore to the northernmost parts of the land. Chr. emphasizes that *all* Israel fled before the Philistines. Verse 1 is more insistent than RSV's "the men of Israel"; rather "each man of Israel" fled. Verse 7 depicts a mass exodus from the richest part of the land.

When we read the accounts of the same events in the Books of Samuel we find a more subtle and differentiated picture. The Philistines probably did not completely overrun the land of Israel—or if they did, their ascendancy was very short-lived. Those who fled following the battle of Gilboa are more narrowly defined in 1 Sam. 31:7. In Sam. too, the Philistine victory is presented against the background of the increasing freedom and strength of David, with victories already behind him (including one over the Philistines themselves, 1 Sam. 23), and Gilboa becomes in fact the turning-point in the long-drawn-out war, after which the Philistines' story is one of decline. It is clear from 2 Sam. 2:8ff. that Israelites loyal to Saul must soon have regained large areas of the territory from which Saul himself had been expelled. Equally clearly Saul's whole house did not die out at the time of his own defeat. Here again, Chr. has telescoped events (v. 6).

Yet Chr. has not been merely careless in its record of historical data. Rather, it has deliberately schematized, in order to bring out more clearly the full implications of Saul's character and actions. How often a real nexus of cause and effect is veiled from general observation by a host of attendant circumstances! An empire, a society, a family, an individual can appear to be at their zenith in terms of success and honour, yet in reality have exhausted all the qualities or ceased to enjoy the conditions which made them great. Decline ensues, yet not obviously related to the real causes. Saul's family might limp on in the benighted reign of Ishbosheth (2 Sam. 2:8ff.; 3:1). But the ultimate displacement of the vestiges of Saul's house was assured, ever since God had vowed that he would raise up "a man after his own heart" (1 Sam. 13:14).

The Chronicler does not want us to miss these connections. Along with other biblical writers (as the author of Ps. 37), though by no means all, he forcefully brings together actions and their consequences. The judgment upon Saul is that he died because of his disobedience to God. With him his whole house died out also (as it really did in the end). His disobedience led not only to the death of himself and his house but, in principle, to the "death" of all Israel, depicted as no longer enjoying the bounty of the land which constituted life. The irony of vv. 11ff. is heavy and sad. Saul had once been the deliverer of Jabesh Gilead (1 Sam. 11:1–11). He had been then at the height of his powers and promise. He passes out of the history of the people of God to the silent tribute of those who lamented one who might have been great.

The central issue in this chapter is the relation between the obedience of God's people and their blessing. That relation may not always appear clearly. Chr. insists that it is immutable. God gave his people a land which was both undeserved and richly adequate (Deut. 6:10ff.; 8:7–10). In Jesus Christ he has revealed how deep and inexhaustible his blessings are (Eph. 1:15ff.). He desires that we as Christians enjoy our inheritance to the full. And the warnings of the writer to the Hebrews lest we be led astray from the path of faith (Heb. 3:7ff.; 6:4–8) find their melancholy echo in the death of Saul.

SAUL'S FAITHLESSNESS—A CLOSER LOOK

1 Chronicles 10:1–14 (*cont'd*)

Verses 13ff. of chapter 10 come from the Chronicler's own pen. His summarized adverse judgment upon Saul falls into three main statements, viz. "he was unfaithful to the Lord", "he did not keep the command of the Lord", and "he did not seek guidance from the Lord"—of which the first may be said to embrace the two following.

The accusation of "faithlessness" is particularly severe. The word used is *ma'al* which is normally reserved for serious sin against God, often associated with idolatry, and carrying with it extreme penalties (e.g. Ezek. 14:13; 15:7f.). It is the seriousness, rather than particular kinds, of sin that the word connotes. It has been pointed out that the Chronicler is responsible for about half of the occurrences of *ma'al* in the OT. In other words it seems that he is particularly concerned to stress that sin of any kind is serious.

This, then, is why Saul died. Perhaps we are tempted to think of Saul primarily as a tragic figure, as weak, irresponsible, impetuous, or in some other way that explains and mitigates his failure to obey God. Chr. is at pains to show that the mere fact of not being with God is tantamount to being against him (cf. the familiar words of Jesus, Matt. 12:30). The proof of this is the fact that Saul's inadequacies lead directly to a situation in which, not only do God's people no longer possess the land, but God's enemies now control it. The Philistines, having despatched Saul, go and boast before their idols (notice that the idols are informed even before the people, v. 9). The Philistines' action has not been a mere neutral, political thing. It is in its essence a rebellion against the living God. There is no such thing as "neutrality" in the attitude of men and women to God. One either "listens to" or "seeks" God (to use the terminology of vv. 13ff.), or one "seeks" or "listens to" an opposite principle. The role of the Philistines in the present section is to press home this point. Saul's failure to "keep the command of the Lord" (1 Sam. 13:13) and to seek guidance from him may have been quiet and inconspicuous. But it unleashed a much greater and more obvious kind of wickedness among and upon God's people. Moral evil is not measured in quantity but in kind. And it has its own "domino" effect.

It is for this reason that the Chronicler selects the action of Saul in requiring the witch of Endor (1 Sam. 28:7ff.) to employ her illicit arts as illustrative of his basic character and disposition. (Isa. 8:19 is explicit in its condemnation of using mediums.) Once again, incidentally, the Chronicler is carefully selecting his material. 1 Sam. 28:6 records that Saul did in fact enquire of the Lord, and it was only because the Lord refused to answer him that he turned to the medium. We must suppose, however, that the Chronicler has rightly discerned the natural and typical tendency of Saul's heart. Saul's seeking the witch stands in sharp contrast to David's enquiring of the Lord, 1 Chr. 14:10. It is possible for those who are fundamentally opposed to God to turn to him in desperation on occasion, yet not in such a way as to alter their basic disposition. (cf. God's complaint in Jer. 2:27.)

Finally, we should not fail to notice that Saul's death in the biblical writer's view was no unlucky accident. Rather, "the Lord slew him" (v. 14(*b*)). I have heard accounts of how military strategists have scrutinized the Gilboa range for clues as to Saul's technical errors in his defeat. No doubt such errors could in principle be identified. But there is a more profound kind of causation in view here. In the mind of God, Saul's time was up. We cannot shirk the implication of judgment. And it is time for the "man after God's own heart" to enter the scene.

THE SEEKER AFTER GOD—I

1 Chronicles 11:1–47

¹Then all Israel gathered together to David at Hebron, and said, "Behold, we are your bone and flesh. ²In times past, even when Saul was king, it was you that led out and brought in Israel; and the Lord your God said to you, 'You shall be shepherd of my people Israel, and you shall be prince over my people Israel.' " ³So all the elders of Israel came to the king at Hebron; and David made a covenant with them at Hebron before the Lord, and they anointed David king over Israel, according to the word of the Lord by Samuel.

⁴And David and all Israel went to Jerusalem, that is Jebus, where the Jebusites were, the inhabitants of the land. ⁵The inhabitants of Jebus said to David, "You will not come in here." Nevertheless David took the stronghold of Zion, that is, the city of David. ⁶David said, "Whoever shall smite the Jebusites first shall be chief and commander." And Joab the son of Zeruiah went up first, so he became chief. ⁷And David dwelt in the stronghold; therefore it was called the city of David. ⁸And he built the city round about from the Millo in complete circuit; and Joab repaired the rest of the city. ⁹And David became greater and greater, for the Lord of hosts was with him.

¹⁰Now these are the chiefs of David's mighty men, who gave him strong support in his kingdom, together with all Israel, to make him king, according to the word of the Lord concerning Israel. ¹¹This is an account of David's mighty men: Jashobe-am, a Hachmonite, was chief of the three; he wielded his spear against three hundred whom he slew at one time.

¹²And next to him among the three mighty men was Eleazar the son of Dodo, the Ahohite. ¹³He was with David at Pas-dammim when the Philistines were gathered there for battle. There was a plot of ground full of barley, and the men fled from the Philistines. ¹⁴But he took his stand in the midst of the plot, and defended it, and slew the Philistines; and the Lord saved them by a great victory.

¹⁵Three of the thirty chief men went down to the rock to David at the cave of Adullam, when the army of Philistines was encamped in the valley of Rephaim. ¹⁶David was then in the stronghold; and the garrison of the Philistines was then at Bethlehem. ¹⁷And David said longingly, "O that some one would give me water to drink from the well of Bethlehem which is by the gate!" ¹⁸Then the three mighty men

broke through the camp of the Philistines, and drew water out of the well of Bethlehem which was by the gate, and took and brought it to David. But David would not drink of it; he poured it out to the Lord, ¹⁹and said, "Far be it from me before my God that I should do this. Shall I drink the lifeblood of these men? For at the risk of their lives they brought it." Therefore he would not drink it. These things did the three mighty men.

²⁰Now Abishai, the brother of Joab, was chief of the thirty. And he wielded his spear against three hundred men and slew them, and won a name beside the three. ²¹He was the most renowned of the thirty, and became their commander; but he did not attain to the three.

²²And Benaiah the son of Jehoiada was a valiant man of Kabzeel, a doer of great deeds; he smote two ariels of Moab. He also went down and slew a lion in a pit on a day when snow had fallen. ²³And he slew an Egyptian, a man of great stature, five cubits tall. The Egyptian had in his hand a spear like a weaver's beam; but Benaiah went down to him with a staff, and snatched the spear out of the Egyptian's hand, and slew him with his own spear. ²⁴These things did Benaiah the son of Jehoiada, and won a name beside the three mighty men. ²⁵He was renowned among the thirty, but he did not attain to the three. And David set him over his bodyguard.

²⁶The mighty men of the armies were Asahel the brother of Joab, Elhanan the son of Dodo of Bethlehem, ²⁷Shammoth of Harod, Helez the Pelonite, ²⁸Ira the son of Ikkesh of Tekoa, Abiezer of Anathoth, ²⁹Sibbecai the Hushathite, Ilai the Ahohite, ³⁰Maharai of Netophah, Heled the son of Baanah of Netophah, ³¹Ithai the son of Ribai of Gibeah of the Benjaminites, Benaiah of Pirathon, ³²Hurai of the brooks of Gaash, Abiel the Arbathite, ³³Azmaveth of Baharum, Eliahba of Shaalbon, ³⁴Hashem the Gizonite, Jonathan the son of Shagee the Hararite, ³⁵Ahiam the son of Sachar the Hararite, Eliphal the son of Ur, ³⁶Hepher the Mecherathite, Ahijah the Pelonite, ³⁷Hezro of Carmel, Naarai the son of Ezbai, ³⁸Joel the brother of Nathan, Mibhar the son of Hagri, ³⁹Zelek the Ammonite, Naharai of Beeroth, the armour-bearer of Joab the son of Zeruiah, ⁴⁰Ira the Ithrite, Gareb the Ithrite, ⁴¹Uriah the Hittite, Zabad the son of Ahlai, ⁴²Adina the son of Shiza the Reubenite, a leader of the Reubenites, and thirty with him, ⁴³Hanan the son of Maacah, and Joshaphat the Mithnite, ⁴⁴Uzzia the Ashterathite, Shama and Jeiel the sons of Hotham the Aroerite, ⁴⁵Jediael the son of Shimri, and Joha his brother, the Tizite, ⁴⁶Eliel the Mahavite, and Jeribai, and Joshaviah, the sons of El-naam, and Ithmah the Moabite, ⁴⁷Eliel, and Obed, and Jaasiel the Mezobaite.

It is important to realize how vital to Chr. is the era of David and Solomon. Between them they occupy the stage from this point until 2 Chr. 9–twenty-eight chapters out of sixty-five. The statistic shows to what extent the Books of Chronicles are *not* a straightforward history of Israel, but rather a search for models for the author's own day. Saul has been weighed in the balance and found wanting, because he did not "seek the Lord". David and Solomon are now presented as, fundamentally, those who *did* seek the Lord (cf. 1 Chr. 14:10, 16). Not that they themselves are perfect. The Chronicler has no interest in idealizing David and Solomon *for their own sake*. He is much more interested in Israel. What is there in Israel's history, he asks, that can profitably be applied to the community of his own day, relatively recently restored from Babylon, its Temple rebuilt, yet itself politically weak and dependent? The splendid days of empire—for it was no less—are recalled, to give a picture of what Israel truly is in the eyes of God. Central to this picture are the Temple, the ark of the covenant, and the organization of right worship. To these things the details of the following chapters are subordinate.

(a) *Promises fulfilled*

The opening picture, vv. 1–3, sets David's accession to the kingship in the context of a promise fulfilled (v. 3, "the word of the Lord by Samuel" may refer to 1 Sam. 15:28; 16:1). David's reign is in fact the crowning of that more fundamental promise—of peaceful possession of the land which is a major theme of the Torah or Pentateuch, especially Deuteronomy (e.g. 11:24f.). And this is the significance of the story of the capture of Jebus (vv. 4–9), home of the Jebusites, one of the peoples listed in Deut. 7:1 as those whom it was Israel's task to expel from the land. Jebus, however, had resisted early Israelite attacks. The fact that it now falls to David is symbolic, therefore, of the fact that the promise to Israel given through Moses is now being completely fulfilled through David.

The various warlike fragments in this and the following chapters have a similar function (especially those concerning the

Philistines, last seen in chapter 10 wreaking havoc in the heartland). As indeed do the list of and stories about David's formidable warriors. The Chronicler has again schematized his available material in order to make his main points. Verses 1–9 cover broadly the account in 2 Sam. 5:1–10. Verses 10–47 are drawn from 2 Sam. 23. In this case he is probably closer to actual historical sequence than the author of Samuel. Most significant, however, is what is omitted from the Sam. narrative, viz. 2 Sam. 1–4. These chapters record how Saul was not *immediately* succeeded by David in the whole land, but rather that there was a period during which Saul's son, Ishbosheth (or Ishbaal) reigned over a large part of Israel (2 Sam. 2:8ff.), and indeed engaged in a long war with David (2 Sam. 3:1). The decline of the Saulides was in fact a gradual affair, and Saulide opposition to David actually continued long after Saul's house had ceased to pose a real threat (2 Sam. 20). Equally gradual was David's subjugation of the enemies of Israel. Chr. passes over here (though it is noted at 1 Chr. 29:27) the fact that David ruled for seven of his forty years at Hebron before he took Jerusalem.

On the contrary, Chr.'s picture is one both of rapid conquest and of an Israel united behind its king. Once again it is important to say that Chr. is not doing violence to history, but rather selecting and simplifying. Even the report of the taking of Jebus is devoid of embellishment (contrast 2 Sam. 5:6ff.); the very curtness of the account shows how futile was all resistance to the fulfilment of God's promise. Even by its omissions, therefore, Chr. wishes to show the inevitability and completeness of that fulfilment. This is not to say that it is *here* complete. The story of the capture of Jebus does not focus on the victory itself. Rather it points forward to the day when, as *Jerusalem*, the place which God has chosen "to put his name there" (Deut. 12:5), it will be the centre of true worship. To that end Joab "repairs"—literally "enlivens"—the city. Its possession will be life. The material structures will serve that end. A fuller revelation of the life that God would give lay yet in the future. But the OT writers knew something of its fullness (cf. Neh. 12:43), and the Chronicler here anticipates it eagerly.

THE SEEKER AFTER GOD—II

1 Chronicles 11:1–47 (*cont'd*)

(b) *The leader*

David was a *real* leader. So much is clear from the people's declaration in v. 2. Even when the trappings of leadership had belonged to Saul, it was in reality David who had led Israel and made progress towards securing the heritage of the people of God. And such is often the case. The holding of office is not synonymous with real power. Presidents and kings have been the puppets of faceless manipulators behind the scenes. Within the church, the possession of dignities is no guarantee or badge of spiritual character (though hardly incompatible with it). But, just as Israel flocked to David, people will find and follow those *in whom is the power of God.* Even in conferring kingship upon him, they recognized that he possessed a kind of authority to lead which it was not theirs to give. And even as king the reason for his increasing greatness is that "the Lord of hosts was with him" (v. 9).

The very words with which David is acclaimed, namely Shepherd and Prince (v. 2), witness to this. "You shall be shepherd" actually translates a verb in the Hebrew (*tir'eh*, "you shall shepherd"; the usual word for "shepherd" in the OT, *ro'eh*, is in fact a participle of the same verb). The idea is significant in two ways. First, in the choice of the idea of shepherding as a model for leadership, with its connotations both of humility and of devoted care. Its frequent application to the kings of Israel only serves to show how badly most of them failed to discharge their real duties, and became obsessed instead with the preservation and increase of their status and power (cf. Jer. 23:1–4). It is an abiding temptation to Christians to seek external marks of distinction, such as the world needs. The pursuit of them can result in the loss of real stature. Secondly, the verbal form reminds us again that any holding of a responsible position, specifically in the Church, without a corresponding activity in pursuit of its aims is an empty charade. The people of Israel do not merely confer an honour on

David (though honour it was—would not Jesus himself take the same title, John 10?), but they express confidence that he actually will be active on their behalf. (The word "prince" echoes the point, in that it is not the word "king". It too indicates real eminence, without connoting the splendours of monarchy.)

(c) *The man after God's own heart*

The account in vv. 15–19 is strange and not often well explained in commentaries. David expresses a desire to drink water from the well at Bethlehem, and "the three mighty men" (see below) break through Philistine ranks in order to get it. David then refuses to drink it and "pours it out to the Lord". The symbolism in the pouring is drawn from the realm of Israel's ritual life. Blood was "poured out upon the earth like water" (Deut. 12:16, 24), because it was reckoned to be or contain the life of the creature (Deut. 12:23, cf. Gen. 9:4; Lev. 17:14) and therefore it should not be consumed. The blood of an animal was always drained off when it was slaughtered, sacrificially or otherwise (in a sacrifice, it was sprinkled on the altar, see e.g. Lev. 1:5). David's point in this case is that, as the water was obtained at the risk of the men's lives, it is as precious as blood, and therefore should not be drunk.

But that is not the whole story. Naturally, there was no ritual *necessity* for David to pour out this water. Had he been in real need of it he would presumably have drunk it. Indeed, it is inconceivable that David should not have made adequate provision for water for himself and his army. His real desire—not perceived by the "three", who resemble here the impetuous apostle Peter in their slowness to plumb their leader's spirituality—is deeper. It is that he should possess Bethlehem. And in this he distinguishes himself yet again as one who is fit to lead God's people. No doubt David's natural yearning for his home is part of the longing he expresses. But in positioning the account here, Chr. is insisting that David is motivated by the fact that Bethlehem belongs to the heritage of Israel. The longing is spiritual. It is that God's people should actually possess all that God has prepared for them. It is a longing that he himself should be all that he ought to be as one chosen by God to be king over God's people in the land given to them. And here too is a model of Christian leadership—a leadership that is marked by a desire that people should discover and make their own the treasures that are in Christ. The letters and prayers of Paul show that he, like David, was such a one (1 Cor. 1:4ff.; Col. 2:1ff.).

(d) *A people united and open*

We have observed above that one of the reasons for the inclusion at this point of lists of warriors is to demonstrate the power of God's people to overcome their enemies, according to his promise. They serve a further purpose, however. I have said that Chr. is not interested in idealizing David or Solomon *for their own sake*. Rather the interest is in *Israel*. The Chronicler, though he omits references to the divisions within Israel which followed the death of Saul, is much aware of them. Indeed he takes a strong stand on the premise that the true Israel is defined by its loyalty to the Davidic house. It is for this reason that the division of the kingdom into two under Rehoboam and Jeroboam constitutes a rebellion on the part of the north (2 Chr. 10:19). But he maintains, nonetheless, that Israel properly understood should be based on the twelve tribes. And the names of David's warriors reflect that broad base of the true Israel, coming as they do from all parts of the country (for details see one of the larger Commentaries). In a further way then, the claim is made that all Israel supported David. The foundation laid here will constitute a basis on which the Chronicler will be able to make a plea for the unity of Israel, despite old divisions and prejudices.

It is also significant that David's followers are not all Israelites, Uriah being a Hittite, v. 41, Ithmah a Moabite, v. 46, and Zelek an Ammonite, v. 39. The people of God are not only united but open. The inclusion of Moabites and Ammonites is particularly striking in view of the rigour of Deut. 23:3, though indeed the exclusion is of limited duration there. Deuteronomy also provided for the equal treatment of aliens who dwelt among the

Israelites (14:29). That spirit is here too, and the true character of the people of God as receiving and international begins to be seen.

(The Three and the Thirty. There are corruptions in the text which make it difficult to know just who the Three were and how they related to the Thirty. RSV is probably right to take Jashobeam as chief of the Three (v. 11)—following the Greek version rather than the Hebrew—the same person, therefore, as Josheb-basshebeth, 2 Sam. 23:8. The other two are Eleazar and Shammah, the latter having dropped out, presumably, of the text of Chr., cf. 2 Sam. 23:11. RSV seems to be right also, again against the Hebrew text, in making Abishai chief of the Thirty, v. 20. But the leadership of the Thirty may actually have changed from time to time, cf. 1 Chr. 12:4, 18.)

YOUR GOD HELPS YOU—I

1 Chronicles 12:1–22

[1]Now these are the men who came to David at Ziklag, while he could not move about freely because of Saul the son of Kish; and they were among the mighty men who helped him in war. [2]They were bowmen, and could shoot arrows and sling stones with either the right or the left hand; they were Benjaminites, Saul's kinsmen. [3]The chief was Ahiezer, then Joash, both sons of Shemaah of Gibeah; also Jeziel and Pelet the sons of Azmaveth; Beracah, Jehu of Anathoth, [4]Ishmaiah of Gibeon, a mighty man among the thirty and a leader over the thirty; Jeremiah, Jahaziel, Johanan, Jozabad of Gederah, [5]Eluzai, Jerimoth, Bealiah, Shemariah, Shephatiah the Haruphite; [6]Elkanah, Isshiah, Azarel, Joezer, and Jashobeam, the Korahites; [7]and Joelah and Zebadiah, the sons of Jeroham of Gedor.

[8]From the Gadites there went over to David at the stronghold in the wilderness mighty and experienced warriors, expert with shield and spear, whose faces were like the faces of lions, and who were swift as gazelles upon the mountains: [9]Ezer the chief, Obadiah second, Eliab third, [10]Mishmannah fourth, Jeremiah fifth, [11]Attai sixth, Eliel seventh, [12]Johanan eighth, Elzabad ninth, [13]Jeremiah tenth, Machbannai eleventh. [14]These Gadites were officers of the army, the lesser over

a hundred and the greater over a thousand. [15]These are the men who crossed the Jordan in the first month, when it was overflowing all its banks, and put to flight all those in the valleys, to the east and to the west.

[16]And some of the men of Benjamin and Judah came to the stronghold to David. [17]David went out to meet them and said to them, "If you have come to me in friendship to help me, my heart will be knit to you; but if to betray me to my adversaries, although there is no wrong in my hands, then may the God of our fathers see and rebuke you." [18]Then the Spirit came upon Amasai, chief of the thirty, and he said,

"We are yours, O David;
    and with you, O son of Jesse!
Peace, peace to you,
    and peace to your helpers!
For your God helps you."

Then David received them, and made them officers of his troops.

[19]Some of the men of Manasseh deserted to David when he came with the Philistines for the battle against Saul. (Yet he did not help them, for the rulers of the Philistines took counsel and sent him away, saying, "At peril to our heads he will desert to his master Saul.") [20]As he went to Ziklag these men of Manasseh deserted to him: Adnah, Jozabad, Jediael, Michael, Jozabad, Elihu, and Zillethai, chiefs of thousands in Manasseh. [21]They helped David against the band of raiders; for they were all mighty men of valour, and were commanders in the army. [22]For from day to day men kept coming to David to help him, until there was a great army, like an army of God.

We have already seen David made king at Hebron (11:3) and in possession of his capital, Jerusalem (11:4ff.). The present chapter, therefore, is of the nature of a flashback, picturing David on the run from Saul. (There is no parallel in Samuel, but for Ziklag as one of David's places of resort during his time on the run, see 1 Sam. 30). The chapter falls into two parts, vv. 1–22 recording how outstanding warriors from certain tribes came to join David, and vv. 23–40 providing a further picture of a united Israel acclaiming him at Hebron.

The function of the first section (vv. 1–22) is to show how David's inexorable rise to eminence had begun even when he seemed to be an also-ran. The theme of this passage is *help*. It is a catalogue of "the mighty men who *helped* him in war" (v. 1). It is not clear why it should be these four tribes (namely Benjamin, Gad, Judah and Manasseh) which are said to have provided men for David during his time at Ziklag. Clearly there is special significance in the mention of Benjamin and Judah (vv. 2, 16ff.). Benjamin was Saul's tribe, and the defection of some of *his* men to David is a sure sign that the pendulum was swinging against him. Judah was David's own tribe. That David should entertain suspicions about his kinsmen reminds us that the "new man" was not instantly accepted by everyone around him, and that the danger of betrayal attended his days in the wilderness (cf. 1 Sam. 25:10). In this case the men of both Judah and Benjamin turned out to be loyal, and the alliance of the two tribes would have spoken strongly to the people of the Chronicler's day, since the restoration community was composed largely of members of them. Gad and Manasseh do not seem to have special significance beyond their representation of wider Israel. The quality of all the warriors is emphasized—the Benjaminites especially dexterous (v. 2), the Gadites able to handle impossible odds (v. 14, where the meaning probably is that even the weakest was *a match for* a hundred etc.). The scattered vignettes which we are allowed of these men—as when (v. 15) the Gadites cross the Jordan in flood in the course of some unspecified military raid—are designed to show their exceptional capacities.

The brief dialogue between David and the men of Benjamin (vv. 16ff.), however, has a deeper purpose. It shows that what we are dealing with is no mere military annal (though some such document probably constitutes Chr.'s source for the present chapter). Rather it is a meditation on the nature of *help*. We have noticed that the idea of help appears in the superscription (v. 1) of our account. The word subsequently appears five times (vv. 17, 18, 19, 21, 22; even some of the names reflect the theme: Ezer, v. 9, means "help"; and Ahiezer, v. 3, "brother of help"). Our word "help" often conjures up far paler ideas than the Hebrew word does. To us it can simply mean "assist", although it undoubtedly covers a wide range. The Hebrew word, however, expresses the sort of idea that the drowning man has in mind, rather than that of the child who is in difficulty with a piece of arithmetic. It is, in other words, tantamount to salvation (usually conceived, in the OT, in immediate and physical terms). Thus Samuel could set up a memorial stone and call it Ebenezer (literally "stone of help", 1 Sam. 7:12) to commemorate a decisive victory over the Philistines.

YOUR GOD HELPS YOU—II

1 Chronicles 12:1–22 (*cont'd*)

Amasai's speech to David makes the crucial point that it is God who is ultimately the source of all help. The OT speaks with different voices about the relationship between human and divine help. In Dan. 11:34, for example, Daniel's predictions about Israel's experiences under the Greek Seleucid empire in the second century B.C. describe the extraordinarily successful Maccabean revolt as "a little help", thus effectively damning it with faint praise. In that place the author, in stressing that real help comes from God, feels it necessary to make the point that people tend to rely on their own strength rather than upon him and that their achievements are not always as great as they seem. Here the point is that even when help emanates evidently and genuinely from human resources, it has no existence of its own but is in reality the outflow of the help of God.

Amasai has observed the chief events in David's flight from Saul—doubtless he knows some of David's early victories (e.g. 1 Sam. 23), or of his defeat of Goliath (1 Sam. 17). He knows that "your God has helped you" (the verb is actually in the past tense, though Amasai no doubt sees that God's past help for David implies that he will continue to help him). And the testimony is significant coming from one who is clearly an outstanding warrior. Here is a picture of men well-equipped, in skill and arms, yet seeing that their strength is nothing if it is not from God. (When it is said, incidentally, (v. 22) that the "great army" was "like an army of God", the implication is that it really *was* an army of God. Yet there is a fleeting picture also of the host of heaven itself gathering to David's cause (cf. 2 Kings 6:17).)

Amasai's speech is notable for two further reasons. The first is the fact that it happens as a result of the Spirit coming upon him—literally "clothing" him—(as also Gideon, Judg. 6:34). The OT's teaching about God's spirit is more muted than that of the NT. The account of Pentecost (Acts 2:1ff.) probably implies an altogether new experience of the Spirit on the part of the early Christians. Yet it is legitimate to read "the Spirit" with RSV (rather than the bland "a spirit", which is, other considerations apart, a legitimate translation of the word *ruach*), because *ruach* has specific associations with God's speech to his people through the prophets. (Ezekiel is the best example, cf. Ezek. 2:2. Contrast 2 Kings 2:9, where "spirit" is better, and which illustrates a relatively rudimentary understanding of how God worked through his early prophets.) Amasai's words, therefore, have the character of prophecy, rather than mere well-wishing, let alone flattery. Through his Spirit, God gives him to discern the truth about David, despite unpromising circumstances. In a day when interest in the work of the Holy Spirit in the Church is at a high level, it is important both to recognize the *fact* of his activity, and to ask how we may expect and know it. Our next point offers a suggestion in this respect.

The Peace of God (1 Chr. 12:18)
(a) The dominant idea in Amasai's speech itself is not actually help but *peace*. This comes as something of a surprise in the mouth of one who has come to lend his weight to David's war-effort. But it has to be understood in the light of God's promises to Israel, and later expressly to David, in which the idea of "rest from enemies" is of central importance (Deut. 12:10f.; 2 Sam. 7:1; 1 Chr. 17:1, and see comment thereon). Peace in the OT (*shalom*) is much more than the absence of hostilities, but rather a positive fullness of life, an experience of well-being which, for the people of the OT, had material as well as spiritual dimensions. For this reason the pronouncement of some churchmen about peace in the weaker sense, while well-meaning, can actually emasculate the real biblical message about the possibilities

for human life. The gospel is not about "not fighting". It is about wholeness of life as God intended it, characterized by security, love and identification with his will. (Security should be understood in our day primarily as a matter of personality, and of *inner* peace. On *shalom* as material blessing see below on vv. 23–40.) (b) We now take up again the matter of Amasai's inspiration by the Spirit. In the light of what we know of God's promises to Israel, and to David, it is evident that Amasai's "word" is less a new revelation than a perception, albeit a special one, of something that God was otherwise revealing, namely, that David would have rest from his enemies. It has also the character of a prayer. In our church life it is right to seek and respond to all activity of the Spirit. But equally it is important to know that there is no work of the Spirit which is not intimately associated with the knowledge of God which his written word is designed to give. There is a need for "testing the spirits" (1 John 4:1), and for the disciplined application to God's word which will give us the equipment to do so. Similarly the sensitive prayer life, individual and corporate, will be that in which a knowledge of the character of God in all his past dealings with his people in general and oneself in particular plays the central role and affords perceptions of his will for given situations.

WITH A WHOLE HEART

1 Chronicles 12:23–40

²³These are the numbers of the divisions of the armed troops, who came to David in Hebron, to turn the kingdom of Saul over to him, according to the word of the Lord. ²⁴The men of Judah bearing shield and spear were six thousand eight hundred armed troops. ²⁵Of the Simeonites, mighty men of valour for war, seven thousand one hundred. ²⁶Of the Levites four thousand six hundred. ²⁷The prince Jehoiada, of the house of Aaron, and with him three thousand seven hundred. ²⁸Zadok, a young man mighty in valour, and twenty-two commanders from his own father's house. ²⁹Of the Benjaminites, the kinsmen of Saul, three thousand, of whom the majority had hitherto kept their allegiance to the house of Saul. ³⁰Of the Ephraimites twenty

thousand eight hundred, mighty men of valour, famous men in their fathers' houses. [31]Of the half-tribe of Manasseh eighteen thousand, who were expressly named to come and make David king. [32]Of Issachar men who had understanding of the times, to know what Israel ought to do, two hundred chiefs, and all their kinsmen under their command. [33]Of Zebulun fifty thousand seasoned troops, equipped for battle with all the weapons of war, to help David with singleness of purpose. [34]Of Naphtali a thousand commanders with whom were thirty-seven thousand men armed with shield and spear. [35]Of the Danites twenty-eight thousand six hundred men equipped for battle. [36]Of Asher forty thousand seasoned troops ready for battle. [37]Of the Reubenites and Gadites and the half-tribe of Manasseh from beyond the Jordan, one hundred and twenty thousand men armed with all the weapons of war.

[38]All these, men of war, arrayed in battle order, came to Hebron with full intent to make David king over all Israel; likewise all the rest of Israel were of a single mind to make David king. [39]And they were there with David for three days, eating and drinking, for their brethren had made preparation for them. [40]And also their neighbours, from as far as Issachar and Zebulun and Naphtali, came bringing food on asses and on camels and on mules and on oxen, abundant provisions of meal, cakes of figs, clusters of raisins, and wine and oil, oxen and sheep, for there was joy in Israel.

(i)

The narrative returns now, with little regard for chronology, to David's coronation at Hebron (cf. 11:1ff.), to give a picture of the unity and single-mindedness of Israel in making him king. Counting the Levites, thirteen tribes are named here. There were never thirteen tribes at any one time in Israel, of course. Levi early ceased to function as a tribe, but rather was scattered among the others. Sometimes it is omitted from the tribal lists, and the number twelve is retained by dividing Joseph into Ephraim and Manasseh (cf. Num. 26:5ff.). When Levi is included, however, Joseph is represented as one (cf. Gen. 35:23–26; 1 Chr. 2:1–2). Chr., again spurning the pedantic detail, here represents Israel in its fullness. No part of Israel failed to give its support to David. Indeed it is interesting to notice that the largest contributions to this tide of support for David came from the north. The numbers given for Ephraim, Zebulun and Asher, in particular, are large in comparison with the relatively low numbers for Judah and Benjamin. This has been taken as evidence for the authenticity of the list on the grounds that Chr. would naturally want to enhance the claims made for the southern tribes, and that their low numbers therefore reflect a scrupulous honesty in recording the way it really was.

Be that as it may, we should not underestimate Chr.'s positive portrayal of a fully united Israel. As in our day, the Chronicler was in a position in which his ideals for a united people of God were far from matched by the conditions he knew. But he continued to hold the ideal before him as something that was supremely desirable.

(ii)

Not only did the people of David's day act in a concerted way, but they did so "with singleness of purpose" (v. 33, cf. v. 38)—or "with a whole heart", as the Hebrew of v. 38 has it. There were no reservations. Now, this singleness of purpose is not actually directed towards the *forging* of unity. Unity is portrayed as forged already. The "whole-heartedness" is directed towards the realization of Yahweh's full blessing for Israel. Chr. reminds us here of the need to be about the business of God's kingdom with complete self-giving. How many churches meander along achieving little in terms of real spiritual change and progress simply because their people's hearts are divided? (cf. James 1:7f.)

The motifs of unity and determination do converge, of course. A real unity contributes to the effectiveness of the action of God's people. Notice how each tribe contributes. Issachar is singled out for its chiefs' "understanding of the times" (v. 32). It has been suggested that this may refer to astrological knowledge (as in Esth. 1:13). Chr. hardly understands it in this way, but rather in terms of the wisdom which is a gift of God. True unity must strengthen the Church simply because of a pooling of God-given resources. The sad story of attempts to achieve visible church unity in recent decades (in Britain) may only prompt the thought that real unity does not necessarily require structural or organizational uniformity. Indeed attempts to achieve this can sometimes merely throw differences into relief. But failures at this level should not deter church people from *actually* seeking to work together in the daily business of bringing people to Christ and building them up in him.

(iii)

The last few verses of the chapter (38–40) afford a glimpse of the luxuriance of OT celebration. The single-minded resolve to realize God's promises (by crowning David) is accompanied by a healthy knowledge of what God's blessing is. Here is the material side of *shalom* in all its gladness. The mouth-watering catalogue of good things casts this depiction of joy precisely in the terms in which God had promised to bless Israel in Moses' time (Deut. 8:7–10). The joy of the people of God is a motif in Chr. (cf. 1 Chr. 29:22; 2 Chr. 7:10; 30:21ff.). Any idea that the OT is a grim and doom-laden thing is wide of the mark. On the contrary, it is hardly an exaggeration to say that joy is its dominant mood (especially in the Psalms, e.g. 81:1–5; 84:1f.; 92:1–4; 100:1f.; 146–150). David's followers could show determination because they had a knowledge of God's blessing as something palpable.

This prompts two thoughts.

(a) It is difficult for us as Christians to appropriate in a balanced way the idea of a material aspect of God's blessing. The ability to distinguish between glad acceptance of what God gives and active seeking of "the good things of life" is essential. The primary goal for the Christian must be that aspect of *shalom* which is identification with the will of God. To set one's sights on material blessing will bypass that first target. As far as material things are concerned we shall do well to believe the words of Jesus in Matt. 6:33, and be chastened by those in Matt. 19:24.

(b) There is nevertheless an indissoluble link between the experience of God's blessing and the kind of purposefulness which we have seen in David's followers. With the coming of Christ and his indwelling in believers (John 14:23) Christians have access to a more profound knowledge of God than his people of OT times enjoyed. Only by cultivating the habit of seeing his hand in our lives is it possible to understand how profound is his desire and capacity to bless—both in material and other ways. And it is only when we truly know God as the One who cares for *me* that we shall ever achieve a real devotion to the doing of his will.

SEEKING THE ARK

1 Chronicles 13:1–14

[1]David consulted with the commanders of thousands and of hundreds, with every leader. [2]And David said to all the assembly of Israel, "If it seems good to you, and if it is the will of the Lord our God, let us send abroad to our brethren who remain in all the land of Israel, and with them to the priests and Levites in the cities that have pasture lands, that they may come together to us. [3]Then let us bring again the ark of our God to us; for we neglected it in the days of Saul." [4]All the assembly agreed to do so, for the thing was right in the eyes of all the people.

[5]So David assembled all Israel from the Shihor of Egypt to the entrance of Hamath, to bring the ark of God from Kiriath-jearim. [6]And David and all Israel went up to Baalah, that is, to Kiriath-jearim which belongs to Judah, to bring up from there the ark of God, which is called by the name of the Lord who sits enthroned above the cherubim. [7]And they carried the ark of God upon a new cart, from the house of Abinadab, and Uzzah and Ahio were driving the cart. [8]And David and all Israel were making merry before God with all their might, with song and lyres and harps and tambourines and cymbals and trumpets.

[9]And when they came to the threshing floor of Chidon, Uzzah put out his hand to hold the ark, for the oxen stumbled. [10]And the anger of the Lord was kindled against Uzzah; and he smote him because he put forth his hand to the ark; and he died there before God. [11]And David was angry because the Lord had broken forth upon Uzzah; and that place is called Perez-uzza to this day. [12]And David was afraid of God that day; and he said, "How can I bring the ark of God home to me?" [13]So David did not take the ark home into the city of David, but took it aside to the house of Obed-edom the Gittite. [14]And the ark of God remained with the household of Obed-edom in his house three months; and the Lord blessed the household of Obed-edom and all that he had.

(i)

The actions of David in this passage contrast expressly with those of Saul in chapter 10. The words "we neglected it", v. 3, referring to the ark, literally mean "we did not seek it". David's confession on behalf of Israel refers to Saul's day. (Saul, we recall, had sought a medium instead of the Lord, 1 Chr. 10:13.) Under Saul the whole people had failed to seek God. Now in contrast the whole people "seeks" the ark under David. (Chr. makes something of the involvement of the whole people in the decision, v. 1. David appears to act much more on his own initiative in 2 Sam. 6:1f.) "Seeking" the ark is tantamount to seeking God. (The verb which means "seek", *darash*, is sometimes translated "care for". Those who *care for* the ark are in reality seeking God.) So the motif of the worthy leader of Israel is further developed here, and specifically in relation to the ark of God.

(ii)

In Israel's traditions the ark symbolized the presence of God. It was constructed to occupy the innermost and holiest part of the tabernacle made long before Chr., and even David, in the desert period. Above this ark was a throne, "the mercy-seat", flanked by cherubim, and upon which the Lord was pictured as dwelling (Exod. 25:10ff., 22). The same conception is reflected in v. 6 of our passage. Clearly it was important to David to have the ark in the city which he was to make his capital, and which was to become the centre of Israel's worship.

The ark's immediate pre-history had been somewhat chequered. The story of its movements in the war against the Philistines is told in 1 Sam. 4:3–7:2. Having been borne into battle by Israel, in an attempt to harness the power of God, it had actually been captured by the enemy. The Lord, however, having been unwilling to be used even by his own people as a kind of lucky mascot, was equally unwilling to have his ark abused by the Philistines, who had consequently suffered from its presence and sent it back, whereupon it was accepted by the people of Kiriath-jearim, an obscure village a few miles west of Jerusalem, where it had remained untended during Saul's reign.

Behind Israel's failure to handle the ark properly in the Philistine wars was the constant danger that they would misunderstand its significance. The idea that God dwelt "above the cherubim" could so easily lead to the belief that he could be manipulated, that he was at the disposal of his people, rather than that *they* should serve *him*.

For this reason certain strands in the OT insist that God is in no way *confined* to the place where the ark is. One way of expressing this concern is the use of the idea of the "name" of God. Deuteronomy, for example, thinks of the sanctuary of God as the place where he has put his name (12:5 and elsewhere), to stress that God himself is not contained there. Deuteronomy also emphasizes the fact that there is nothing magical about the ark by insisting on the fact that in itself it is merely a container of the tablets of the law (10:1f.).

The Chronicler attempts to retain both perspectives upon the ark. On the one hand he says that the ark is called by the "name" of God, in line with his own insistence that nothing on earth can contain him (cf. 2 Chr. 6:10, 18). Yet on the other he insists that the ark really does signify God's presence, for God does "sit enthroned above the cherubim". So the conception of God's presence as material remains in some sense in Chr., and this explains what we read about the ark in relation first to Uzzah then to Obed-Edom.

(iii)

The death of Uzzah is one of those incidents which has been thought to show the OT God as vindictive in his execution of vengeance, and interpreters have adopted various stratagems to try to mitigate the full force of the statement that "the Lord smote him". Yet the full force of the passage depends upon taking the statement at its face value. Two points must be made. In his dealings with Israel, i.e. before the coming of Christ, God attached his presence (with the reservations expressed above) to places and things, in a way which the New Testament tells us no longer obtains (see Matt. 27:51; Heb. ch. 8). The fate of Uzzah is not isolated in the OT, but in line with that of all those who infringed (or were warned not to infringe) the regulations pertaining to the symbols of God's holiness. Exod. 19:21ff. is an analogous case, speaking of a danger to the people arising from simple uninformed curiosity. The mode of God's revelation and presence in the OT—a presence much sought and graciously granted (Exod. 33:3, 12–23; 34:9ff.)—brought with it the need to deal carefully with it. (cf. also the fate of Korah and his followers, Num. 16.)

Israel's respect for her God, in accordance with her nature as a physically defined entity, was marked by her attention to the outward manifestations and symbols of God's Covenant (although this is by no means substituted for the devotion of the heart, cf. Deut. 30:10.) The importance of right attention to the trappings of worship, however, placed a huge responsibility on the religious leaders. And this is the correct perspective on the Uzzah story. It is irrelevant to speculate whether Uzzah died coincidentally from natural causes, or even what his own state of mind was as he reached out, presumably quite spontaneously, to steady the ark. The point is that Uzzah is the victim of a carelessness on the part of his leaders, ultimately David himself, as is made clear in 1 Chr. 15:13—and in spite of the gesture made in this regard by the provision of a "new cart" (v. 7). In 15:13 David prescribes rigorous attention to the regulations that pertain to the bearing of the ark, in recognition that there had been a failure in this respect before. The death of Uzzah, therefore, while seeming to come grimly to us from an alien thought-world, has a message for us in terms of careful attention to our own God-given role within the Church. God has given gifts and apportioned responsibilities within the Church (Eph. 4:11ff., 1 Cor. 12), *for the good of the whole body*. Our failure to exercise and fulfil them must result in loss on the part of our Christian brothers and sisters.

David's anger and fear in connection with the Uzzah incident is that of one who has been discovered in a fault. Perhaps he had come to assume that the Lord was irreversibly with him, and had become casual in his devotion. Perhaps he had come to trust in his own strength. In any case his exclamation in v. 12 is less pure enquiry than petulant self-justification. His naming of the place

Perez-Uzzah belongs to his attempt to deflect the blame for the incident upon God. Even his stationing of the ark at Kiriath-jearim rather than taking it on to Jerusalem may reflect the same temper. Thus the disturbed conscience prefers to find means of excuse rather than seek immediate restitution. David is great enough to overcome his pique in the end (chapter 15). But the immediate effect of his attitude is delay and frustration (however great the temporary advantage of Obed-Edom, who was it seems a Levite, cf. 26:8, and whose experience represents the other side of the coin from that of Uzzah).

NOBODY'S PERFECT

1 Chronicles 14:1–17

¹And Hiram king of Tyre sent messengers to David, and cedar trees, also masons and carpenters to build a house for him. ²And David perceived that the Lord had established him king over Israel, and that his kingdom was highly exalted for the sake of his people Israel.

³And David took more wives in Jerusalem, and David begot more sons and daughters. ⁴These are the names of the children whom he had in Jerusalem: Shammua, Shobab, Nathan, Solomon, ⁵Ibhar, Elishua, Elpelet, ⁶Nogah, Nepheg, Japhia, ⁷Elishama, Beeliada, and Eliphelet.

⁸When the Philistines heard that David had been anointed king over all Israel, all the Philistines went up in search of David; and David heard of it and went out against them. ⁹Now the Philistines had come and made a raid in the valley of Rephaim. ¹⁰And David inquired of God, "Shall I go up against the Philistines? Wilt thou give them into my hand?" And the Lord said to him, "Go up, and I will give them into your hand." ¹¹And he went up to Baal-perazim, and David defeated them there; and David said, "God has broken through my enemies by my hand, like a bursting flood." Therefore the name of that place is called Baal-perazim. ¹²And they left their gods there, and David gave command, and they were burned.

¹³And the Philistines yet again made a raid in the valley. ¹⁴And when David again inquired of God, God said to him, "You shall not go up after them; go around and come upon them opposite the balsam trees. ¹⁵And when you hear the sound of marching in the tops of the

balsam trees, then go out to battle; for God has gone out before you to smite the army of the Philistines." ¹⁶And David did as God commanded him, and they smote the Philistine army from Gibeon to Gezer. ¹⁷And the fame of David went out into all lands, and the Lord brought the fear of him upon all nations.

This passage, which introduces Hiram king of Tyre, lists David's sons born to him in Jerusalem and records certain victories over the Philistines, is deliberately placed by Chr. *after* the narrative of the bringing of the ark to Kiriath-jearim, though it preceded it in Samuel. See 2 Sam. 5:13ff. The transposition is made to throw into relief the contrast with Saul. David, unlike Saul, has sought the ark, and now is portrayed in victory over the Philistines. The two things are brought into a causal connection. In OT terms this is close to the words of Jesus: "seek first God's kingdom and his righteousness, and all these things shall be yours as well" (Matt. 6:33). There is a further dimension in our story, however, because David's obedience is related to progress towards realizing God's promise and the establishment of his reign. Verse 17 speaks of a world-wide fame achieved by David, and the fear of him that is spoken of there is a hint of the universal dominion that was finally to be achieved by that greater King who was yet to be revealed.

The affirmation in this chapter that David is, after all, proceeding inexorably towards the establishment of his kingdom puts the setback of chapter 13 in its true perspective. There we saw a chink in the armour of the man of God. Here we see God's purposes continuing to be worked out in him. There are, therefore, two contrasts in this chapter. The first, and more important, is between Saul and David; and the second between David's relation to God in this and the previous chapter.

(a) The contrast with Saul is worked out in some detail. There is significance in the listing of David's sons because of the association of Jerusalem, the new royal centre, with Solomon. Solomon would be to David what Jonathan never was to Saul—an heir to sit on the throne. Once again David is portrayed in victory over the Philistines while Saul was shown in defeat. David's burning of the Philistine gods and expulsion of them from the land is in triumphant contrast to the events of chapter 10.

(b) The contrast with David's setback in chapter 13 is effected by the repeated use of the verb *parats*. In the bearing of the ark to Kiriath-jearim God had broken forth (*parats*) upon Uzzah (13:11) hence the name Perez (-ts)-Uzza). Now the same verb is used to describe God's breaking through the Philistines, at Baal-Peraz(-ts-)im. The effect is an affirmation of the fact that God is still fundamentally intent upon the establishment of his purpose through David. He has not turned against David in any way that threatens his underlying commitment to him. David's basic orientation in chapter 13 has, of course, been right, even if the practice was not perfect, and Chr. is anxious to insist that David's "seeking" of the ark betrays his real character as one who "seeks" the Lord. Yet he is far from irreproachable, and the Lord's bearing with him is a measure of his patience and grace. This is a bigger theme in the Books of Samuel, especially 2 Sam. 9–20, which Chr. has omitted. But Chr. has not abandoned realism. And the combination of the two contrasts which we have seen in this chapter is a powerful testimony to God's persistence in his plan of salvation despite the great shortcomings of his chosen human instruments.

(c) Every Christian is part of God's continuing plan for the redemption of the world. It may be that, even in rightly identifying the way in which God could advance his purposes through us, we are often less than satisfactory in the practice of it. But here we have a picture of a God who kindly overrules, sets us back on the path and refreshes our vision.

A final point is in place. God does, of course, involve us in his service simply because of the favour which he bestows upon us as individuals. But that favour is never in isolation from our belonging to the community of his people. This is the point of v. 2. David's kingdom is established *for the sake of his people Israel*. The high distinction bestowed upon David has the overarching purpose of blessing all the people of God. So it is with every gift of distinction which a Christian enjoys. Here is another contrast with the tragic case of Uzzah. There a responsibility was poorly discharged and someone else suffered. But God does and will use us on behalf of his people in spite of our failures. That is a perspective which should motivate us whenever we feel closeted with our inadequacies, and spur us to exercise our gifts for the immediate good of the people of God and the ultimate establishment of his kingdom.

A NEW OPPORTUNITY...

1 Chronicles 15:1–29

¹David built houses for himself in the city of David; and he prepared a place for the ark of God, and pitched a tent for it. ²Then David said, "No one but the Levites may carry the ark of God, for the Lord chose them to carry the ark of the Lord and to minister to him for ever." ³And David assembled all Israel at Jerusalem, to bring up the ark of the Lord to its place, which he had prepared for it. ⁴And David gathered together the sons of Aaron and the Levites: ⁵of the sons of Kohath, Uriel the chief, with a hundred and twenty of his brethren; ⁶of the sons of Merari, Asaiah the chief, with two hundred and twenty of his brethren; ⁷of the sons of Gershom, Joel the chief, with a hundred and thirty of his brethren; ⁸of the sons of Elizaphan, Shemaiah the chief, with two hundred of his brethren; ⁹of the sons of Hebron, Eliel the chief, with eighty of his brethren; ¹⁰of the sons of Uzziel, Amminadab the chief, with a hundred and twelve of his brethren. ¹¹Then David summoned the priests Zadok and Abiathar, and the Levites Uriel, Asaiah, Joel, Shemaiah, Eliel, and Amminadab, ¹²and said to them, "You are the heads of the fathers' houses of the Levites; sanctify yourselves, you and your brethren, so that you may bring up the ark of the Lord, the God of Israel, to the place that I have prepared for it. ¹³Because you did not carry it the first time, the Lord our God broke forth upon us, because we did not care for it in the way that is ordained." ¹⁴So the priests and the Levites sanctified themselves to bring up the ark of the Lord, the God of Israel. ¹⁵And the Levites carried the ark of God upon their shoulders with the poles, as Moses had commanded according to the word of the Lord.

¹⁶David also commanded the chiefs of the Levites to appoint their brethren as the singers who should play loudly on musical instruments, on harps and lyres and cymbals, to raise sounds of joy. ¹⁷So the Levites appointed Heman the son of Joel; and of his brethren Asaph the son of Berechiah; and of the sons of Merari, their brethren, Ethan the son of

Kushaiah; [18]and with them their brethren of the second order, Zechariah, Jaaziel, Shemiramoth, Jehiel, Unni, Eliab, Benaiah, Maaseiah, Mattithiah, Eliphelehu, and Mikneiah, and the gatekeepers Obed-edom and Jeiel. [19]The singers, Heman, Asaph, and Ethan, were to sound bronze cymbals; [20]Zechariah, Aziel, Shemiramoth, Jehiel, Unni, Eliab, Maaseiah, and Benaiah were to play harps according to Alamoth; [21]but Mattithiah, Eliphelehu, Mikneiah, Obed-edom, Jeiel, and Azaziah were to lead with lyres according to the Sheminith. [22]Chenaniah, leader of the Levites in music, should direct the music, for he understood it. [23]Berechiah and Elkanah were to be gatekeepers for the ark. [24]Shebaniah, Joshaphat, Nethanel, Amasai, Zechariah, Benaiah, and Eliezer, the priests, should blow the trumpets before the ark of God. Obed-edom and Jehiah also were to be gatekeepers for the ark.

[25]So David and the elders of Israel, and the commanders of thousands, went to bring up the ark of the covenant of the Lord from the house of Obed-edom with rejoicing. [26]And because God helped the Levites who were carrying the ark of the covenant of the Lord, they sacrified seven bulls and seven rams. [27]David was clothed with a robe of fine linen, as also were all the Levites who were carrying the ark, and the singers, and Chenaniah the leader of the music of the singers; and David wore a linen ephod. [28]So all Israel brought up the ark of the covenant of the Lord with shouting, to the sound of the horn, trumpets, and cymbals, and made loud music on harps and lyres.

[29]And as the ark of the covenant of the Lord came to the city of David, Michal the daughter of Saul looked out of the window, and saw King David dancing and making merry; and she despised him in her heart.

(i)

Following the unfortunate first attempt to bring the ark up to Jerusalem (chapter 13), David is now determined to do the thing properly. We noticed above that the fate of Uzzah was associated with David's earlier failure in respect of cultic rectitude. The first few verses of our chapter do not appear in the corresponding 2 Sam. 6, and their concern is to picture David paying careful attention precisely to those things which he had neglected before. This concern is evident first in vv. 1–3, where Chr. makes explicit certain preparations for bringing the ark to Jerusalem, which the author of 2 Sam 6:12ff. merely presupposes. He first prepares a "place" for it, not, obviously, the Temple which has not yet been constructed but presumably a separated part of the city, respecting the requirements of the law regarding distinctions between holy and profane (see, for example, Lev. 17:3ff.). In that place, he pitches a "tent", perhaps corresponding to the Tent of Meeting which, in the wilderness period, had contained ark and tabernacle (Exod. 26: 7ff.). The actual Tent of Meeting still stood at Gibeon (cf. 2 Chr. 1:3). David, therefore, chooses not to move the Tent of Meeting itself. (We are told in 1 Kings 8:4 that Solomon later brought the Tent of Meeting, along with the ark, into the Temple. Whether the original tent at Gibeon is meant, or David's newer substitute, is not clear.) But his course of action is in any case motivated by a concern to discharge his duties properly in relation to God's law.

Most significantly (v. 2), he ensures, with some attention to detail, that the ark will be borne in the appointed manner, by Levites only (Deut. 10:8; cf. Num. 4:1–15, and, for the regulation about the poles, Exod. 25:13f.). Their "sanctification" (vv. 12, 14) refers to ritual preparation, the terms of this possibly being contained in Exod. 19:14f., 22, where the idea of God "breaking out" (*parats*) upon the people provides a link with the fate of Uzzah, a recurrence of which David's preparations are designed to avoid (see above on chapters 13, 14). The story of David's concern for correct practice in relation to ark-bearing reaches its climax in v. 26, which tells (as does 2 Sam. 6) how sacrifices of thanksgiving were made when the ark was seen to have successfully resumed its journey to Jerusalem. Unlike the Samuel passage, Chr. spells out that the success has been due to God "helping" the Levites, his help coming in return for ritual faithfulness. (On the theme of "help", see above on 1 Chr. 12.)

Second time round, therefore, David gets it right. Second opportunities, in the grace of God, do come. For Christians they will not be in terms of close attention to the details of ritual regulation, since these no longer apply directly. But the lives of many Christians are littered with missed opportunities of one sort or another—whether in terms of the fostering of relationships within the Church and outside it with a view to ministry and witness; or the use of a God-given talent in the context of the Church's work; or assent to a particular course of action to which we know God has been calling us.

Opportunity has been figuratively depicted as a man who runs past. He only runs past once, and must be grasped at the crucial moment. From his forehead hangs a forelock of hair by which he must be caught. There is nothing to lay hold of at the back of his head. Once past, he is gone forever. No doubt such a picture accurately portrays some, perhaps much, human experience. But it is not a Christian picture of life. Rather it derives from a view of reality according to which human experience is subject to forces that are impersonal, insensitive, even cynical. The God of the Bible is very different. He forgives indefinitely (cf. Matt. 18:21f.); and he piles opportunity upon opportunity. Some Christians squander useful time and emotional energy in what Dr. Martyn Lloyd-Jones in his book *Spiritual Depression* has called "vain regrets". In his relations with human beings God is supremely the one who "lets bygones be bygones", in a completely unqualified way. That is what the cross means to the repentant sinner. And it means that *today* we can concentrate our energies on seeking and taking the fresh opportunities which God lays before us, rather than lamenting uselessly those that we missed in the past.

...AND NEW DUTIES

1 Chronicles 15:1–29 (*cont'd*)

(ii)

We have noticed at an earlier stage how the worship of the God of Israel is a joyful thing (12:40). Joy also attends this the most significant event in David's reign (v. 25). In fact, so much does David recognize that his God is a God of joy that he more or less institutionalizes it by establishing a choir and orchestra whose charter is precisely "to raise sounds of joy" (v. 16). David is rightly hailed, then, as the fountainhead of Israelite song, though he is seen here as a delegator rather than a composer in his own right. (Notice especially the name of Asaph, which often occurs in Psalm headings, e.g. Ps. 82. It is often said, on the other hand, that the Psalm heading "A Psalm of David" could equally well mean "A Psalm *for* David". This better reflects the picture we have here—although clearly David is elsewhere portrayed as a musician himself, 1 Sam. 16:14ff.)

We are bound to say that the present passage falls short of being a charter for church choirs! We cannot transpose the regulations for Israel's temple worship so simply to that of our churches—just as we cannot in any simple way assimilate her laws into our ethics. The duty of song as specifically laid upon the Levites is part of irreversibly obsolete arrangements. But if there is no specific legislation here, yet we must nevertheless sing, just because God is the God of joy, and because he has given music to humanity as one of her chief ways of expressing it (notice how quickly our primeval forefathers cottoned on, Gen. 4:21). Chr., furthermore, often stresses the need for excellence in the service of God, as we have seen in relation to David's warriors (12:2, 32; on singers, cf. also 25:7). And this leads us back, by a circuitous route, to saying that the pursuit of excellence in church music is a good in itself (though not of course an *end* in itself). Where the resources exist, therefore, it is right that those who are appropriately gifted should lead in that ministry and achieve the highest possible standards. Yet because the worship of the Temple does not *legislate* for church music, so we must not think the worship of smaller and relatively poorly equipped assemblies of God's people inferior because of its technical defects. If God looks upon the heart in relation to the character of our lives, he will also look upon our intentions in relation to the outward expression of our worship.

(iii)

A further point has to be made in relation to the Levites' musical duties. These duties were a new departure for them. It is occasioned by the fact that the ark, which has now found a permanent resting-place, no longer needs to be carried, and therefore the Levites have lost an important part of their raison d'être. In God's purposes, however, they acquire a new role, and resources are found among them to discharge it adequately. If there were those among the Levites who found it difficult or distasteful to adapt to new duties we learn nothing of it from Chr. The need to change the pattern of one's life, sometimes in a fundamental way, can come to Christians as to others. And while the Levites in our passage evince nothing of it there is often a natural resistance to it, whether advancing years have made change of any sort difficult to accept, or because a mode of living that once was fresh and vital and relevant, corresponding to a call and vision from God, has now become *merely* a mode of living, an end in itself. Here is one practical implication of what it is to "seek God" (one of Chr.'s great themes). It is a mistake to think that a Christian's calling, or ministry, or life-style is fixed once for all by some determinative early experience of God, after which the question of life-direction need no longer be raised. The failure to realize this can result in years wasted in irrelevancy, while new and exhilarating fields might have been explored and vital services rendered to God. We cannot be content with the memory of a voice heard once, long ago. Rather, the Christian must listen to what God is saying *today*, and let him challenge every aspect of his life-pattern, so that he lives each day in the light of a *fresh* vision of God's purposes for him.

(iv)

Like the author of 2 Sam., Chr. inserts a footnote on the sullen Michal (v. 29). Chr.'s point about Michal is rather different from that of 2 Sam. 6:20ff. There the reader senses a frustration and a jealousy, related to David's uninhibited celebration among the servant-girls, and her own childlessness. Here Michal's contempt appears to relate to the honour in which David holds the ark. The cameo makes the point that the character of Saul—whom Chr. has presented as typical of those who do *not* seek the things of God—has been transmitted to his family. So it is with sin. It is misguided to suppose that there are sins which "do nobody any harm". The effects of sin are not described exhaustively when those which are immediate and obvious have been observed. We do not do our duty to those whom we influence simply by minding our "p's and q's", but rather by cultivating character. And the principle is most applicable in relation to our children.

BLESSED BE THE LORD—I

1 Chronicles 16:1–43

¹And they brought in the ark of God, and set it inside the tent which David had pitched for it; and they offered burnt offerings and peace offerings before God. ²And when David had finished offering the burnt offerings and the peace offerings, he blessed the people in the name of the Lord, ³and distributed to all Israel, both men and women, to each a loaf of bread, a portion of meat, and a cake of raisins.

⁴Moreover he appointed certain of the Levites as ministers before the ark of the Lord, to invoke, to thank, and to praise the Lord, the God of Israel. ⁵Asaph was the chief, and second to him were Zechariah, Jeiel, Shemiramoth, Jehiel, Mattithiah, Eliab, Benaiah, Obed-edom, and Jeiel, who were to play harps and lyres; Asaph was to sound the cymbals, ⁶and Benaiah and Jahaziel the priests were to blow trumpets continually, before the ark of the covenant of God.

⁷Then on that day David first appointed that thanksgiving be sung to the Lord by Asaph and his brethren.

⁸O give thanks to the Lord, call on his name,
    make known his deeds among the peoples!
⁹Sing to him, sing praises to him,
    tell of all his wonderful works!
¹⁰Glory in his holy name;
    let the hearts of those who seek the Lord rejoice!
¹¹Seek the Lord and his strength,
    seek his presence continually!
¹²Remember the wonderful works that he has done,
    the wonders he wrought, the judgments he uttered,
¹³O offspring of Abraham his servant,
    sons of Jacob, his chosen ones!

¹⁴He is the Lord our God;

his judgments are in all the earth.
¹⁵He is mindful of his covenant for ever,
of the word that he commanded, for a thousand generations,
¹⁶the covenant which he made with Abraham,
his sworn promise to Isaac,
¹⁷which he confirmed as a statute to Jacob,
as an everlasting covenant to Israel,
¹⁸saying, "To you I will give the land of Canaan,
as your portion for an inheritance."

¹⁹When they were few in number,
and of little account, and sojourners in it,
²⁰wandering from nation to nation,
from one kingdom to another people,
²¹he allowed no one to oppress them;
he rebuked kings on their account,
²²saying, "Touch not my anointed ones,
do my prophets no harm!"

²³Sing to the Lord, all the earth!
Tell of his salvation from day to day.
²⁴Declare his glory among the nations,
his marvellous works among all the peoples!
²⁵For great is the Lord, and greatly to be praised,
and he is to be held in awe above all gods.
²⁶For all the gods of the peoples are idols;
but the Lord made the heavens.
²⁷Honour and majesty are before him;
strength and joy are in his place.

²⁸Ascribe to the Lord, O families of the peoples,
ascribe to the Lord glory and strength!
²⁹Ascribe to the Lord the glory due his name;
bring an offering, and come before him!
Worship the Lord in holy array;
³⁰ tremble before him, all the earth;
yea, the world stands firm, never to be moved.
³¹Let the heavens be glad, and let the earth rejoice,
and let them say among the nations, "The Lord reigns!"
³²Let the sea roar, and all that fills it,
let the field exult, and everything in it!
³³Then shall the trees of the wood sing for joy

before the Lord, for he comes to judge the earth.
³⁴O give thanks to the Lord, for he is good;
   for his steadfast love endures for ever!

³⁵Say also:
   "Deliver us, O God of our salvation,
      and gather and save us from among the nations,
   that we may give thanks to thy holy name,
      and glory in thy praise.
³⁶Blessed be the Lord, the God of Israel,
   from everlasting to everlasting!"

Then all the people said "Amen!" and praised the Lord.
   ³⁷So David left Asaph and his brethren there before the ark of the
covenant of the Lord to minister continually before the ark as each day
required, ³⁸and also Obed-edom and his sixty-eight brethren; while
Obed-edom, the son of Jeduthun, and Hosah were to be gatekeepers.
³⁹And he left Zadok the priest and his brethren the priests before the
tabernacle of the Lord in the high place that was at Gibeon, ⁴⁰to offer
burnt offerings to the Lord upon the altar of burnt offering continually
morning and evening, according to all that is written in the law of the
Lord which he commanded Israel. ⁴¹With them were Heman and
Jeduthun, and the rest of those chosen and expressly named to give
thanks to the Lord, for his steadfast love endures for ever. ⁴²Heman
and Jeduthun had trumpets and cymbals for the music and instruments
for sacred song. The sons of Jeduthun were appointed to the gate.
   ⁴³Then all the people departed each to his house, and David went
home to bless his household.

The account of the bringing up of the ark now reaches its climax
with its coming to rest in the tent which David has pitched for it.
The atmosphere continues to be one of celebration. David pre-
sides over the whole affair, evidently directing, or temporarily
taking over, the priestly duty of "blessing the people" (v. 2; cf.
Deut. 10:8). The distribution of various foods is no mere royal
bounty, but has a symbolic character, re-affirming to the people
God's good intention to let them enjoy the good things of the
promised land.
   The bulk of the chapter consists of the great Psalm of praise
which is sung by Asaph and his brethren. Chr. not only tells us
that David organized the music, but it gives us an example of it.

The writer almost certainly does not mean that the people used *only* these words in the course of what must have been a major celebration. Nor does the Psalm *merely* exemplify the art of David's musicians, or the temple liturgy. Rather the Chronicler makes the point that he is recording one of the major events with which his whole work is concerned. (Notice how great events in Israel's history are typically marked by celebration with music, cf. Exod. 15; Neh. 12.)

All the elements of the psalm are drawn from the Psalter. (Verses 8–22 = Ps. 105:1–15; vv. 23–33 = Ps. 96:1–13; v. 34 = Ps. 106:1; vv. 35f. = Ps. 106:47f. For that reason no attempt is made here to give a full exposition. The reader is referred to the volumes in this series on the Psalms.) In examining the Psalm we must ask why this particular material is presented to us from so much that might have been used on the occasion in question.

BLESSED BE THE LORD—II

1 Chronicles 16:1–43 (*cont'd*)

Notice first how the Psalm gives expression to themes which we have already seen to characterize Chr. in general.

(a) Verses 8–18 focus the attention on God's deeds, and exhort the hearers to remember them (v. 12). The Chronicler's whole history is designed precisely to set before the restoration community the great things which God has done in Israel heretofore. The exhortation to "seek the Lord", v. 11, is generally significant in Chr., and in this context makes the necessary qualification that the enjoyment of God's favour depends upon devotion to him.

Verses 15–18 go on to specify God's deeds in terms of covenant, and the promise of land made to the patriarchs long ago. The focus on the land as the substance of the promise (v. 18), and the description of the Covenant as "everlasting" (v. 17), will have had special significance for the small and sometimes beleaguered restoration community. The invocation of the patriarchal name and promises in this poetic and rhetorical style is an effective complement to Chr.'s normal historiography, and participation in the singing of words like these must have helped the people of the restoration really to experience the things they knew in their minds to be true.

(b) Verses 19–22 centre on Israel's small numbers. This theme is central to the OT's theology of election (cf. Deut. 7:6ff., as well as Ps. 105). We have seen the Chronicler reflect upon it particularly in the genealogies. And once again it has particular reverberations for the community of his own day, so obviously vulnerable, and dependent on the goodwill of its neighbours. *This* community, he urges, is still the people of God, and enjoys his protection.

(c) Verses 23–36. The election of Israel has as its implication God's reign over all the nations. The point is made in different ways. First, there is a contrast between the Lord and the gods of other nations, in line with the numerous OT passages which insist that Israel's God alone has real life and power (cf. Isa. 40:18ff.). The point recalls how Saul's disobedience (1 Chr. 10) sold Israel into the power of other gods (as would that of, for example, Ahaz, 2 Chr. 28:23). There is thus a powerful assurance, at this crucial moment, that ultimately the true power of God must prevail over the shadow of it possessed by other gods. Secondly, there is an appeal to the nations to honour Israel's God, an appeal which is given substance by Chr.'s record elsewhere of how the nations give recognition to him (cf. Hiram, 2 Chr. 2:12; the Queen of Sheba, 2 Chr. 9:8; Cyrus, 2 Chr. 36:23).

We have noticed on a number of occasions that the choice of Psalm-material would have spoken strongly to the community of the Chronicler's day. But he has in addition actually made changes to the Psalm-texts which he used. Verse 13, for example, should read "O offspring of Israel" rather than "of Abraham", RSV having misguidedly preserved that text as it is in the Book of Psalms (105:6), thus missing the Chronicler's point, namely that the community of his day is true Israel. RSV has similarly suppressed his alteration of "He is mindful" (v. 15; 105:8) to "Be mindful!" The note of exhortation is consistent with Chr.'s ubiquitous warning that God's people at any time only enjoy his benefits as long as they truly seek him. (For these and other changes to the Psalms' texts see the larger Commentaries.) Finally, vv. 35f. are readily comprehensible as the prayer of a people restored from exile, and sensing that their position among the nations is precarious.

How much the record of this act of praise became part of the Chronicler's work as he wrote is reflected in v. 41, where, though he has returned to prose, he cannot help introducing again the refrain from the Psalm "for his steadfast love endures for ever" when he names the Lord. Thus the praise of one generation inspires another, and modern Christians can appropriate it in the same way. Many must identify with the sense of fewness and vulnerability felt by the restoration community. Chr. directs us to ponder again on the great things God has done. For Christians such pondering will begin at the cross, continue with the times in their own experience when they have known God's mercies in a special way, and culminate in the final victory of Christ, when every knee shall bow in adoration of him.

DYNASTY—I

1 Chronicles 17:1–27

¹Now when David dwelt in his house, David said to Nathan the prophet, "Behold, I dwell in a house of cedar, but the ark of the covenant of the Lord is under a tent." ²And Nathan said to David, "Do all that is in your heart, for God is with you."

³But that same night the word of the Lord came to Nathan, ⁴"Go and tell my servant David, 'Thus says the Lord: You shall not build me a house to dwell in. ⁵For I have not dwelt in a house since the day I led up Israel to this day, but I have gone from tent to tent and from dwelling to dwelling. ⁶In all places where I have moved with all Israel, did I speak a word with any of the judges of Israel, whom I commanded to shepherd my people, saying, "Why have you not built me a house of cedar?"' ⁷Now therefore thus shall you say to my servant David, 'Thus says the Lord of hosts, I took you from the pasture, from following the sheep, that you should be prince over my people Israel; ⁸and I have been with you wherever you went, and have cut off all your enemies

from before you; and I will make for you a name, like the name of the great ones of the earth. ⁹And I will appoint a place for my people Israel, and will plant them, that they may dwell in their own place, and be disturbed no more; and violent men shall waste them no more, as formerly, ¹⁰from the time that I appointed judges over my people Israel; and I will subdue all your enemies. Moreover I declare to you that the Lord will build you a house. ¹¹When your days are fulfilled to go to be with your fathers, I will raise up your offspring after you, one of your own sons, and I will establish his kingdom. ¹²He shall build a house for me, and I will establish his throne for ever. ¹³I will be his father, and he shall be my son; I will not take my steadfast love from him, as I took it from him who was before you, ¹⁴but I will confirm him in my house and in my kingdom for ever and his throne shall be established for ever.'" ¹⁵In accordance with all these words, and in accordance with all this vision, Nathan spoke to David.

¹⁶Then King David went in and sat before the Lord, and said, "Who am I, O Lord God, and what is my house, that thou hast brought me thus far? ¹⁷And this was a small thing in thy eyes, O God; thou hast also spoken of thy servant's house for a great while to come, and hast shown me future generations, O Lord God! ¹⁸And what more can David say to thee for honouring thy servant? For thou knowest thy servant. ¹⁹For thy servant's sake, O Lord, and according to thy own heart, thou hast wrought all this greatness, in making known all these great things. ²⁰There is none like thee, O Lord, and there is no God besides thee, according to all that we have heard with our ears. ²¹What other nation on earth is like thy people Israel, whom God went to redeem to be his people, making for thyself a name for great and terrible things, in driving out nations before thy people whom thou didst redeem from Egypt? ²²And thou didst make thy people Israel to be thy people for ever; and thou, O Lord, didst become their God. ²³And now, O Lord, let the word which thou hast spoken concerning thy servant and concerning his house be established for ever, and do as thou hast spoken; ²⁴and thy name will be established and magnified for ever, saying, 'The Lord of hosts, the God of Israel, is Israel's God,' and the house of thy servant David will be established before thee. ²⁵For thou, my God, hast revealed to thy servant that thou wilt build a house for him; therefore thy servant has found courage to pray before thee. ²⁶And now, O Lord, thou art God, and thou hast promised this good thing to thy servant; ²⁷now therefore may it please thee to bless the house of thy servant, that it may continue for ever before thee; for what thou, O Lord, hast blessed is blessed for ever."

(i)

With the bringing of the ark to Jerusalem there is a sense in which David has already made his major contribution to the establishment of God's kingdom in Israel. Although Solomon himself does not properly take the stage until 2 Chr. 1, everything now points forward to the time when he will do so. The central issue in this chapter—vital in the theology of Chr.—is: who will build the house of the Lord? It is David's desire to do this himself (v. 1). God replies, however, that it is not to be David's task, but rather that of Solomon. (This is the real implication of v. 4, i.e. *not* that a house is not to be built at all.) Elsewhere (1 Chr. 22:8) the explanation of why David is not God's choice for building the Temple is given in terms of his great shedding of blood in war. In Chr.'s theology, therefore, David, that man of war, can do no more than prepare for the *peaceful* reign of his son Solomon, in which the Temple will be built.

David's warlike activities, it should be said, are not made the cause of a general condemnation of the man. On the contrary, we have seen how God gave him victories in direct consequence of his faithfulness in seeking him (14:10ff.). And the achievements of David cannot be underestimated. His "dwelling in his house" in Jerusalem was the fruit of brilliant manoeuvring, in terms of inner-Israelite politics as well as military might, for the northern and southern halves of David's kingdom were no natural bedfellows, as subsequent events would show. The point is rather that there are varieties of service within God's purposes.

And this is true not only in a general sense of the Church at any given time. But there are different times: a time for conquest, and a time for consolidation; a time for stern resistance to worldly pressures, and a time for standing alongside the unchurched in compassion and winsomeness. Often we may have to accept that the work which we would dearly like to perform in terms of Christian service is not that for which we are best equipped, and not that to which God has in fact called us. It may be, like David's, a preparatory work, leading to something more obviously grand. Recognition and acceptance of our true measure is the first and necessary step towards seeing the significance of what, in God's purposes, we really can achieve and have achieved.

(ii)

There is, in fact, an "education" of David in this chapter. We have seen before (in relation to Uzzah, 13:9ff.) that the great David, though the instrument of God's purposes, was capable of misunderstanding and negligence, and how he was brought to a better understanding. Here too we see a movement. The incompleteness of David's understanding is reflected in his conception of God's "house". His idea is purely material. He will, he thinks, build for the Lord a house like his own. Now the Chronicler by no means despises the desire to build a house, in the bricks-and-mortar sense, for the Lord. The Lord's refusal to allow David to build presupposes that a house will nevertheless be built sometime. But the point of vv. 5ff. is that the relationship which God has with his people, through their leaders, has never depended, and can never depend, upon the mere construction of a building. (The parallel passage in 2 Sam. 7 makes this point more strongly and may actually express a fundamental distaste on the Lord's part for the very idea of a Temple. In the Chronicler's day, of course, the issue of *whether* there should be a Temple in Israel is long dead. The idea has been accepted into Israel's religion and attitudes to it can become a symbol of faithfulness or otherwise; cf. the prophet Haggai's exhortation to re-build the Temple in the immediate wake of exile, Hag. 1:2ff.)

To this end the Lord subtly shifts the meaning of the word "house". In vv. 7–10 he reassures David of his protection of his people, and his establishment of them in a "place" (v. 9) of their own, free from the ravages of enemies. (Perhaps the need for some outward sign of a divine guarantee was at the back of David's mind in his desire to build the Temple.) But then (v. 10) he shows that the building of a house is more than this. "The *Lord* will build *you* a house," he says, in a remarkable reversal of David's plan (v. 1). To this extent had David failed to appreciate that it was the Lord who was the real architect of the continuing healthy relationship between himself and his people. "House" gradually becomes synonymous with "kingdom" (v. 14), and both belong to the Lord. The establishment of Solomon, and the building of a bricks-and-mortar house by that king, will be the outward sign that the promise has been realized.

DYNASTY—II

1 Chronicles 17:1–27 (*cont'd*)

(iii)

It is the recognition of the Lord's own kingship in the affairs of his people that dominates David's prayer (vv. 16–27). The prayer itself is the greatest of those which David prays in 1 Chr. (along with 29:10ff.), and this is a measure of the importance of the subject-matter of the chapter. Two points may be noted.

(a) David has become sensitive to his actual humility before God. There is, in vv. 16–20, an awe at the greatness of God and an amazement that God should so elevate him. (The last clause of v. 17 is obscure, but may well be best rendered: ". . . and [thou] hast regarded me after the manner of a man of high degree".) The fact that God "knows" him enhances the astonishment. David has thus gained (or regained) a right proportion. It is interesting that in v. 23 he prays: "do as thou hast spoken." This is almost certainly a deliberate reflection of Nathan's "Do all that is in your heart", addressed to David in v. 2. That first response of Nathan to David's plan to build up the Temple is puzzling, in view of the fact that it is immediately overruled by a word that comes to the prophet that very night. Did Nathan simply get it wrong the first time? Whatever was in Nathan's mind, this first response plays a more profound role in the chapter than a mere error. The contrast between v. 2 and v. 23 shows that David has come to appreciate that to ask God to do according to his word is better than to act precipitately according to his own perceptions, even if highly intentioned. Of course, we must always ultimately act on the basis of our perceptions. But they must be informed, and transformed, by unremitting exposure to the word of God.

(b) David's perspective has now broadened so that he sees God not only as *his* God, but as God of the people of Israel. His concept of his own leadership is now set in the context of God's plan to make his glory known before the world by means of all that he has done for Israel. Notice the repetition of the phrase "for ever". The people belong to God "for ever" (v. 22); David prays that his dynasty will be established "for ever" (v. 23); and thus the Lord's name will be magnified "for ever" (v. 24) in the eyes of all the world. We must discuss the exact meaning of this phrase in a moment. Let us notice for now that it is God's firm and enduring purpose to display before the world that he is God. (cf. prophetic statements such as Isa. 2:2–4; 45:22f.) David's servant-role in preparing for Solomon and the Temple is subordinate to this overarching servant-role which he shares with all God's people before and since.

(iv)

It remains to ask in what sense the promise to David and his sons can rightly be said to be "for ever". The promise here and in 2 Sam. 7 is often said by commentators to be unconditional, and to stand therefore in stark contrast to the Covenant with Moses at Sinai (cf. Exod. chs. 20–23; Deut. ch. 28). Indeed, it may be that a belief in an unconditional promise of God's dwelling with David and Israel underlay much of the complacency which the prophets found in relation to God's laws. (cf. Jer. 7:1–15, where the prophet castigates the people's trust in the mere possession of the trappings of religion, especially the Temple, and their contempt for the moral demands of God.) 1 Chr. 17 can even appear more thoroughly unconditional than 2 Sam. 7 because Chr. omits the warning in 2 Sam. 7:14 that God will chasten any member of the dynasty who does wrong.

Two points must be made, however.

(a) The commitment "for ever" is never quite unconditional. In 1 Sam. 2:30 the Lord, addressing Eli the priest, refers to a promise made to his forefather Levi that his descendants should serve as priests "for ever". But even in mentioning that commitment, the Lord abrogates it, declaring: "Far be it from me; for those who honour me I will honour, and those who despise me shall be lightly esteemed." The real force of the Lord's promise "for ever" is that on *his* side the commitment is absolute and enduring. But every such commitment carries with it the condition, expressed or not, of man's obedient response.

(b) The context of Chr. as a whole makes it clear that the need for such response is taken for granted here. We have seen that the whole point of the contrast between Saul and David was to illustrate the need for "seeking" God. And the immediate context of chapter 17 itself makes its own contribution to the theme, because of the way in which the promise—and David's fuller realization of all that God has done in the past—*produces* his prayer. This causal relationship is no accident. It is made explicit in v. 25, where David says that he has found (literally) the *heart* to pray as a direct result of God's word to him. And we have thus an important perspective upon the nature of human response to God. Other contexts (e.g. Deut. 28) major upon sanctions as a motive to response, and this represents one side of biblical teaching. But the whole biblical psychology of response lays much stress upon the kindling of gratitude and the conditioning of the heart by means of the persuasion that God, in all his majesty, has acted and will act on the individual's behalf, beyond all reason or merit. David, with his new-found wonder at God's commitment to him, can still pray for the continuation of his own line (v. 27). But notice that there is no thought of it continuing for its own sake. Rather he prays that it may continue for ever "before thee". And this carries with it the assertion that it will conform to God's desires for it. Here is a right response to the recognition of gifts from God—the resolution to put them at his disposal without reservation. The unconditionality in the chapter is on both sides.

(v)

But it may be that we have not finally answered the question what we, with the advantages of our historical perspective, are to make of a promise "for ever" to a dynasty which did in fact cease to exist a few centuries after David. Part of the answer lies in the conditionality which we have already recognized in the promise.

But there is a further perspective. It could be argued that one of the Chronicler's purposes in devoting so much space to both David and Solomon is to show that it was their combined reigns which established God's promise. 1 Chr. 28:7 shows that Solomon in particular was expected to obey God. The subsequent depiction of Solomon's reign (2 Chr. 1–9) is intended to show that he did in fact do so. And, therefore, despite the vagaries of subsequent kings, the promise is seen as finally established (cf. 2 Chr. 13:5). We have to remember that not only do we have hindsight but that the Chronicler too is writing his account, and spelling out the significance of the royal promise, a couple of centuries after the actual demise of the monarchy. If, then, the royal promise has abiding relevance, but was not manifested in his day, it must have a still future significance. In one sense, from his viewpoint, his writings come to his small, politically disadvantaged community with the message that it is still the people of God and must respond as such here and now—a message that is ever relevant to the Church. But equally, the hope is extended that there is yet a glorious future for the people of God. And that is a perspective which we too must not lose.

DAVID'S WARS—I

1 Chronicles 18:1–20:8

18 ¹After this David defeated the Philistines and subdued them, and he took Gath and its villages out of the hand of the Philistines.

²And he defeated Moab, and the Moabites became servants to David and brought tribute.

³David also defeated Hadadezer king of Zobah, toward Hamath, as he went to set up his monument at the river Euphrates. ⁴And David took from him a thousand chariots, seven thousand horsemen, and twenty thousand foot soldiers; and David hamstrung all the chariot horses, but left enough for a hundred chariots. ⁵And when the Syrians of Damascus came to help Hadadezer king of Zobah, David slew twenty-two thousand men of the Syrians. ⁶Then David put garrisons in Syria of Damascus; and the Syrians became servants to David, and brought tribute. And the Lord gave victory to David wherever he went.

⁷And David took the shields of gold which were carried by the servants of Hadadezer, and brought them to Jerusalem. ⁸And from Tibhath and from Cun, cities of Hadadezer, David took very much bronze; with it Solomon made the bronze sea and the pillars and the vessels of bronze.

⁹When Tou king of Hamath heard that David had defeated the whole army of Hadadezer, king of Zobah, ¹⁰he sent his son Hadoram to King David, to greet him, and to congratulate him because he had fought against Hadadezer and defeated him; for Hadadezer had often been at war with Tou. And he sent all sorts of articles of gold, of silver, and of bronze; ¹¹these also King David dedicated to the Lord, together with the silver and gold which he had carried off from all the nations, from Edom, Moab, the Ammonites, the Philistines, and Amalek.

¹²And Abishai, the son of Zeruiah, slew eighteen thousand Edomites in the Valley of Salt. ¹³And he put garrisons in Edom; and all the Edomites became David's servants. And the Lord gave victory to David wherever he went.

¹⁴So David reigned over all Israel; and he administered justice and equity to all his people. ¹⁵And Joab the son of Zeruiah was over the army; and Jehoshaphat the son of Ahilud was recorder; ¹⁶and Zadok the son of Ahitub and Ahimelech the son of Abiathar were priests; and Shavsha was secretary; ¹⁷and Benaiah the son of Jehoiada was over the Cherethites and the Pelethites; and David's sons were the chief officials in the service of the king.

19 ¹Now after this Nahash the king of the Ammonites died, and his son reigned in his stead. ²And David said, "I will deal loyally with Hanun the son of Nahash, for his father dealt loyally with me." So David sent messengers to console him concerning his father. And David's servants came to Hanun in the land of the Ammonites, to console him. ³But the princes of the Ammonites said to Hanun, "Do you think, because David has sent comforters to you, that he is honouring your father? Have not his servants come to you to search and to overthrow and to spy out the land?" ⁴So Hanun took David's servants, and shaved them, and cut off their garments in the middle, at their hips, and sent them away; ⁵and they departed. When David was told concerning the men, he sent to meet them, for the men were greatly ashamed. And the king said, "Remain at Jericho until your beards have grown, and then return."

⁶When the Ammonites saw that they had made themselves odious to David, Hanun and the Ammonites sent a thousand talents of silver to

hire chariots and horsemen from Mesopotamia, from Aram-maacah, and from Zobah. [7]They hired thirty-two thousands chariots and the king of Maacah with his army, who came and encamped before Medeba. And the Ammonites were mustered from their cities and came to battle. [8]When David heard of it, he sent Joab and all the army of the mighty men. [9]And the Ammonites came out and drew up in battle array at the entrance of the city, and the kings who had come were by themselves in the open country.

[10]When Joab saw that the battle was set against him both in front and in the rear, he chose some of the picked men of Israel, and arrayed them against the Syrians; [11]the rest of his men he put in the charge of Abishai his brother, and they were arrayed against the Ammonites. [12]And he said, "If the Syrians are too strong for me, then you shall help me; but if the Ammonites are too strong for you, then I will help you. [13]Be of good courage, and let us play the man for our people, and for the cities of our God; and may the Lord do what seems good to him." [14]So Joab and the people who were with him drew near before the Syrians for battle; and they fled before him. [15]And when the Ammonites saw that the Syrians fled, they likewise fled before Abishai, Joab's brother, and entered the city. Then Joab came to Jerusalem.

[16]But when the Syrians saw that they had been defeated by Israel, they sent messengers and brought out the Syrians who were beyond the Euphrates, with Shophach the commander of the army of Hadadezer at their head. [17]And when it was told David, he gathered all Israel together, and crossed the Jordan, and came to them, and drew up his forces against them. And when David set the battle in array against the Syrians, they fought with him. [18]And the Syrians fled before Israel; and David slew of the Syrians the men of seven thousand chariots, and forty thousands foot soldiers, and killed also Shophach the commander of their army. [19]And when the servants of Hadadezer saw that they had been defeated by Israel, they made peace with David, and became subject to him. So the Syrians were not willing to help the Ammonites any more.

20 [1]In the spring of the year, the time when kings go forth to battle, Joab led out the army, and ravaged the country of the Ammonites, and came and besieged Rabbah. But David remained at Jerusalem. And Joab smote Rabbah, and overthrew it. [2]And David took the crown of their king from his head; he found that it weighed a talent of gold, and in it was a precious stone; and it was placed on David's head. And he brought forth the spoil of the city, a very great amount. [3]And he

brought forth the people who were in it, and set them to labour with saws and iron picks and axes; and thus David did to all the cities of the Ammonites. Then David and all the people returned to Jerusalem.

⁴And after this there arose war with the Philistines at Gezer; then Sibbecai the Hushathite slew Sippai, who was one of the descendants of the giants; and the Philistines were subdued. ⁵And there was again war with the Philistines; and Elhanan the son of Jair slew Lahmi the brother of Goliath the Gittite, the shaft of whose spear was like a weaver's beam. ⁶And there was again war at Gath, where there was a man of great stature, who had six fingers on each hand, and six toes on each foot, twenty-four in number; and he also was descended from the giants. ⁷And when he taunted Israel, Jonathan the son of Shimea, David's brother, slew him. ⁸These were descended from the giants in Gath; and they fell by the hand of David and by the hand of his servants.

The main point of chapters 18–20 is to confirm that the previous chapter identifies the role of David, in contrast to Solomon, as the warrior who by his victories achieved the peace which was to characterize his successor's reign. That David is not blamed for being a man of war is clear from the comment that appears twice in chapter 18: "And the Lord gave victory to David wherever he went" (vv. 6, 13). Indeed David's warlike exploits, paradoxically, contribute to the final success of the Temple project, since the booty acquired in them is used in the beautification of the building (v. 8; cf. 2 Chr. 5:1).

The account of David's wars in chapters 18–20 is drawn from various parts of 2 Sam. chs. 8–21. The unity of theme that is thus achieved is a result of the omission of a large amount of material in 2 Samuel. There, the Ammonite war, for example (2 Sam. chs. 10–11), is primarily a backcloth for the story of David's adultery with Bathsheba and related murder of Uriah. Those actions in turn spark off a series of events which are far from glorifying to the house of David (mainly Ammon's rape of Tamar, ch. 13, and Absalom's rebellion, chs. 15ff.). The omission of this block of material is as instructive as that which is included, for it shows that Chr. is determined to develop the theme of David's positive contribution to the establishment of God's kingdom in Israel, a purpose which would not have been served by the inclusion of evidence of his deficiencies. We saw at an earlier stage (concerning Uzzah and David's subsequent successes against the Philistines, chs. 13f.) how the Lord was prepared to continue with David as the instrument for achieving his purposes despite the negligence which had caused Uzzah's demise. The omission of the huge misdemeanours reported in 2 Sam. 9–20, with all their debilitating consequences for the kingdom, is further dramatic evidence of God's willingness to use even the most inconstant of people in his service. Christians often become obsessed by their failures. It is a measure of the grace of God that he is willing to put the best interpretation upon the most vacillating life of faith.

DAVID'S WARS—II

1 Chronicles 18:1–20:8 (*cont'd*)

The reader will have observed how difficult it is, in speaking of God's dealings with the people of OT times, to distinguish between his kingdom in a spiritual sense, and the human kingdom over which David was placed. In its former sense, of course, the word carries far more profound connotations, the kingdom, or kingship of God connoting something of his character and natural relationship to men. Yet the significance of the fact that he did actually bind himself to the nation Israel in OT times (Deut. 7:6–12) cannot be over-estimated. Indeed the implications of the fact that in the OT the people of God was also—for the greatest part of the period—a policital entity are usually overlooked when certain ethical aspects of the OT are examined.

The nationhood of God's people is a vital factor in the understanding of the presentation of war in the OT. As Christians, with access to the New Testament, we are accustomed, rightly, to think of the people of God as a spiritual entity, and this implies that our concepts both of the conflict with evil and of the business of proclaiming the kingdom of God are spiritual. In the OT the materiality of the people of God (though this does not carry with it an "unspirituality") implies that there is a material dimension to both these aspects of its life (i.e conflict and proclamation). The opposition of the Philistines, Moabites, Ammonites, etc., to Israel is opposition to God. (cf. the attitude to other nations in Deut. 7 when Israel's first possession of the land is envisaged.) Hanun's insult to David's servants (19:3–5) is an insult to God. It is against this backcloth that God's commissioning of David to fight must be viewed. It is not a justification of war as such. Nor can the OT be appealed to in any simple way as a vindication of any modern war. The idea of a "holy war" in the modern world is ruled out, in principle and absolutely, by virtue of the fact that the people of God is no longer a political entity. (This applies equally to "Christian" countries which use crusading language to justify wars which are really politico-ideological, and to the military enterprises of the modern state of Israel, which many Christians persist in thinking of as the "real" people of God, in the face of New Testament teaching to the effect that all men are now on an equal footing before him, Eph. 2:11–22.)

I have joined together above the ideas of conflict and proclamation. This is because the particular conflicts in which David's armies engage have the purpose of demonstrating the supremacy and reality of Israel's God. It would be absurd to think of the warriors of David, or indeed of David himself, as the champions of good ranged against the hosts of evil in any absolute sense. As men, the armies of Israel were no better than anyone else. They become the champions of right only inasmuch as they are the chosen people of God and the bearers of his name. The aim of battle, furthermore, despite its undeniable blood-thirstiness (19:18) is not destruction in itself, but the establishment, or re-establishment, of a right order in the world, i.e. an order in which the nations serve the true people of God (19:19), and therefore, implicitly, recognize God himself. (20:3 probably also pictures the mere subjugation of the Ammonites, as per RSV, rather than the cruel tortures which are suggested by some translations both of this verse and of 2 Sam. 12:31. The problem of interpretation arises from a corrupt text.)

There are several other problems of interpretation in chapters 18–20, which can only be adequately dealt with in a more technical Commentary. These are (i) the lineage of Zadok (18:16); (ii) the function of David's sons (18:17), and (iii) the identity of the slayer of Goliath (20:5). On the former two consult such a Commentary. The last requires some attention.

The story of David's remarkable defeat of the giant Goliath has come to epitomize any hugely ill-balanced contest in which the weaker party overcomes the stronger. It is known to the modern reader largely from 1 Sam. 17. Alongside this story the Books of Samuel also record that one Elhanan slew "Goliath the Gittite", a Philistine giant (2 Sam. 21:19). Chr. gives us yet another permutation, according to which Elhanan killed not Goliath himself but his brother, called Lahmi. The difference between 2 Sam. 21:19 and our passage is explicable, at least partly, on the grounds of textual corruption. But the question remains, Elhanan or David? A possible remedy for the problem is the postulation of a second Goliath and a second contest. Against this stands the mention of Goliath's spear, whose shaft was "like a weaver's beam". That this phrase exactly corresponds to the description of the more famous Goliath's spear (1 Sam. 17:7) suggests that it is in fact the same man. In favour of the possibility of a second Goliath, on the other hand, is the suggestion in 20:4–8 that Gath was renowned for its giants. That the name Goliath might have been borne by more than one giant is suggested not only by the character of the population of Gath, but more specifically by an inscription recently found on the tomb of a family named Goliath in Philistine territory, with the comment that its members were of unusually large stature.

It is ultimately impossible to resolve the problems, as indeed it is to be dogmatic one way or the other. It is easy to become unwarrantably rationalistic in the pursuit either of the defence of or an attack upon the integrity and reliability of the Bible. It is well known that the actual events of history can never be recovered by historical research, for they are far too diverse and intractable—quite apart from the fallibility of our human perception of them. The way of faith, when confronted with perplexing phenomena in the Bible, is to stand back, admit that fallibility, and trust that the Lord's word is indeed truth.

THE TEMPLE SITE LOCATED

1 Chronicles 21:1–22:1

[1]Satan stood up against Israel, and incited David to number Israel. [2]So David said to Joab and the commanders of the army, "Go, number Israel, from Beersheba to Dan, and bring me a report, that I may know their number." [3]But Joab said, "May the Lord add to his people a hundred times as many as they are! Are they not, my lord the king, all of them my lord's servants? Why then should my lord require this? Why should he bring guilt upon Israel?" [4]But the king's word prevailed against Joab. So Joab departed and went throughout all Israel, and came back to Jerusalem. [5]And Joab gave the sum of the numbering of the people to David. In all Israel there were one million one hundred thousand men who drew the sword, and in Judah four hundred and seventy thousand who drew the sword. [6]But he did not include Levi and Benjamin in the numbering, for the king's command was abhorrent to Joab.

[7]But God was displeased with this thing, and he smote Israel. [8]And David said to God, "I have sinned greatly in that I have done this thing. But now, I pray thee, take away the iniquity of thy servant; for I have done very foolishly." [9]And the Lord spoke to Gad, David's seer, saying, [10]"Go and say to David, 'Thus says the Lord, Three things I offer you; choose one of them, that I may do it to you.'" [11]So Gad came to David and said to him, "Thus says the Lord, 'Take which you will: [12]either three years of famine; or three months of devastation by your foes, while the sword of your enemies overtakes you; or else three days of the sword of the Lord, pestilence upon the land, and the angel of the Lord destroying throughout all the territory of Israel.' Now decide what answer I shall return to him who sent me." [13]Then David said to Gad, "I am in great distress; let me fall into the hand of the Lord, for his mercy is very great; but let me not fall into the hand of man."

[14]So the Lord sent a pestilence upon Israel; and there fell seventy thousand men of Israel. [15]And God sent the angel to Jerusalem to destroy it; but when he was about to destroy it, the Lord saw, and he repented of the evil; and he said to the destroying angel, "It is enough;

now stay your hand." And the angel of the Lord was standing by the threshing floor of Ornan the Jebusite. ¹⁶And David lifted his eyes and saw the angel of the Lord standing between earth and heaven, and in his hand a drawn sword stretched out over Jerusalem. Then David and the elders, clothed in sack-cloth, fell upon their faces. ¹⁷And David said to God, "Was it not I who gave command to number the people? It is I who have sinned and done very wickedly. But these sheep, what have they done? Let thy hand, I pray thee, O Lord my God, be against me and against my father's house; but let not the plague be upon thy people."

¹⁸Then the angel of the Lord commanded Gad to say to David that David should go up and rear an altar to the Lord on the threshing floor of Ornan the Jebusite. ¹⁹So David went up at Gad's word, which he had spoken in the name of the Lord. ²⁰Now Ornan was threshing wheat; he turned and saw the angel, and his four sons who were with him hid themselves. ²¹As David came to Ornan, Ornan looked and saw David and went forth from the threshing floor, and did obeisance to David with his face to the ground. ²²And David said to Ornan, "Give me the site of the threshing floor that I may build on it an altar to the Lord—give it to me at its full price—that the plague may be averted from the people." ²³Then Ornan said to David, "Take it; and let my lord the king do what seems good to him; see, I give the oxen for burnt offerings, and the threshing sledges for the wood, and the wheat for a cereal offering. I give it all." ²⁴But King David said to Ornan, "No, but I will buy it for the full price; I will not take for the Lord what is yours, nor offer burnt offerings which cost me nothing." ²⁵So David paid Ornan six hundred shekels of gold by weight for the site. ²⁶And David built there an altar to the Lord and presented burnt offerings and peace offerings, and called upon the Lord, and he answered him with fire from heaven upon the altar of burnt offering. ²⁷Then the Lord commanded the angel; and he put his sword back into its sheath.

²⁸At that time, when David saw that the Lord had answered him at the threshing floor of Ornan the Jebusite, he made his sacrifices there. ²⁹For the tabernacle of the Lord, which Moses had made in the wilderness, and the altar of burnt offering were at that time in the high place at Gibeon; ³⁰but David could not go before it to inquire of God, for he was afraid of the sword of the angel of the Lord. ¹Then David said, "Here shall be the house of the Lord God and here the altar of burnt offering for Israel."

The theme of the preparations for the building of the Temple continues. We have seen the promise to David that Solomon would be the builder (ch. 17), and how David's wars would contribute to the project (18–20). Now, in chapter 21, the site of the Temple is located. There is so much other important material in this chapter that its central purpose can be missed at first reading. Yet the Chronicler has taken pains (more than the author of 2 Sam. 24, the parallel passage) to show how all the events of the chapter serve that purpose. And in the end we see that the discovery of the location of the Temple site is only won through a scenario of sin, in all its mysteriousness, judgment and mercy. (Each of the following three subsections may be treated as a suitable portion for a daily meditation.)

THE SIN AND ITS CAUSES (21:1–6)

(a) The sin of David is remarkable both for its character and for the manner in which it is introduced. Suddenly Satan is on the stage. His entrance is the more striking because of the few appearances he makes in the OT (only here, in Job 1, 2 and Zech. 3:1f.). His name announces him as the accuser, but his essential crookedness is revealed here, by the way in which he seduces to the misdemeanours of which he would like to accuse. (cf. his role in Job.)

With the introduction of Satan we are faced not simply with an account of a particular sin, but with a statement about the origins of sin itself. Our passage bears a resemblance in this respect to that greater treatment of the origins of sin, Gen. 3, where the serpent (not explicitly identified with Satan) appears on the scene in a way that is not explained. There as here the existence of a being that has some undefined interest in the ruin of men is simply taken for granted. The Bible offers us little explicit help on the philosophical question how evil can exist in a world created by a good and omnipotent God. It is more concerned to show how, in fact, it came once, in a definitive way, to exercise influence over humanity (Gen. 3) and how that influence persisted (as in a passage like this one). We have seen David, the "man after God's own heart", fall before. Here we have a glimpse of the chain of cause and effect behind his actions. The letter to the Ephesians knows that flesh and blood is involved in a spiritual battle (6:10ff.), and is vulnerable on three fronts—viz. "to the world, the flesh and the devil" (2:2f.). In the matter of the census, David allows Satan one of his victories. Christians are as vulnerable as David. The hallmark of the battle is its secretiveness. So let us be aware that we are in one.

(b) As if the origin of sin were not difficult enough to comprehend there is an added complication in that Chr. here diverges from its source in 2 Sam. 24:1 which tells us that it was the Lord himself who incited David. We are sometimes told that Chr. marks the beginning of a trend in Judaism towards a dualism in which the devil was thought to exercise an independent power in opposition to God, a clash between warring principles of good and evil such as is known in Persian and Greek religion. The comparison of 2 Sam. 24:1 and 1 Chr. 21:1 does not lead to such a conclusion, however. Rather it shows, as indeed does the prologue of Job, that behind and above the spiritual agent of evil God reigns. This is the antithesis of dualism, for it amounts to an assertion that all evil, however vicious and potent, is subject ultimately to the power of good. It is important to keep this aim in mind when faced with the allegation that the OT makes God the author of sin (as in a passage like 2 Sam. 24:1). Passages which seem to speak this way are really saying that the God of Israel brooks no rival in his sway over the world he has made, and they exist to offer a sure hope to those besieged by the power of evil. (cf. the unrelieved gloom of Ps. 88, where nevertheless the mere fact of address to God is a lifeline resisting the influence of any other power.) The veil that conceals the actual origins of evil at places like Gen. 3 and 1 Chr. 21 is never completely drawn back. The triumph of the goodness of God in a situation of judgment is a theme that is developed in the present chapter, as we shall see later.

(c) The point has further to be made that the reference to Satan's incitement of David is in no sense intended to exonerate him from guilt, as has sometimes been suggested.

On the contrary, David himself confesses twice in the chapter (vv. 8, 17) that he alone is responsible for the judgment that falls upon his people. It is human not only to err, but to try to avoid the blame (cf. Adam, Gen. 3:12). Perhaps the one thing that impresses more than David's sins in his life are his repentances (cf. 2 Sam. 12:13ff., and, associated in its heading with the same incident, Ps. 51). We do well to let his willingness to come fully to terms with his deficiencies inform our own responses to our moral failures before God. A similar issue arises in Rom. 7:20 where Paul pleads that when he does what he does not want to do "it is no longer I that do it but sin which dwells within me". This too, however, is in a wider context which freely recognizes personal responsibility for sin: e.g. Rom. 2:6–16.

But what, finally, was the nature of David's sin on this occasion? The text gives no clear answer to this. To take a census was evidently not a wrong thing in itself (cf. Exod. 30:12; Num. 1:2). It can hardly even be argued that the probable military purpose of the census (suggested by the fact that it is undertaken by Joab and the commanders, v. 2) is the reason for its sinfulness, since the census in Num. 1 also had such a purpose and we have seen that David's warlike activities are generally commended. If we are to discover a reasonable explanation at all, we must look to motive. Presumably the implication of the passage is that David had come to pride himself upon his military strength and place his reliance upon his own prowess as a general—a natural human reaction, no doubt, following so many victories. Joab's words (v. 3) certainly suggest that the numerical strength of the people is the Lord's affair, and that David should content himself with his delegated role. The irony of David's self-admiration is that it leads directly to a *depletion* of his visible resources when the judgment falls (v. 14). The way of real strength, and strengthening, is the recognition that it comes from God.

So it is that what appear to be our strengths can easily become our weaknesses. It is said that a minister, on going to a new and talented congregation, lamented that he had no opportunity to practise what he regarded as his strengths, and that he received the surprising advice to "praise the Lord" for the circumstance! The Lord no doubt equips his people for different roles (cf. Eph. 4:11f.; 1 Cor. 12) and we must exercise our gifts. But the greatest strength of all comes with the recognition of our weaknesses (2 Cor. 12:10).

JUDGMENT AND MERCY (21:7–17)

In the remainder of the chapter there is a complex interplay between the themes of judgment and mercy—both essential, in the end, to an understanding of the purpose of the Temple. The theme of judgment is the more obvious, with the pestilence which destroys seventy thousand "men of Israel" (v. 14). The record of the number shows that the punishment is tailored to the particular offence of David. Here again, as with Uzzah, David's sin had disastrous implications for those in his charge.

Yet despite the severity of the punishment there is a sense in which the real subject here is mercy. Supremely this is because the goal of the chapter is the establishment of the Temple, which is for Chr. the great symbol of God's presence with his people. But in these verses we see it in two other ways.

(a) *God repents*. We have noticed David's repentance already (vv. 1–6). Now we see that this is paralleled by God who "repents of the evil" which he is about to do to Jerusalem. There is thus an extended balance in the chapter between what David does and what God does: David "numbers" the people in his census and repents of his sin; God "numbers" the people in judgment, and repents of the evil. As the judgment is traceable to the sin, the withholding of God's hand is traceable to the repentance. The whole question of the relationship between particular suffering and particular sin cannot be gone into here (though we shall find it again in Chr.). Jesus' words in John 9:3 (as indeed the Book of Job) warn us against erecting the experience of David into a principle that is true in every circumstance. Yet, perhaps it is right to point to the chastening or educative dimension of suffering (Rom. 5:3ff.), since there seems to be something of this in God's dealings with David in Chr. Christians may expect God to fit them for his service in various ways, which may include an element of discipline. Where hardship is in fact productive in terms of character we should not baulk at the thought of God's chastening hand.

The idea of God "repenting" of evil can constitute an intellectual difficulty for some people, because of the apparent implications (i) that he has somehow mismanaged things and (ii) that he is morally blameworthy. In fact both of these are illusory. When it is said that God "repents" the meaning is that from now on he intends to proceed in a different way. As ever, the Bible does not address the philosophical question which is suggested to our minds but which we can never finally answer: viz., how do we reconcile the omniscience of God with his rather "human" response and reaction to ever new situations? Rather it makes a moral appeal to man's heart, an appeal which assures any approach to God in penitence will find a merciful response.

The suspicion, on the other hand, of moral imperfection on God's part rests on a misunderstanding of the word "evil" (*ra'ah*). It is true that the word *can* refer to moral evil. But equally it can simply mean "catastrophe". (The same ambiguity exists in the English "evil", since a natural disaster, for example, might be described as such—an evil in the experience of those whom it affects.) There is then no implication of divine guilt. Verse 15 simply means that God has ceased to act in judgment.

(b) The mercy of God is further affirmed in these verses in the choice of punishment that is offered to David, and in David's reply that he would rather fall into the hands of God than of man, because "his mercy is very great" (vv. 11–13). There might appear to be something rather hollow about this offer. Indeed it is not easy to see, in a book which so strongly emphasizes God's control in all of Israel's—and the nations'—affairs, a sense in which famine and devastation by enemies might be any less a divine visitation than the plague which David actually chooses.

There is, however, a danger of over-rationalizing the exchange between David and the prophet Gad. The point of it is not to distinguish between the causes of different kinds of disaster, but to produce the affirmation of God's mercy—and indeed of his mercy right in the teeth of judgment. That affirmation is not bland or half-hearted. On the contrary it is considered and resolute (literally: "many are his mercies, very much", the word "many" occupying an emphatic initial position, and the word meaning "very much" appended to make sure that the point is not lost). David is content to fall into the hands of God because he knows that God's true nature is to have mercy. At critical points in the Christian's experience too it is his knowledge of God in the past which equips him for the present. Similarly it is our seeking and learning of God here and now that fortifies us for all future eventualities.

This is not to diminish the fact that there is judgment in the air in these verses. Although we know from v. 15 of God's decision to spare Jerusalem, the angel's sword remains drawn through to v. 27. For David and the elders (v. 16) that sword signifies the possibility of judgment, and they are driven to more earnest prayers. In a sense, too, the picture is designed to convey the justice of judgment. The prayers of David and the elders, together with the provisions for sacrificial offering which immediately follow, explain why judgment did not fall. God in his mercy responds to the cry of the human heart, here in the form of intercession, and provides a means whereby sin can be atoned for.

THE PROVISION FOR SIN (21:18–22:1)

The final section of chapter 21 now identifies the place where Solomon would build the Temple, the area still known to Jews in Jerusalem as the Temple Mount, though now it bears two Muslim mosques. In David's time there was evidently no tradition of worship having been offered there. The place is merely a threshing-floor and has to be bought. The central statement of this section is in v. 24, where David says, "I will not . . . offer burnt offerings which cost me nothing". Commentators note an interesting parallel between David's transaction with Ornan and that of Abraham with Ephron the Hittite in Gen. 23, where the field of Machpelah is at stake. There too a bargain is struck after the seller has initially offered to make a gift of the land (Gen. 23:15; 1 Chr. 21:23), possibly out of nothing more than conventional eastern politeness. As the purchase of Machpelah was a seal upon the possession of Canaan for Abraham's descendants, though in a higher sense that possession was granted by God, so the purchase of the threshing-floor of Ornan is an indication of the costly commitment of Israel to the place of her future worship—though that too is a gift of God. It is one of the great themes of Israel's prophets that the mere possession of the trappings of religion is valueless without a response of whole-hearted obedience to God (cf. Isa. 1:11ff.; Amos 5:21ff.; Ps. 50:7ff.). Malachi exposes the fraudulent religion of those who make offerings of animals that are of no value anyway (Mal. 1:13f.). David knows instinctively what was later so devastatingly expounded by Jesus himself, that discipleship is a sham if it is not costly (Luke 9:23–25).

It remains simply to make a distinction, in terms of enjoying an undisturbed relationship with God, between cost that is *sub*jective and cost that is *ob*jective. In David's penitence, intercession and purchase of the threshing-floor we have seen the *sub*jective cost, the cost experienced by the person who would be in fellowship with God. The objective cost is symbolized by the Temple and the sacrificial system for which it was intended. That system was not new. It dated from Moses' period (v. 29), and was currently being carried on at the high place (or sanctuary) of Gibeon. But there is a reaffirmation in this chapter that God has provided a way of atonement for the sin of his people. The rituals testify to God's decision to deal with sin. That decision, independent of any human penitence etc., has ever been an essential feature of reconciliation between God and man. We know that it culminated in the death of Christ and that the rituals of the OT were passing shadows (cf. Heb. 10:1–18). Yet God's decision regarding OT times was for those times real and effective. And when David built the altar and called upon the Lord (v. 26), the angel's sword was finally returned to its sheath (v. 27).

Note

The numbers in this chapter differ somewhat from those in 2 Sam. 24. The figure for the census is 1,100,000 rather than 1,300,000. And the price of the threshing-floor is 600 shekels of gold rather than 50 of silver. Chr. appears here to use numbers in a stylized way. The 1,100,000 probably represents a round figure of 100,000 on average for the eleven tribes numbered (Joseph being divided into two, Ephraim and Manasseh, and Levi and Benjamin being omitted). The figure of 600 shekels, on the other hand, is based on a figure of 50 for each tribe, emphasizing that Jerusalem belongs to an ideal all-Israel, not just the tribes actually represented in the restoration period.

SOLOMON'S ORDERS—I

1 Chronicles 22:2–19

2David commanded to gather together the aliens who were in the land of Israel, and he set stonecutters to prepare dressed stones for building the house of God. 3David also provided great stores of iron for nails for the doors of the gates and for clamps, as well as bronze in quantities beyond weighing, 4and cedar timbers without number; for the Sidonians and Tyrians brought great quantities of cedar to David. 5For David said, "Solomon my son is young and inexperienced, and the house that is to be built for the Lord must be exceedingly magnificent, of fame and glory throughout all lands; I will therefore make preparation for it." So David provided materials in great quantity before his death.

6Then he called for Solomon his son, and charged him to build a house for the Lord, the God of Israel. 7David said to Solomon, "My son, I had it in my heart to build a house to the name of the Lord my God. 8But the word of the Lord came to me, saying, 'You have shed much blood and have waged great wars; you shall not build a house to my name, because you have shed so much blood before me upon the earth. 9Behold, a son shall be born to you; he shall be a man of peace. I will give him peace from all his enemies round about; for his name shall be Solomon, and I will give peace and quiet to Israel in his days. 10He shall build a house for my name. He shall be my son, and I will be his father, and I will establish his royal throne in Israel for ever.' 11Now, my son, the Lord be with you, so that you may succeed in building the house of the Lord your God, as he has spoken concerning you. 12Only, may the Lord grant you discretion and understanding, that when he gives you charge over Israel you may keep the law of the Lord your God. [13]Then you will prosper if you are careful to observe the statutes and the ordinances which the Lord commanded Moses for Israel. Be strong, and of good courage. Fear not; be not dismayed. [14]With great pains I have provided for the house of the Lord a hundred thousand talents of gold, a million talents of silver, and bronze and iron beyond weighing, for there is so much of it; timber and stone too I have provided. To these you must add. [15]You have an abundance of workmen: stonecutters, masons, carpenters, and all kinds of craftsmen without number, skilled in working [16]gold, silver, bronze, and iron. Arise and be doing! The Lord be with you!"

[17]David also commanded all the leaders of Israel to help Solomon his son, saying [18]"Is not the Lord your God with you? And has he not given you peace on every side? For he has delivered the inhabitants of the land into my hand; and the land is subdued before the Lord and his people. [19]Now set your mind and heart to seek the Lord your God. Arise and build the sanctuary of the Lord God, so that the ark of the covenant of the Lord and the holy vessels of God may be brought into a house built for the name of the Lord."

The remainder of 1 Chr. is concerned with David's charge to Solomon to build the Temple and his specific instructions to him regarding the organization of worship. There is a considerable amount of material common to chs. 22 and 28–29, the main difference being that in the latter two chapters the charge to Solomon is public, whereas in ch. 22 it is private. The intervening chs. 23–27 contain detailed information about the performance of temple-duties.

(i)

The fact that Chr. lingers so long over David's charge to Solomon shows how important it was considered to be. What was implicit in ch. 17, namely that Solomon is the one divinely appointed for the task of building the Temple, is now made explicit, and furnished with an explanation (v. 8). We have seen (in ch. 17) that the designation of David as a "man of wars" (cf. 28:3) does not imply culpability. Similarly the description of Solomon as a "man of rest" (better than RSV's "man of peace") is not meant to congratulate him upon a moral quality. The contrast between David and Solomon simply shows that in God's purposes the time has come for the Temple to be built. The point of v. 9 can only be understood by reference to Deut. 12:10f. which, addressed to an earlier generation of Israel on the verge of what was then the "promised land", commanded them to seek "the place which the Lord your God will choose" in order to make their offerings there. This "seeking" was to be consequent upon the Lord giving them "rest from all your enemies round about" (Deut. 12:10). The word "rest" in that place is now taken up in relation to Solomon. (The second occurrence of the word "peace" in v. 9, RSV, should, like the first, be rendered "rest", showing how closely Deut. 12:10 is here reproduced.) All this reinforces what was said in relation to ch. 17 about the way in which different people are called to different kinds of service, fitting in their own individual way into God's greater purposes.

This theme is taken a step further now. Chr. has concentrated hitherto on the disqualification of David for the task of building the Temple. Here we see that there is a disqualification which applies to Solomon also (v. 5). If David was not the man to build, Solomon was not the man to plan. David's description of him as "young and inexperienced" is quite a strong repudiation of his ability in this respect. Indeed RSV's "inexperienced" does not adequately convey the weakness, or even timidity, which is meant. How much this deficiency was merely a factor of his youth is hard to discern. But it is something more than youthfulness itself. The point is stressed, therefore, that the task of building the Temple required the combined gifts and abilities of both David and Solomon, even if the latter would inevitably come to have the glory of the Temple reflect particularly upon him and his reign. All service of God is in this sense co-operative. This is one of the implications of God having called out for himself a Church, rather than a sum of individuals. There is no "freelance" Christianity. (cf. the New Testament's description of the Church as a "body", 1 Cor. 12:12ff.) As we have noticed before, the principle of complementary service may often mean taking what looks like the inferior part. But that part is bound to be vital. (For a treatment of the theme of "togetherness", see B. Milne, *We Belong Together,* IVP.)

SOLOMON'S ORDERS—II

1 Chronicles 22:2–19 (*cont'd*)

(ii)

Having stressed the complementarity of David and Solomon, there is nevertheless a sense in which a goal is to be reached with Solomon. The goal has two aspects.

(a) It is God's intention that his people should enjoy "rest". In the concrete terms of the monarchy this is conceived as rest from war. Elsewhere, in what we know as the fourth commandment, there is the idea of rest from labour (Exod. 20:11. Here admittedly, a different word is used, viz., *shabbat*, underlying the English "sabbath". But this need not affect our point.) In no case does "rest" imply the mere absence of exertion. Its implications are best seen against the background of Genesis 1–3, the story of the disruption of human life as it was created to be. The OT idea of rest is anything which tends towards the re-establishment of that unalloyed *enjoyment* of God and his creation (see Gen. 2:9). The Sabbath was a respite from that curse of labour which was a consequence of the first disobedience (Gen. 3:17–19). So now, rest from enemies is the necessary precondition of the enjoyment of the land which God has given to Israel. (For a reflection of the general richness of creation in the promised land in particular see Deut. 8:7–9. This picture certainly underlies the idea of rest in Deut. 12:10 which, as we have seen, informs our present passage.)

That the Chronicler's idea of rest has all these positive connotations is confirmed by his care to point out (v. 2) that David's conscription of labour for the construction of the Temple applied only to "aliens" in the land (though such scrupulousness was in practice to be short lived). This kind of distinction strikes the modern reader as unfair. But it is consistent with the OT's insistence that God's blessings came first and foremost to his own people. (Again, Deuteronomy lays the basis here. For the distinction between Israelites and others see Deut. 15:2f. That this was no oppressive "apartheid" emerges from, for example, Deut. 14:29—where the word "sojourner" is the same as that translated "alien" in our passage. But the dominant factor in the deuteronomic theology which is informing the Chronicler at this point is the realization of God's ultimate purposes through his people, Deut. 7:6ff. We cannot forget, however, that the "all nations" perspective of Gen. 12:1–3 provides the ultimate context.) A right understanding of rest, then, for God's people now as then, must always imply enjoyment of his creation with an acknowledgment that it is indeed his—and, moreover, enjoyment of God himself. The ultimate "rest" for the Christian is beyond the present world (Heb. 4:9f). Yet rest in the sense described can be a reality in this life too.

(b) The goal for God's people which is reached with Solomon has also a dimension of witness. This is a theme which will become prominent in the descripton of Solomon's reign (2 Chr. 1–9). Let us simply notice, at this stage, that the Temple is to be "exceedingly magnificent, of fame and glory *throughout all lands* . . ." (v. 5). This too is part of the context of the rest which the people are said to enjoy. An essential part of their raison d'être as God's people is to demonstrate before all the world that God alone is worthy of worship. (We have referred a moment ago to Gen. 12:1–3.) The splendour of the Temple is not self-indulgent, nor dedicated to the greater glory of King Solomon—but a symbol, in a world in which such symbols were important, that the God of Israel was King over all the earth. The Church can never understand its "rest" as the right to keep its knowledge of God to itself. Indeed, real knowledge and celebration of God cannot be hidden.

(iii)

David's charge to Solomon (vv. 11–16) is a model for all who are about to enter upon a new task or sphere of work in God's service—and for those who commission them. It has three elements: (a) assurance, (b) exhortation, and (c) prayer.

(a) The assurance of God's presence frames the charge, occurring at vv. 11 and 16. It is expressly related to the task which is being laid upon Solomon, and it is God's presence which ensures that that task will be brought to successful completion. We have seen that David's successes have been consistently attributed to God's hand: (cf. 12:18, "your God helps you", and 18:6, "The Lord gave David victory wherever he went"). The assurance of God's presence here is no vague wish. It is a statement of the fact that God is unremittingly involved with those who serve him in their serving. It always has purposes in view. Ultimately it is the purpose of salvation itself. (cf. the famous prophecy in Isa. 7:14, where Immanuel means "God with us", and the less well-known development of the idea in Isa. 8:8,10.)

(b) While the link between service of God and the divine guarantee of its success is indissoluble, the assurance that is thus given is never independent of the requirement of obedience. (Isa. 8:8, just cited, shows disquietingly that the presence of God *can* be disastrous!) Verse 13 contains a more explicit exhortation in this respect than any we have yet seen addressed to the monarch in Chr. The language used is strongly reminiscent of Deuteronomy (e.g. 12:1; specifically, influence has been traced from Josh. 1:7–9 (Williamson) in the context of an extended parallel between the passing of authority from Moses to Joshua and its passing from David to Solomon.)

Obedience to God is defined as obedience to his "statutes and ordinances which the Lord commanded Moses for Israel". The reference here is to the large body of regulations contained in the Torah (Pentateuch), of which the best known are the Ten Commandments, Exod. 20:1–17. Alongside Solomon's particular task of temple-construction, therefore, is the general necessity to be subject to God's standards. Too often, in our day, the will of God is sought in the context of special revelations, and obedience conceived as response to these. But in the Bible, New Testament as well as Old, guidance and obedience are presented much more in terms of conformity to the standards of God. (See e.g. Ps. 25. It is impossible to discuss at length, here, the New Testament's attitude to Old Testament law; but see Rom. 3:31; Gal. 5:13–26.) The primary concern of Christians must be to have their character formed by the character of God (Rom. 12:2). In the OT, kings, far from being exempt from this requirement, were specially exhorted to be subject to God's commands (cf. Deut. 17:14–20). So in Christian leadership, the godliness of the leader is always more important than the task of the moment. Let me share with you a confession of Kierkegaard:

> I once contemplated the possibility of not letting myself be taken over by Christianity, to do nothing else but expound and interpret it, myself not a Christian in the final and most decisive sense of the word, yet leading others to Christianity.
>
> And only now, with the help of heavy sufferings and the bitterness of repentance, have I perhaps learned enough about dying away from the world that I can rightly speak of finding my whole life and my salvation through the forgiveness of sins.
>
> (quoted from M. Muggeridge, *A Third Testament,* Collins)

(c) Last, but not least, in the context of our commissioning to service, is prayer. In v. 12 David prays that the Lord will give Solomon "discretion and understanding". This is very much in keeping with Solomon's own prayer in 2 Chr. 1:10, which is so signally answered, Solomon's wisdom becoming one of the hall-marks of his reign, and indeed proverbial. The nature of wisdom is here closely associated with the law-keeping which we have just discussed, though generally in the OT it is wider than that, a mixture of intelligence, general competence and self-control. (Joseph and Daniel illustrate the qualities well.) The essential point here, however, is that any great undertaking needs a solid foundation of prayer, which the possession of great abilities does not render superfluous. It is noteworthy that God's actual grant-ing of wisdom to Solomon (who, we recall, was apparently ill-fitted for great responsibility in himself; see on v. 5) was preceded not only by Solomon's own prayer, but at an earlier stage by David's too.

GATEKEEPERS—AND OTHERS (TEXT)

1 Chronicles 23:1–27:34

23 ¹When David was old and full of days, he made Solomon his son king over Israel.

²David assembled all the leaders of Israel and the priests and the Levites. ³The Levites, thirty years old and upward, were numbered, and the total was thirty-eight thousand men. ⁴"Twenty-four thousand of these," David said, "shall have charge of the work in the house of the Lord, six thousand shall be officers and judges, ⁵four thousand gatekeepers, and four thousand shall offer praises to the Lord with the instruments which I have made for praise." ⁶And David organized them in divisions corresponding to the sons of Levi: Gershom, Kohath, and Merari.

⁷The sons of Gershom were Ladan and Shimei. ⁸The sons of Ladan: Jehiel the chief, and Zetham, and Joel, three. ⁹The sons of Shimei: Shelomoth, Haziel, and Haran, three. These were the heads of the fathers' houses of Ladan. ¹⁰And the sons of Shimei: Jahath, Zina, and Jeush, and Beriah. These four were the sons of Shimei. ¹¹Jahath was the chief, and Zizah the second; but Jeush and Beriah had not many sons, therefore they became a father's house in one reckoning.

¹²The sons of Kohath: Amram, Izhar, Hebron, and Uzziel, four. ¹³The sons of Amram: Aaron and Moses. Aaron was set apart to consecrate the most holy things, that he and his sons for ever should burn incense before the Lord, and minister to him and pronounce blessings in his name for ever. ¹⁴But the sons of Moses the man of God were named among the tribe of Levi. ¹⁵The sons of Moses: Gershom and Eliezer. ¹⁶The sons of Gershom: Shebuel the chief. ¹⁷The sons of Eliezer: Rehabiah the chief; Eliezer had no other sons, but the sons of Rehabiah were very many. ¹⁸The sons of Izhar: Shelomith the chief. ¹⁹The sons of Hebron: Jeriah the chief, Amariah the second, Jahaziel the third, and Jekameam the fourth. ²⁰The sons of Uzziel: Micah the chief and Isshiah the second.

²¹The sons of Merari: Mahli and Mushi. The sons of Mahli: Eleazar and Kish. ²²Eleazar died having no sons, but only daughters; their kinsmen, the sons of Kish, married them. ²³The sons of Mushi: Mahli, Eder, and Jeremoth, three.

²⁴These were the sons of Levi by their fathers' houses, the heads of fathers' houses as they were registered according to the number of the names of the individuals from twenty years old and upward who were to do the work for the service of the house of the Lord. ²⁵For David said, "The Lord, the God of Israel, has given peace to his people; and he dwells in Jerusalem for ever. ²⁶And so the Levites no longer need to carry the tabernacle or any of the things for its service"—²⁷for by the last words of David these were the number of the Levites from twenty

years old and upward— ²⁸"but their duty shall be to assist the sons of Aaron for the service of the house of the Lord, having the care of the courts and the chambers, the cleansing of all that is holy, and any work for the service of the house of God; ²⁹to assist also with the showbread, the flour for the cereal offering, the wafers of unleavened bread, the baked offering, the offering mixed with oil, and all measures of quantity or size. ³⁰And they shall stand every morning, thanking and praising the Lord, and likewise at evening, ³¹and whenever burnt offerings are offered to the Lord on sabbaths, new moons, and feast days, according to the number required of them, continually before the Lord. ³²Thus they shall keep charge of the tent of meeting and the sanctuary, and shall attend the sons of Aaron, their brethren, for the service of the house of the Lord."

24 ¹The divisions of the sons of Aaron were these. The sons of Aaron: Nadab, Abihu, Eleazar, and Ithamar. ²But Nadab and Abihu died before their father, and had no children, so Eleazar and Ithamar became the priests. ³With the help of Zadok of the sons of Eleazar, and Ahimelech of the sons of Ithamar, David organized them according to the appointed duties in their service. ⁴Since more chief men were found among the sons of Eleazar than among the sons of Ithamar, they organized them under sixteen heads of fathers' houses of the sons of Eleazar, and eight of the sons of Ithamar. ⁵They organized them by lot, all alike, for there were officers of the sanctuary and officers of God among both the sons of Eleazar and the sons of Ithamar. ⁶And the scribe Shemaiah the son of Nethanel, a Levite, recorded them in the presence of the king, and the princes, and Zadok the priest, and Ahimelech the son of Abiathar, and the heads of the fathers' houses of the priests and of the Levites; one father's house being chosen for Eleazar and one chosen for Ithamar.

⁷The first lot fell to Jehoiarib, the second to Jedaiah, ⁸the third to Harim, the fourth to Seorim, ⁹the fifth to Malchijah, the sixth to Mijamin, ¹⁰the seventh to Hakkoz, the eighth to Abijah, ¹¹the ninth to Jeshua, the tenth to Shecaniah, ¹²the eleventh to Eliashib, the twelfth to Jakim, ¹³the thirteenth to Huppah, the fourteenth to Jeshebeab, ¹⁴the fifteenth to Bilgah, the sixteenth to Immer, ¹⁵the seventeenth to Hezir, the eighteenth to Happizzez, ¹⁶the nineteenth to Pethahiah, the twentieth to Jehezkel, ¹⁷the twenty-first to Jachin, the twenty-second to Gamul, ¹⁸the twenty-third to Delaiah, the twenty-fourth to Maaziah. ¹⁹These had as their appointed duty in their service to come into the house of the Lord according to the procedure established for

them by Aaron their father, as the Lord God of Israel had commanded him. ²⁰And of the rest of the sons of Levi: of the sons of Amram, Shubael; of the sons of Shubael, Jehdeiah. ²¹Of Rehabiah: of the sons of Rehabiah, Isshiah the chief. ²²Of the Izharites, Shelomoth; of the sons of Shelomoth, Jahath. ²³The sons of Hebron: Jeriah the chief, Amariah the second, Jahaziel the third, Jekameam the fourth. ²⁴The sons of Uzziel, Micah; of the sons of Micah, Shamir. ²⁵The brother of Micah, Isshiah; of the sons of Isshiah, Zechariah. ²⁶The sons of Merari: Mahli and Mushi. The sons of Jaaziah: Beno. ²⁷The sons of Merari: of Jaaziah, Beno, Shoham, Zaccur, and Ibri. ²⁸Of Mahli: Eleazar, who had no sons. ²⁹Of Kish, the sons of Kish: Jerahmeel. ³⁰The sons of Mushi: Mahli, Eder, and Jerimoth. These were the sons of the Levites according to their fathers' houses. ³¹These also, the head of each father's house and his younger brother alike, cast lots, just as their brethren the sons of Aaron, in the presence of King David, Zadok, Ahimelech, and the heads of fathers' houses of the priests and of the Levites.

25 ¹David and the chiefs of the service also set apart for the service certain of the sons of Asaph, and of Heman, and of Jeduthun, who should prophesy with lyres, with harps, and with cymbals. The list of those who did the work and of their duties was: ²Of the sons of Asaph: Zaccur, Joseph, Nethaniah, and Asharelah, sons of Asaph, under the direction of Asaph, who prophesied under the direction of the king. ³Of Jeduthun, the sons of Jeduthun: Gedaliah, Zeri, Jeshaiah, Shimei, Hashabiah, and Mattithiah, six, under the direction of their father Jeduthun, who prophesied with the lyre in thanksgiving and praise to the Lord. ⁴Of Heman, the sons of Heman: Bukkiah, Mattaniah, Uzziel, Shebuel, and Jerimoth, Hananiah, Hanani, Eliathah, Giddalti, and Romamtiezer, Joshbekashah, Mallothi, Hothir, Mahazioth. ⁵All these were the sons of Heman the king's seer, according to the promise of God to exalt him; for God had given Heman fourteen sons and three daughters. ⁶They were all under the direction of their father in the music in the house of the Lord with cymbals, harps, and lyres for the service of the house of God. Asaph, Jeduthun, and Heman were under the order of the king. ⁷The number of them along with their brethren, who were trained in singing to the Lord, all who were skilful, was two hundred and eighty-eight. ⁸And they cast lots for their duties, small and great, teacher and pupil alike.

⁹The first lot fell for Asaph to Joseph; the second to Gedaliah, to

him and his brethren and his sons, twelve; ¹⁰the third to Zaccur, his sons and his brethren, twelve; ¹¹the fourth to Izri, his sons and his brethren, twelve; ¹²the fifth to Nethaniah, his sons and his brethren, twelve; ¹³the sixth to Bukkiah, his sons and his brethren, twelve; ¹⁴the seventh to Jesharelah, his sons and his brethren, twelve; ¹⁵the eighth to Jeshaiah, his sons and his brethren, twelve; ¹⁶the ninth to Mattaniah, his sons and his brethren, twelve; ¹⁷the tenth to Shimei, his sons and his brethren, twelve; ¹⁸the eleventh to Azarel, his sons and his brethren, twelve; ¹⁹the twelfth to Hashabiah, his sons and his brethren, twelve; ²⁰to the thirteenth, Shubael, his sons and his brethren, twelve; ²¹to the fourteenth, Mattithiah, his sons and his brethren, twelve; ²²to the fifteenth, to Jeremoth, his sons and his brethren, twelve; ²³to the sixteenth, to Hananiah, his sons and his brethren, twelve; ²⁴to the seventeenth, to Joshbekashah, his sons and his brethren, twelve; ²⁵to the eighteenth, to Hanani, his sons and his brethren, twelve; ²⁶to the nineteenth, to Mallothi, his sons and his brethren, twelve; ²⁷to the twentieth, to Eliathah, his sons and his brethren, twelve; ²⁸to the twenty-first, to Hothir, his sons and his brethren, twelve; ²⁹to the twenty-second, to Giddalti, his sons and his brethren, twelve; ³⁰to the twenty-third, to Mahazioth, his sons and his brethren, twelve; ³¹to the twenty-fourth, to Romamtiezer, his sons and his brethren, twelve.

26 ¹As for the divisions of the gatekeepers: of the Korahites, Meshelemiah the son of Kore, of the sons of Asaph. ²And Meshelemiah had sons: Zechariah the first-born, Jediael the second, Zebadiah the third, Jathniel the fourth, ³Elam the fifth, Jehohanan the sixth, Eliehoenai the seventh. ⁴And Obed-edom had sons: Shemaiah the first-born, Jehozabad the second, Joah the third, Sachar the fourth, Nethanel the fifth, ⁵Ammiel the sixth, Issachar the seventh, Peullethai the eighth; for God blessed him. ⁶Also to his son Shemaiah were sons born who were rulers in their fathers' houses, for they were men of great ability. ⁷The sons of Shemaiah: Othni, Rephael, Obed, and Elzabad, whose brethren were able men, Elihu and Semachiah. ⁸All these were of the sons of Obed-edom with their sons and brethren, able men qualified for the service; sixty-two of Obed-edom. ⁹And Meshelemiah had sons and brethren, able men, eighteen. ¹⁰And Hosah, of the sons of Merari, had sons: Shimri the chief (for though he was not the first-born, his father made him chief), ¹¹Hilkiah the second, Tebaliah the third, Zechariah the fourth: all the sons and brethren of Hosah were thirteen.

¹²These divisions of the gatekeepers, corresponding to their chief men, had duties, just as their brethren did, ministering in the house of the Lord; ¹³and they cast lots by fathers' houses, small and great alike, for their gates. ¹⁴The lot for the east fell to Shelemiah. They cast lots also for his son Zechariah, a shrewd counsellor, and his lot came out for the north. ¹⁵Obed-edom's came out for the south, and to his sons was allotted the storehouse. ¹⁶For Shuppim and Hosah it came out for the west, at the gate of Shallecheth on the road that goes up. Watch corresponded to watch. ¹⁷On the east there were six each day, on the north four each day, on the south four each day, as well as two and two at the storehouse; ¹⁸and for the parbar on the west there were four at the road and two at the parbar. ¹⁹These were the divisions of the gatekeepers among the Korahites and the sons of Merari.

²⁰And of the Levites, Ahijah had charge of the treasuries of the house of God and the treasuries of the dedicated gifts. ²¹The sons of Ladan, the sons of the Gershonites belonging to Ladan, the heads of the fathers' houses belonging to Ladan the Gershonite: Jehieli.

²²The sons of Jehieli, Zetham and Joel his brother, were in charge of the treasuries of the house of the Lord. ²³Of the Amramites, the Izharites, the Hebronites, and the Uzzielites—²⁴and Shebuel the son of Gershom, son of Moses, was chief officer in charge of the treasuries. ²⁵His brethren: from Eliezer were his son Rehabiah, and his son Jeshaiah, and his son Joram, and his son Zichri, and his son Shelomoth. ²⁶This Shelomoth and his brethren were in charge of all the treasuries of the dedicated gifts which David the king, and the heads of the fathers' houses, and the officers of the thousands and the hundreds, and the commanders of the army, had dedicated. ²⁷From spoil won in battles they dedicated gifts for the maintenance of the house of the Lord. ²⁸Also all that Samuel the seer, and Saul the son of Kish, and Abner the son of Ner, and Joab the son of Zeruiah had dedicated—all dedicated gifts were in the care of Shelomoth and his brethren.

²⁹Of the Izharites, Chenaniah and his sons were appointed to outside duties for Israel, as officers and judges. ³⁰Of the Hebronites, Hashabiah and his brethren, one thousand seven hundred men of ability, had the oversight of Israel westward of the Jordan for all the work of the Lord and for the service of the king. ³¹Of the Hebronites, Jerijah was chief of the Hebronites of whatever genealogy or fathers' houses. (In the fortieth year of David's reign search was made and men of great ability among them were found at Jazer in Gilead.) ³²King

David appointed him and his brethren, two thousand seven hundred men of ability, heads of fathers' houses, to have the oversight of the Reubenites, the Gadites, and the half-tribe of the Manassites for everything pertaining to God and for the affairs of the king.

27 ¹This is the list of the people of Israel, the heads of fathers' houses, the commanders of thousands and hundreds, and their officers who served the king in all matters concerning the divisions that came and went, month after month throughout the year, each division numbering twenty-four thousand:

²Jashobeam the son of Zabdiel was in charge of the first division in the first month; in his division were twenty-four thousand. ³He was a descendant of Perez, and was chief of all the commanders of the army for the first month. ⁴Dodai the Ahohite was in charge of the division of the second month; in his division were twenty-four thousand. ⁵The third commander, for the third month, was Benaiah, the son of Jehoiada the priest, as chief; in his division were twenty-four thousand. ⁶This is the Benaiah who was a mighty man of the thirty and in command of the thirty; Ammizabad his son was in charge of his division. ⁷Asahel the brother of Joab was fourth, for the fourth month, and his son Zebadiah after him; in his division were twenty-four thousand. ⁸The fifth commander, for the fifth month, was Shamhuth, the Izrahite; in his division were twenty-four thousand. ⁹Sixth, for the sixth month, was Ira, the son of Ikkesh the Tekoite; in his division were twenty-four thousand. ¹⁰Seventh, for the seventh month, was Helez the Pelonite, of the sons of Ephraim; in his division were twenty-four thousand. ¹¹Eighth, for the eighth month, was Sibbecai the Hushathite, of the Zerahites; in his division were twenty-four thousand. ¹²Ninth, for the ninth month, was Abiezer of Anathoth, a Benjaminite; in his division were twenty-four thousand. ¹³Tenth, for the tenth month, was Maharai of Netophah, of the Zerahites; in his division were twenty-four thousand. ¹⁴Eleventh, for the eleventh month, was Benaiah of Pirathon, of the sons of Ephraim; in his division were twenty-four thousand. ¹⁵Twelfth, for the twelfth month, was Heldai the Netophathite, of Othniel; in his division were twenty-four thousand.

¹⁶Over the tribes of Israel, for the Reubenites Eliezer the son of Zichri was chief officer; for the Simeonites, Shephatiah the son of Maacah; ¹⁷for Levi, Hashabiah the son of Kemuel; for Aaron, Zadok; ¹⁸for Judah, Elihu, one of David's brothers; for Issachar, Omri the son of Michael; ¹⁹for Zebulun, Ishmaiah the son of Obadiah; for Naphtali,

Jeremoth the son of Azriel; [20]for the Ephraimites, Hoshea the son of Azaziah; for the half-tribe of Manasseh, Joel the son of Pedaiah; [21]for the half-tribe of Manasseh in Gilead, Iddo the son of Zechariah; for Benjamin, Jaasiel the son of Abner; [22]for Dan, Azarel the son of Jeroham. These were the leaders of the tribes of Israel. [23]David did not number those below twenty years of age, for the Lord had promised to make Israel as many as the stars of heaven. [24]Joab the son of Zeruiah began to number, but did not finish; yet wrath came upon Israel for this, and the number was not entered in the chronicles of King David.

[25]Over the king's treasuries was Azmaveth the son of Adiel; and over the treasuries in the country, in the cities, in the villages and in the towers, was Jonathan the son of Uzziah; [26]and over those who did the work of the field for tilling the soil was Ezri the son of Chelub; [27]and over the vineyards was Shimei the Ramathite; and over the produce of the vineyards for the wine cellars was Zabdi the Shiphmite. [28]Over the olive and sycamore trees in the Shephelah was Baalhanan the Gederite; and over the stores of oil was Joash. [29]Over the herds that pastured in Sharon was Shitrai the Sharonite; over the herds in the valleys was Shaphat the son of Adlai. [30]Over the camels was Obil the Ishmaelite; and over the she-asses was Jehdeiah the Meronothite. Over the flocks was Jaziz the Hagrite. [31]All these were stewards of King David's property.

[32]Jonathan, David's uncle, was a counsellor, being a man of understanding and a scribe; he and Jehiel the son of Hachmoni attended the king's sons. [33]Ahithophel was the king's counsellor, and Hushai the Archite was the king's friend. [34]Ahithophel was succeeded by Jehoiada the son of Benaiah, and Abiathar. Joab was commander of the king's army.

GATEKEEPERS—AND OTHERS (COMMENTARY)—I

1 Chronicles 23:1–27:34 (*cont'd*)

David foresaw that the Temple which he was planning would require a considerable personnel to maintain it. He now proceeds, therefore, to organize the priests and Levites in accordance with the new kinds of demands that Temple-service will bring. Chapter 23:26 makes reference to the fact that the bringing of the ark to Jerusalem has inaugurated a new era in Levitical service, since the central Levitical duty is presented in Num. chs. 3–4 as the tending of the accoutrements of the now obsolete mobile sanctuary. David divides the Levites on the one hand according to traditional family groupings (Gershom, Kohath and Merari), and on the other according to their new functions, viz. officers and judges, gatekeepers and musicians.

It is impossible to deal with all the critical issues which arise in relation to these chapters within the scope of the present work. Suffice it to mention that their unity has been widely called into question for various reasons. Chapter 27, for example, does not specifically belong to the organization of the priests and Levites, but more generally to the military and civil organization of Israel. The Levites' qualifying-age for service varies within ch. 23 (vv. 3, 24, 27). The arrangement whereby duty-rotas were decided by lot (24:5) has been held to be incompatible with the picture of David personally appointing the different groups to their duties.

Some of these points may be felt to be more convincing than others. There are two options when interpreting the material of these chapters. Either we attempt to harmonize the details which have been felt to be mutually incompatible, and attribute all the arrangements outlined here to David's time, or we take the view that there has been elaboration of the basic material to reflect later periods, perhaps even later than Chr. itself. On the latter view, the different ages given for Levitical service would reflect different periods; and the casting of lots would date from the second Temple rather than the first. On the former view, there were general Levitical duties (vv. 28ff.) and more specific ones (vv. 4f.) for which a higher age was required; and David's appointment of the priestly groups left room for details to be worked out, as by a system of lots.

In any case it is hard to deny a fundamental unity of theme. Chapter 27, which we have seen is often held to be out of place, has the purpose, in context, of relating the administration of the Temple to that of the nation as a whole. Formally, this is done by means of a rota system corresponding to that of the priestly divisions (27:1; cf. 24:1). It is thus emphasized that the character of the nation's life is fundamentally religious, even mundane matters being ultimately controlled by the worship of God.

Let us now draw out some general points from these chapters as a whole.

(i)

Essentially what we have before us is a picture of the people of God organized for the life of service. As we have noticed before, the fact that the people of God in the OT is a nation is significant for our interpretation. Because it is a tangible, political entity there is a sense in which its worship has external things more at its centre than Christian worship can ever rightly have. This is why the Temple itself is important in Israel. And it also explains why the life of service can be described so much in terms of organization and ritual. In particular the OT recognizes a distinction between the realms of the "holy" and the profane, things which are holy requiring special classes of people to handle them (see the consecration of Aaron and his sons as priests, Exod. chs. 28–29). This is why priests and Levites are so prominent here. But more important than arrangements for obsolete rituals is the essential fact that here we have a statement about God's centrality in all of life. Chapter 27, with its list of the ministers in David's government (vv. 25ff.) is a reminder that the whole creation is God's and that he has made it over to mankind both for enjoyment and stewardship. This is not to make a trite ecological point, but rather to show that in its service of God Israel was representative of the whole creation. There is in these dry catalogues a reminder that the function of humanity and creation as a whole is to worship God. Israel was entrusted for a time with a duty which lies ultimately upon all. She could only picture God's kingdom in terms which she understood. (Ezek. chs. 40–48 is close to our chapters, with its highly temple-centred vision of the future, yet depicting God's presence as a source of life, in images which remind strongly of Eden, and therefore God's primary purpose to bless and enrich all mankind; Ezek. 47:1–12; cf. Gen. 2:10–14.) The task of the Christian Church is to lead all humanity back to its duty of worship, a worship in which the earth itself, by its abundance, will participate.

GATEKEEPERS—AND OTHERS (COMMENTARY)—II

1 Chronicles 23:1–27:34 (*cont'd*)

(ii)

There are a number of features of the priests' and Levites' service which may be noticed with profit.

(a) *The dignity of service.* When a church's elders or stewards take their turn to do the duty of welcoming Sunday worshippers, and say jocularly that they are "gatekeepers in the house of the Lord", they use a phrase which has become a byword for lowly service. Many of the daily duties of the Levites (who were of an inferior rank to the priests) must have been routine and mundane (23:28ff.). They were, in an almost literal sense, glorified housekeepers. The "holiness" of the Temple decreed that there must be "holy" persons to be busied with its work. That work, however, must often be menial. The lists in those chapters no doubt veil a vast amount of work that was unseen and unsung. The readiness of small and great alike to be subject to the random decree of the "lot" (25:8) is testimony to a great humility. Yet the very association of such tasks with the service of God lent it a glory. Such work continues in the day-to-day life of our churches. We too should be prepared to submerge the difference between "small and great", remembering that those who undertake humble tasks faithfully shall know a recognition which possibly eludes them now.

It is not clear, of course, that all the tasks of the Levites were equally mundane. The business of being officers, judges, gatekeepers and musicians undoubtedly had its own dignity. (The importance of music in the life of Israel is evident from the Psalms.) If the suggestion made above that there were different qualifying ages for different kinds of duties is correct then there may have been a kind of "career-structure".

The advancement to higher duties need not be a model for modern careers. But it is instructive to observe the fastidious care with which the tasks of the Temple's service are surrounded.

(b) *Order and excellence.* Almost more important than the subject-matter of the Levites' duties is the orderliness which is here associated with them (cf. 1 Chr. 6:32). Everyone played his part, it seems, exactly as it was laid down that he should. From this it emerges that the search for "decency and order" in worship was not the invention of Paul (1 Cor. 14:40), but is something inherent in worship itself. Worship can be sublime and spiritual without becoming disorganized; and the converse is probably not true.

Associated with orderliness is the pursuit of excellence. Notice how many references there are in these chapters to skill and ability (e.g. 25:7; 26:6, 9, 30ff.; 27:32). This skill is particularly associated with the musical duties of the Levites, and is therefore easy for us to identify with. There is clear warrant in these verses for the pursuit of excellence in every department of church life. If we would have ministers in our churches let us ensure that they are adequately trained. It must be counter-productive for any church, in seeking to trim its budget, to think first of the theological college, or the length of the training programme. If we would have administrators, secretaries, treasurers, let us ensure that they bring the highest standards to their tasks—providing training in these areas if necessary. If we would have music let us channel all available talent into it, see that the musicians have sufficient resources for their task, and that a proper atmosphere exists for them to make their contribution. (For a reservation, see above on chapter 15.)

Let us, therefore, give our best, remembering all the time that true worship is spiritual (John 4:24) and not yielding to the delusion that spiritual genuineness is the same as professional excellence.

(c) *Adaptability.* We have noticed above that the duties of the Levites inevitably changed with the construction of the Temple and its corollary that the ark was no longer mobile. This capacity to adapt is an object lesson both for established groups within the Church and for individuals. There is probably a greater awareness today than in previous generations of the fact that the ministry of the Church belongs to the body as a whole. This undoubtedly means that the traditional minister has had, and still has, to re-think his own role. One minister, alive to this principle, claimed in a presbytery meeting that he saw his task as the attempt to work himself out of a job. His words provoked some opposition. It is in fact highly unlikely that the growing concept of "body ministry" threatens the full-time, ordained ministry as an institution. On the contrary the church-member who finds himself more and more applying the word of God to others will probably feel a growing need to refer to someone better trained and more experienced.

It must be stressed that the point applies not to the minister only, but to all church-members. The essence of real adaptability is the ability to sense and read new situations, see where the needs really lie, and bring existing resources to bear upon them. Mere contentment to perpetuate inherited institutions and ways of doing things is death to a church.

SOLOMON'S ORDERS—AGAIN—I

1 Chronicles 28:1–21

[1]David assembled at Jerusalem all the officials of Israel, the officials of the tribes, the officers of the divisions that served the king, the commanders of thousands, the commanders of hundreds, the stewards of all the property and cattle of the king and his sons, together with the palace officials, the mighty men, and all the seasoned warriors. [2]Then King David rose to his feet and said: "Hear me, my brethren and my people. I had it in my heart to build a house of rest for the ark of the covenant of the Lord, and for the footstool of our God; and I made preparations for building. [3]But God said to me, 'You may not build a house for my name, for you are a warrior and have shed blood.' [4]Yet the Lord God of Israel chose me from all my father's house to be king over Israel for ever; for he chose Judah as leader, and in the house of

Judah my father's house, and among my father's sons he took pleasure in me to make me king over all Israel. ⁵And of all my sons (for the Lord has given me many sons) he has chosen Solomon my son to sit upon the throne of the kingdom of the Lord over Israel. ⁶He said to me, 'It is Solomon your son who shall build my house and my courts, for I have chosen him to be my son, and I will be his father. ⁷I will establish his kingdom for ever if he continues resolute in keeping my commandments and my ordinances, as he is today.' ⁸Now therefore in the sight of all Israel, the assembly of the Lord, and in the hearing of our God, observe and seek out all the commandments of the Lord your God; that you may possess this good land, and leave it for an inheritance to your children after you for ever.

⁹"And you, Solomon my son, know the God of your father, and serve him with a whole heart and with a willing mind; for the Lord searches all hearts, and understands every plan and thought. If you seek him, he will be found by you; but if you forsake him, he will cast you off for ever. ¹⁰Take heed now, for the Lord has chosen you to build a house for the sanctuary; be strong, and do it."

¹¹Then David gave Solomon his son the plan of the vestibule of the temple, and of its houses, its treasuries, its upper rooms, and its inner chambers, and of the room for the mercy seat; ¹²and the plan of all that he had in mind for the courts of the house of the Lord, all the surrounding chambers, the treasuries of the house of God, and the treasuries for dedicated gifts; ¹³for the divisions of the priests and of the Levites, and all the work of the service in the house of the Lord; for all the vessels for the service in the house of the Lord, ¹⁴the weight of gold for all golden vessels for each service, the weight of silver vessels for each service, ¹⁵the weight of the golden lampstands and their lamps, the weight of gold for each lampstand and its lamps, the weight of silver for a lampstand and its lamps, according to the use of each lampstand in the service, ¹⁶the weight of gold for each table for the showbread, the silver for the silver tables, ¹⁷and pure gold for the forks, the basins, and the cups; for the golden bowls and the weight of each; for the silver bowls and the weight of each; ¹⁸for the altar of incense made of refined gold, and its weight; also his plan for the golden chariot of the cherubim that spread their wings and covered the ark of the covenant of the Lord. ¹⁹All this he made clear by the writing from the hand of the Lord concerning it, all the work to be done according to the plan.

²⁰Then David said to Solomon his son, "Be strong and of good

courage, and do it. Fear not, be not dismayed; for the Lord God, even my God, is with you. He will not fail you or forsake you, until all the work for the service of the house of the Lord is finished. [21]And behold the divisions of the priests and the Levites for all the service of the house of God; and with you in all the work will be every willing man who has skill for any kind of service; also the officers and all the people will be wholly at your command."

Chapters 28–29 continue and complete the process of the transfer of the kingship from David to Solomon begun in ch. 22. We now have a public charge to Solomon, with a proclamation of God's purpose that he and not David should build the Temple, the handing over of David's detailed plans (ch. 28), his gifts for the construction (29:1–9), prayer for the people's continued faithfulness (29:10–19), a ceremony, involving sacrifices, to mark Solomon's accession (29:20–22*a*), and summarizing remarks about David's reign (29:22*b*–30).

The chapters are an important watershed in Chr., being concerned with the occasion when one of the great model figures of the work gives way to the other.

Chapter 28 rehearses themes which we have met before: David's disqualification to build (v. 3); the electing activity of God from the patriarch Judah through to David himself, and then, out of David's many sons, Solomon (vv. 4f.); the dependence of God's continued blessing upon a willingness on the part of king and people to obey his laws (vv. 7f.); the exhortation to Solomon to go about his task with strength, fearing nothing because he knows God is with him (vv. 9f., 20f.), and the provision for all available skills to be brought to the Temple's construction. (See above, mainly on ch. 22, but also on chs. 1–9, for election.)

There are, however, a number of new points in the chapter.

(i)

To begin with something that we sense rather than adduce firm evidence for, there is an underlying pathos in the father's relinquishment of the reins in favour of his son. David, nearing the end of his life, reflects, perhaps more than on death itself, on the measure of his life. When he discloses how he had desired to build the house of God (v. 2), this is more than a mere statement of fact. It is a confession of what he had seen as a fitting culmination of the achievements of his life. The detailed character of the plans which he is able to impart to Solomon show how far the desire had developed in his mind. So David is depicted as having to accept that his own perception of the measure of his life has been misguided, and having to hand over to another something which was close to his heart.

The moment cannot but have been tinged with regret of another sort. Verse 5 ostensibly makes a simple point about how the Lord chose Solomon from among David's numerous sons. This in itself is nothing remarkable. Had not David's own career begun with his selection from among his brothers, though he was the unlikeliest-looking of the bunch (1 Sam. 16:1–13)? Solomon's selection had been rather different, however. Our statement in v. 5 at once hints at and draws a veil over the unsavoury events catalogued in the so-called Succession Narrative (2 Sam. 9–20, 1 Kings 1–2), which suggest that in reality Solomon—himself the fruit of his father's adulterous liaison with Bathsheba (2 Sam. 11–12, especially 12:24)—acceded to the throne in the midst and as the result of court intrigue. Putting the election of Solomon in a line beginning with that of Judah reinforces the point, for the patriarch too was no moral paragon (Gen. 38).

We have noticed before that even Chr.'s rather idealized picture of David is not an attempt to present him as perfect, and seen how God's gracious purposes overruled the man's faults. Here we see David's mature acceptance of this fact. It is one thing to observe, in a detached way and especially about other people, that God is indulgent and continues to accept the service of the sincere and penitent despite their faults. But it is quite another actually to come to terms with one's own limitations, accept that one's role in life and the Kingdom might be relatively meagre, and rejoice that this is from the hand of God. It is especially hard to pass on any task or project to another. But it is part of the acceptance of our own measure that our stake in the service of the

Kingdom never amounts to our personal possession of any aspect of it.

SOLOMON'S ORDERS—AGAIN—II

1 Chronicles 28:1–21 (*cont'd*)

(ii)

The public reiteration of the charge to Solomon has its own significance. It emphasizes that the responsibilities which fall to the new king do not belong to a private relationship between him and God. Rather, he is to exercise his leadership in the sight and on behalf of his people. Indeed, up to v. 8, the exhortations of David are in the plural, and therefore addressed to the assembled company of the representatives of Israel. They are all to obey God's commands, so that their children may continue to possess the land. The terminology here is strongly reminiscent of Deuteronomy's theology of obedience to God and enjoyment of the land. That theology provides the context for the view of kingship (Deut. 17:14–20) which underlies our passage, viz., that the king is a brother in Israel and subject to God's laws along with the mass of the people. The weight here falls, however, on the responsibility of the people to see that the one who is charged with the highest responsibility faithfully discharges it.

For this reason it is good, as a general principle, to have public affirmation and acknowledgment when a member of a church takes up a new responsibility. No position in the church is primarily an honour or a privilege, nor indeed an opportunity to build an empire. The individual's tenure of it is for the good of the people as a body, and is subject to the test of daily faithfulness to them and to God.

(iii)

Two of the major ideas in the chapter are (a) that of rest for the ark (v. 2) and (b) the mutual "seeking" of God and Solomon (v. 9); and the two ideas are connected. Hitherto we have spoken of a rest which has been granted by God to his people (e.g. 22:9, and see comment on that passage). But the rest which relates to the "ark of the covenant of the Lord" is tantamount to a rest to which the Lord himself comes. The idea of a rest for the ark is found also in Ps. 132 (at vv. 8, 14), upon which the present chapter is often said to be a meditation, or even sermon (Von Rad). There as here it is in the context of David's bringing the ark to its permanent home in Jerusalem: and it is only in these two places that it is called the Lord's footstool (cf. Ps. 132:7). There is an interesting reversal, then, in both 1 Chr. 28 and Ps. 132, of the well known idea that David's conquest of his enemies would usher in a time of "rest" for the people. It is Ps. 132 which shows clearly that we should not shrink from the idea of God himself resting. (The word translated "resting-place" in RSV, vv. 8, 14, is simply the word for rest, *menuchah*, which elsewhere relates to Israel.)

This is an important dimension of the relationship between God and his people. We can add to our understanding of this relationship by turning now to v. 9. In that place RSV submerges the fact that the word translated "searches" in the phrase "the Lord searches all hearts" is the same as that translated "seek" a line or two later, in the phrase "if you seek him . . ." (viz. *darash*). In favour of the translation "searches" is the fact that the phrase in which it occurs stands alongside an allusion to God's *understanding* every thought. Yet the use of the verb *darash* of the activity of God as well as of man (of God another verb, *chaqar*, would more unequivocally have meant "search", as in Ps. 139:1) must suggest a seeking on God's part which corresponds to the seeking he demands of his people.

We have then two glimpses into the heart of God in relation to men, revealing how much he has committed himself to their cause and well-being. It may be helpful to think once again of the early chapters of Genesis. When God made man in his image (Gen. 1:26) it was not a case of making a *replica* of himself, but rather one who would have a relationship with him which would be in every way mutual. This means that, by virtue of the creation-commitment, God's heart naturally goes out to man (seeking), and finds rest only when *he* finds rest. God's activity in v. 9 is therefore the seeking of a responsive heart (which inevitably embraces the ideas of "searching" and understanding). The possibility of Solomon's being "cast off for ever" is not, therefore, a meaningless or vindictive threat. It arises from the fact that the only right, or even conceivable, relationship between God and an individual is one in which there is commitment to the relationship on the part of the human party as well as on God's side. The word translated "cast you off" means, more precisely, "reject you as abominable". (The root-meaning of the word suggests something evil-smelling.) The translation "cast you off" misses the fact that something is being said about the *object* of the casting off, not just the subject. The one who does not seek God is unworthy, in the strongest possible sense, of God's commitment to him, because he does not conform to God's own ancient and enduring decree concerning what constitutes true humanity.

It remains simply to notice that the idea of God's commitment to humanity in creation comes to its ultimate expression in the Incarnation. There is a sense in which the Incarnation is not a new intensity of commitment to humanity on God's part. The radical nature of that commitment was implied in the act of creation itself. It is because creation is *for relationship* that it brings in its train such possibilities, on the one hand, for *enjoying* God, and on the other—by the refusal to respond to him—for causing him offence.

THE LORD IS KING—I

1 Chronicles 29:1–30

[1] And David the king said to all the assembly, "Solomon my son, whom alone God has chosen, is young and inexperienced, and the work is great; for the palace will not be for man but for the Lord God. [2] So I have provided for the house of my God, so far as I was able, the gold for the things of gold, the silver for the things of silver, and the bronze for the things of bronze, the iron for the things of iron, and wood for the things of wood, besides great quantities of onyx and stones for setting, antimony, coloured stones, all sorts of precious stones, and marble. [3] Moreover, in addition to all that I have provided for the holy

house, I have a treasure of my own of gold and silver, and because of my devotion to the house of my God I give it to the house of my God: ⁴three thousand talents of gold, of the gold of Ophir, and seven thousand talents of refined silver, for overlaying the walls of the house, ⁵and for all the work to be done by craftsmen, gold for the things of gold and silver for the things of silver. Who then will offer willingly, consecrating himself today to the Lord?''

⁶Then the heads of fathers' houses made their freewill offerings, as did also the leaders of the tribes, the commanders of thousands and of hundreds, and the officers over the king's work. ⁷They gave for the service of the house of God five thousand talents and ten thousand darics of gold, ten thousand talents of silver, eighteen thousand talents of bronze, and a hundred thousand talents of iron. ⁸And whoever had precious stones gave them to the treasury of the house of the Lord, in the care of Jehiel the Gershonite. ⁹Then the people rejoiced because these had given willingly, for with a whole heart they had offered freely to the Lord; David the king also rejoiced greatly.

¹⁰Therefore David blessed the Lord in the presence of all the assembly; and David said: "Blessed art thou, O Lord, the God of Israel our father, for ever and ever. ¹¹Thine, O Lord, is the greatness, and the power, and the glory, and the victory, and the majesty; for all that is in the heavens and in the earth is thine; thine is the kingdom, O Lord, and thou art exalted as head above all. ¹²Both riches and honour come from thee, and thou rulest over all. In thy hand are power and might; and in thy hand it is to make great and to give strength to all. ¹³And now we thank thee, our God, and praise thy glorious name.

¹⁴"But who am I, and what is my people, that we should be able thus to offer willingly? For all things come from thee, and of thy own have we given thee. ¹⁵For we are strangers before thee, and sojourners, as all our fathers were; our days on the earth are like a shadow, and there is no abiding. ¹⁶O Lord our God, all this abundance that we have provided for building thee a house for thy holy name comes from thy hand and is all thy own. ¹⁷I know, my God, that thou triest the heart, and hast pleasure in uprightness; in the uprightness of my heart I have freely offered all these things, and now I have seen thy people, who are present here, offering freely and joyously to thee. ¹⁸O Lord, the God of Abraham, Isaac, and Israel, our fathers, keep for ever such purposes and thoughts in the hearts of thy people, and direct their hearts toward thee. ¹⁹Grant to Solomon my son that with a whole heart he may keep thy commandments, thy testimonies, and thy statutes, per-

forming all, and that he may build the palace for which I have made provision.''

20Then David said to all the assembly, ''Bless the Lord your God.'' And all the assembly blessed the Lord, the God of their fathers, and bowed their heads, and worshipped the Lord, and did obeisance to the king. 21And they performed sacrifices to the Lord, and on the next day offered burnt offerings to the Lord, a thousand bulls, a thousand rams, and a thousand lambs, with their drink offerings, and sacrifices in abundance for all Israel; 22and they ate and drank before the Lord on that day with great gladness.

And they made Solomon the son of David king the second time, and they anointed him as prince for the Lord, and Zadok as priest. 23Then Solomon sat on the throne of the Lord as king instead of David his father; and he prospered, and all Israel obeyed him. 24All the leaders and the mighty men, and also all the sons of King David, pledged their allegiance to King Solomon. 25And the Lord gave Solomon great repute in the sight of all Israel, and bestowed upon him such royal majesty as had not been on any king before him in Israel.

26Thus David the son of Jesse reigned over all Israel. 27The time that he reigned over Israel was forty years; he reigned seven years in Hebron, and thirty-three years in Jerusalem. 28Then he died in a good old age, full of days, riches, and honour; and Solomon his son reigned in his stead. 29Now the acts of King David, from first to last, are written in the Chronicles of Samuel the seer, and in the Chronicles of Nathan the prophet, and in the Chronicles of Gad the seer, 30with accounts of all his rule and his might and of the circumstances that came upon him and upon Israel, and upon all the kingdoms of the countries.

(a) Verses 1–9. *Dedication of Self and Substance*

The Temple, when it is built, will be not only a dwelling-place of God and a house of prayer, but also a monument to the self-giving of David and Israel. It is not the glitter of the wealth itself which we should see in these verses. Rather it is the extent to which the people are called upon to pour themselves into the project. When it is said (v. 6) that ''the heads of fathers' houses made their freewill offerings'', the expression externalizes their action much more than the Hebrew warrants, for the idea is in reality that they made offerings of themselves, in line with the appeal in v. 5.

David leads the way in the act of self-dedication, offering a "treasure of his own" (v. 3). The word is *segullah*, better known in its use to describe the people of Israel as God's "own possession" (Exod. 19:5). A *segullah* was a treasure of special importance to an ancient eastern monarch because it was a kind of personal security against times of political hardship or disaster. David's gift, therefore, is more than simply a gesture of great generosity. (It certainly is that. The figures involved are enormous. On large figures in Chr. see the Introduction.) It amounts to a forfeit of an important visible guarantee of his personal security. In an age when many people channel large proportions of their substance into safeguarding their future David's example here is salutary. Jesus too took up the theme of voluntary vulnerability in a number of his sayings (Matt. 8:20–22; 16:24–26), and in his Incarnation left us with the supreme example of faithfulness to the challenge. The gospel calls into jeopardy not only the "fringe benefits" or the "little luxuries" of life, but its centre and substance. Often the extent to which we are prepared to put at risk our material well-being is a measure of the seriousness with which we take our discipleship.

How much the self-offering which is the theme of these verses belongs to the true nature of man (and is therefore in his own interest—an interest that is only spiritually perceived) is evident from the fact that it becomes the occasion of rejoicing, v. 9. (There is no significant distinction between leaders and people here.) We noticed in relation to 28:9 that there was a mutual "seeking" between God and man which was explicable in terms of man's creation in God's image. The same theology helps us here. People are closest to God-likeness in self-giving, and the nearer they approach God-likeness the more genuinely and rightly they become capable of rejoicing. Contrary to popular belief, the OT's presentation of man's relationship with God is above all in terms of joy. And it is always inseparable from affirmations that his truest interests lie in the way of wholehearted acceptance of God's lordship (cf. Neh. 12:44–47; Ps. 100:1f.). The search for true happiness cannot be along the path of self-gratification. That way lies, at best, momentary exhilaration followed by disappointment and a keen sense of the ephemeral character of pleasure as it is commonly understood. Joy and self-giving are inherently and invariably factors of each other. (Notice that there is no thought of material return on David's part here. The giving is real and unconditional.)

THE LORD IS KING—II

1 Chronicles 29:1–30 (*cont'd*)

(b) Verses 10–30. *Thine is the Kingdom, O Lord!*

(i) David's prayer, whose greatness is attested by the fact that its tones still reverberate in our churches, has the primary purpose of ascribing to God those attributes which appearances might attach to himself, and more importantly, to Solomon. The position of the prayer within Chr. as a whole is important. It has been well pointed out that it takes up themes also present in ch. 16, the praises which attended the bringing of the ark to Jerusalem. There as here there is an emphasis on the fact that the greatness of Israel does not lie within, but rather is granted by God. Particularly striking is David's use of the terms "stranger" and "sojourner" (v. 15), invoking the analogy of the patriarchs, who had never possessed the land as future generations would. The prayers of chs. 16 and 29, therefore, mark two of the great events of David's reign, the bringing of the ark and the commissioning of Solomon to carry out his plans for the Temple. More importantly, perhaps, this prayer serves as a prelude to Solomon's reign. That reign was to be the most magnificent in Israel's history, and the temptations of its grandeur and wealth would weigh heavily upon Solomon.

The prayer puts all power in a right perspective at the outset. Verse 11 is central. The word-order of the statement beginning: "Thine, O Lord, is the greatness . . ." places the emphasis on the Lord, as much as to say: "It is Thou, O Lord, who art great and not I, nor even Solomon." The list of qualities well suits a mighty king: "power" is the power of a warrior; "glory" is the ornamental magnificence of a Louis XIV; "victory" and possession of the earth are the ambition of every autocrat. The climax, "thine is the kingdom", crystallizes what David is saying. (Notice that the Temple is called a "palace" in this chapter, v. 1.) Any human greatness which fancies that it is self-existent, underived, is a delusion and an offence to God. The spirit that is challenged here, moreover, is not confined to ancient monarchs. Who can deny that it exactly describes twentieth-century self-regarding obsession with achievement and progress?

(ii) A consequence of the fact that all wealth belongs to and derives from God is the inevitable recognition that men cannot in any real sense give materially to him. The second part of v. 14, so aptly used at the dedication of church offerings, guards against any feeling of self-congratulation in the act of giving. Not only do we not possess anything independently of God, but we have no natural right to do so. David's rhetorical question, in the first half of v. 14, expresses his feeling of unworthiness to be in the successful position he is in. It is a mark of his right perspective on wealth that his possession of it drives him to his knees in humility rather than kindling pride in his eminence. The use of the terms "strangers" and "sojourners" emphasizes this lack of entitlement to the wealth of which he disposes. The word translated "stranger" (*ger*) is widely used in the OT precisely to distinguish from Israelites, heirs to the promised land, those non-Israelites who were resident in the land yet only by the goodwill of the rightful inhabitants. The application of the term to Israelites, therefore, is pointed. In the history of Israel which yet lay ahead of David it was to be one of her chronic faults to take for granted as of right those things which were in reality the marks of God's unmerited goodness (land, Temple, even the law; Jer. 7:4; 8:8). David's prayer that they would recognize who was their true King and the source of all they had, by honest devotion to him (v. 17), applies to the modern Church as much as to those who first heard his words.

(iii) The point can be made from a rather different angle. In the Chronicler's day, less glorious than David's, and in our own, when the cause of the Church can often seem to be as good as lost in a world which enthrones human things, God was and is still King. In the Chronicler's purposes David's prayer probably served to assure his contemporaries of this. In these "latter days" we have seen even greater evidence of God's kingship than the Chronicler, with the resurrection of Christ, and the promise of his coming again in glory. There have been many "days of small things" (Zech. 4:10) in the history of the Church. But none can alter the one eternal and unchanging truth of the universe: the kingship of God.

The First Book of Chronicles closes with a report of the celebrations attending Solomon's accession, in the form of worship of God. The people bless and sacrifice to the one who has given them a visible symbol of his enduring presence with them (vv. 20–22), and the allegiance given to Solomon (v. 24) is really given to God who, in Solomon's reign, will display his power more than ever before (v. 25). David is retired honourably (vv. 26ff.) to make way for his greater (but not greatest) son. (*Note*: The "second time" of v. 22 is obscure. It is absent from some ancient versions and may not be original.)

THE SECOND BOOK OF CHRONICLES

THE NEW MAN—I

2 Chronicles 1:1–17

[1]Solomon the son of David established himself in his kingdom, and the Lord his God was with him and made him exceedingly great.

[2]Solomon spoke to all Israel, to the commanders of thousands and of hundreds, to the judges, and to all the leaders in all Israel, the heads of fathers' houses. [3]And Solomon, and all the assembly with him, went to the high place that was at Gibeon; for the tent of meeting of God, which Moses the servant of the Lord had made in the wilderness, was there. [4](But David had brought up the ark of God from Kiriathjearim to the place that David had prepared for it, for he had pitched a tent for it in Jerusalem.) [5]Moreover the bronze altar that Bezalel the son of Uri, son of Hur, had made, was there before the tabernacle of the Lord. And Solomon and the assembly sought the Lord. [6]And Solomon went up there to the bronze altar before the Lord, which was at the tent of meeting, and offered a thousand burnt offerings upon it.

[7]In that night God appeared to Solomon, and said to him, "Ask what I shall give you." [8]And Solomon said to God, "Thou hast shown great and steadfast love to David my father, and hast made me king in his stead. [9]O Lord God, let thy promise to David my father be now fulfilled, for thou hast made me king over a people as many as the dust of the earth. [10]Give me now wisdom and knowledge to go out and come in before this people, for who can rule this thy people, that is so great?" [11]God answered Solomon, "Because this was in your heart, and you have not asked possessions, wealth, honour, or the life of those who hate you, and have not even asked long life, but have asked wisdom and knowledge for yourself that you may rule my people over whom I have made you king, [12]wisdom and knowledge are granted to you. I will also give you riches, possessions, and honour, such as none of the kings had who were before you, and none after you shall have the like." [13]So Solomon came from the high place at Gibeon, from before the tent of meeting, to Jerusalem. And he reigned over Israel.

¹⁴Solomon gathered together chariots and horsemen; he had four-teen hundred chariots and twelve thousand horsemen, who he stationed in the chariot cities and with the king in Jerusalem. ¹⁵And the king made silver and gold as common in Jerusalem as stone, and he made cedar as plentiful as the sycamore of the Shephelah. ¹⁶And Solomon's import of horses was from Egypt and Kue, and the king's traders received them from Kue for a price. ¹⁷They imported a chariot from Egypt for six hundred shekels of silver, and a horse for a hundred and fifty; likewise through them these were exported to all the kings of the Hittites and the kings of Syria.

(i) *Continuity and Discontinuity*

The Second Book of Chronicles continues from the first without a break. Solomon, having acceded to the throne in the previous chapter (vv. 2f.), now gathers the leaders of Israel together for a great act of worship to mark the beginning of his reign (vv. 2ff.). The new regime both continues from and excels that of David. The continuity is expressed in a number of ways. As God is said to have been *with* David at the beginning of his reign (1 Chr. 11:9), so now he is *with* Solomon, v. 1. In each case the practical effect of God's attendance is that the king becomes greater and greater (see the same verses). It was, furthermore, central to David's prayer for Solomon that the Lord would be with him, with the specific purpose that he should be able to build the Temple (1 Chr. 22:11). This prayer amounted to David's recognition that there was a total purpose for himself and Solomon together (see on 1 Chr. 17) which could only be achieved in Solomon's reign. It was Solomon who must build. Would he be adequate to the task?

As a preliminary answer to that question Solomon is now presented as being involved in the contrast which was made early in 1 Chr. between David and Saul. Unlike Saul, David "sought" the ark (1 Chr. 13:3; 15:13). Now Solomon too "seeks" the altar (v. 5—rather than RSV's imprecise "sought the Lord". See further below.) He thus shares with David the basic qualification of faithfulness to God (symbolized by the attitude to the ark) for becoming an instrument in the achievement of his purposes. The fact that Solomon assembles the leaders of Israel as David had done in the past (1 Chr. 28–29) announces that the stage is set for the final acts of the David–Solomon drama to be performed.

The fact of continuity with David does not imply that there is nothing new with Solomon. On the contrary it is explicitly said that Solomon would be wealthy beyond all the kings who were before him (v. 12; cf. 1 Chr. 29:25). In effect the reference can only be to Saul, his son Ishbosheth, whom Chr. does not even mention, and David. The superiority of Solomon relates particularly, however, to David. The real apogee of Israel's greatness comes not with him, but with Solomon. To stress that greatness and a sense in which Israel enters upon a new phase in its life, an extended analogy is drawn here and in the chapters that follow between Solomon's presiding over the building of the Temple and the construction of the tabernacle in the days of Moses. Solomon's resort to the Tent of Meeting at Gibeon (vv. 3ff.) brings into the foreground a symbol of the old order which was about to give way dramatically to the new. And the reminiscence about the tabernacle's master-craftsman Bezalel (cf. Exod. 31:2ff.) prepares for the introduction of the equally dexterous Huram-abi who will devote his talents to the fine work that will be done on the Temple (2 Chr. 2:13).

(ii) *Chr.'s Portrayal of Solomon*

Finally, by way of introduction to 2 Chr., it has to be said that Chr.'s portrayal of Solomon, in order to achieve this picture of greatness, omits a great deal that is recorded about him in the Books of Kings, and does so consistently to his advantage. When we take into account all that is said about Solomon in the biblical accounts it is clear that he had great faults, and the memory of his reign is blemished in various ways. There is no mention here of his harsh suppression of residual Saulide opposition (1 Kings 2); nor of his press-ganging of Israelites for the Temple-building (1 Kings 5:13ff.); nor of the fact that he spent thirteen years building his own house while it took him only seven to build the Temple (1 Kings 6:38; 7:1); nor of his susceptibility to the allurements of women, especially foreign women. 1 Kings 11:3 numbers his harem as seven hundred wives and three hundred concubines, who "turned away his heart", and for these liaisons he is explicitly condemned in that context (v. 2). Here perhaps more than anywhere in Chr. we have to come to terms with the extent to which the biblical writers selected their material in order to pursue their own theological purposes. The Chronicler's aim in his portrayal of Solomon is to show how God governed the events of history to impart to the kingdom of Israel, at least once, a splendour which was fit to symbolize his own. There may be argument as to how far this picture is legitimate in what purports to be a work of history. In defence of the Chronicler's responsibility as a historian it may be pointed out that 1 Kings gives the impression of a *late* decline in Solomon's character, locating his infidelity to the Lord particularly in the time of his old age (1 Kings 11:4). Kings too can present Solomon as wise and just (1 Kings 3). Perhaps, therefore, we can say that Chr. has simply taken the most positive view possible of Solomon's actual career. The Kings and Chronicles accounts, taken together, become another testimony—alongside the whole biblical picture of David—to the way in which God deigns to use great sinners in the work of his kingdom, so much so that the OT's latest picture of Solomon does not even remember his sins.

THE NEW MAN—II

2 Chronicles 1:1–17 (*cont'd*)

(iii) *The Features of Solomon's Reign*

Chapter 1 has been helpfully sub-divided into three parts: vv. 2–6, dealing with Solomon's worship, vv. 7–13 with his wisdom, and vv. 14–17 with his wealth. This sub-division, furthermore, serves to introduce Solomon's reign with three programmatic statements about its main features (Williamson). All three features bear upon the building of the Temple.

(a) *Worship* (vv. 2–6). Not only does Solomon gather the people for worship, he also leads them in it (v. 6). The question whether Solomon himself assumes priestly responsibilities is probably irresolvable and need not concern us. The point is that at the outset of his reign he affirms in signal fashion that everything he does will be in the context of worship and service. Despite his great office and the prestige attached to it he declares that he is subservient to the highest authority. (cf. again the ideal of kingship in Deut. 17:14–20.) Herein lies his worthiness to be responsible for the construction of the house of worship.

The note in v. 4 is rightly bracketed by RSV. It is a parenthetic explanation of the fact that Solomon's visit to Gibeon cannot correctly be described as "seeking the ark". The ark, having been brought to Jerusalem, is still in a kind of limbo. While the Temple remains unbuilt, the major place of worship remains the highplace at Gibeon where the tabernacle is. In the circumstances, therefore, Solomon's "seeking" the altar counts as a seeking of the ark in Chr.'s terms.

(b) *Wisdom* (vv. 7–13). Solomon is perhaps best known for his wisdom. The Book of Proverbs is traditionally ascribed to him, and there are other indications that he was in fact the originator of wise sayings (1 Kings 4:32). His wisdom extended also to the giving of judgment in cases of difficult civil litigation (1 Kings 3:16–28). We are more concerned, however, with the way in which he acquired wisdom, and what its nature was.

The impressive thing about Solomon's acquisition of wisdom is the fact that he seeks it from the Lord in response to the Lord's own question, "Ask what I shall give you" (v. 7). With the world thus at his feet the temptation to self-aggrandizement must have been great. But Solomon is overwhelmed by the magnitude of his responsibility. In his feeling of inadequacy before the greatness, and perhaps unruliness, of Israel, he echoes the reaction of Moses, who never wanted to lead Israel in the first place (Exod. 4:1,10–13), and whose experience with them confirmed his fears as to their recalcitrance (Num. 11:11–15, especially v. 14). Solomon sees the nature of the task and the need for God's special enabling for it, and has the moral stature to make such enabling his primary request of God. There is a simplicity and a spirituality about Solomon's reasoning which is perhaps seldom matched by modern Christians. The tendency to embark upon a path of Christian service upon *condition* that God will take care of the material necessities of life (perhaps even specified) reflects both a lack of faith and of perception. Embarkation comes first. God's consequent faithfulness in all things, experienced once by Solomon, is confirmed as an abiding principle by Jesus (Matt. 6:33).

Wisdom in the OT is above all a practical thing, not an abstract quality. Wisdom is the prerequisite of effective action. It is close to skill or ability. Bezalel, the architect of the tabernacle, mentioned in v. 5, is an outstanding exponent of it, his workmanlike arts having been imparted, we are told, by the Spirit of God (Exod. 31:3). Solomon's wisdom, therefore, is first and foremost a wisdom to rule, both effectively and according to God's own standards (cf. David's prayer, 1 Chr. 22:12, where wisdom to rule is expressly linked with law-keeping). There is nothing in this wisdom of Machiavellian guile. The Bible does not warrant a separate code of ethical conduct for politicians (or businessmen) on the grounds that the affairs with which they deal are momentous. On the contrary, its model for effective ability as honest simplicity is provided right at the top, in a king.

(c) *Wealth* (vv. 14–17). The high premium put by the OT on wealth can be a problem for some, an excuse for self-indulgence for others. When it is said that "the king made silver and gold as common in Jerusalem as stone . . ." (v. 15) and when we are told of the immensity and monetary value of his armoury, it is all clearly part of the presentation of Solomon as one who was fit to build God's house. The riches are expressly given by God as a reward for Solomon's selflessness. The tone seems to be a far cry from Jesus' warning that "it is easier for a camel to go through the eye of a needle than for a rich man to enter the kingdom of God" (Matt. 19:24).

Here as on other occasions it is of paramount importance to realize that both the contemporary canons of greatness and the externality of the people of God as an entity in the OT affect values. Blessing and welfare are often seen in material terms. And the Books of Chronicles clearly understand the wealth of Solomon's kingdom as appropriate to what they present as a reflection of the divine kingdom and glory upon earth. There is, therefore, something essentially time-bound about the place given to wealth in Chr. Since the modern Church is *not* a political entity, and is not seeking to win converts to God by an outward demonstration of greatness, it—and we—cannot take Chr. as a model for how we value wealth.

The task of assessing the place of material prosperity in Christian living is, in fact, delicate. What we do justifiably take from the OT's view of wealth is a positive attitude to created things as good, in contrast to those religions which have regarded all matter as evil (a tendency which has led, paradoxically, both to asceticism—as a denial of the material world, and to unrestrained licentiousness— on the grounds that matter is evil anyway!) Solomon's choice, however, still serves as a guideline in regard to material things. The resolution to serve God whatever the implications for status or income is a biblical response. The belief that wealth is an invariable mark of blessing is an unbiblical delusion and becomes a pseudo-religious justification of rapacity. The readiness to allow God his freedom in the matter of our material well-being is a true mark of discipleship.

THE LORD'S SUPREMACY

2 Chronicles 2:1–18

¹Now Solomon purposed to build a temple for the name of the Lord, and a royal palace for himself. ²And Solomon assigned seventy thousand men to bear burdens and eighty thousand to quarry in the hill country, and three thousand six hundred to oversee them. ³And Solomon sent word to Huram the king of Tyre: "As you dealt with David my father and sent him cedar to build himself a house to dwell in, so deal with me. ⁴Behold, I am about to build a house for the name of the Lord my God and dedicate it to him for the burning of incense of sweet spices before him, and for the continual offering of the showbread, and for burnt offerings morning and evening, on the sabbaths

and the new moons and the appointed feasts of the Lord our God, as ordained for ever for Israel. [5]The house which I am to build will be great, for our God is greater than all gods. [6]But who is able to build him a house, since heaven, even highest heaven, cannot contain him? Who am I to build a house for him, except as a place to burn incense before him? [7]So now send me a man skilled to work in gold, silver, bronze, and iron, and in purple, crimson, and blue fabrics, trained also in engraving, to be with the skilled workers who are with me in Judah and Jerusalem, whom David my father provided. [8]Send me also cedar, cypress, and algum timber from Lebanon, for I know that your servants know how to cut timber in Lebanon. And my servants will be with your servants, [9]to prepare timber for me in abundance, for the house I am to build will be great and wonderful. [10]I will give for your servants, the hewers who cut timber, twenty thousand cors of crushed wheat, twenty thousand cors of barley, twenty thousand baths of wine, and twenty thousand baths of oil.''

[11]Then Huram the king of Tyre answered in a letter which he sent to Solomon, ''Because the Lord loves his people he has made you king over them.'' [12]Huram also said, ''Blessed be the Lord God of Israel, who made heaven and earth, who has given King David a wise son, endued with discretion and understanding, who will build a temple for the Lord, and a royal palace for himself.

[13]''Now I have sent a skilled man, endued with understanding, Huram-abi, [14]the son of a woman of the daughters of Dan, and his father was a man of Tyre. He is trained to work in gold, silver, bronze, iron, stone, and wood, and in purple, blue, and crimson fabrics and fine linen, and to do all sorts of engraving and execute any design that may be assigned him, with your craftsmen, the craftsmen of my lord, David your father. [15]Now therefore the wheat and barley, oil and wine, of which my lord has spoken, let him send to his servants; [16]and we will cut whatever timber you need from Lebanon, and bring it to you in rafts by sea to Joppa, so that you may take it up to Jerusalem.''

[17]Then Solomon took a census of all the aliens who were in the land of Israel, after the census of them which David his father had taken; and there were found a hundred and fifty-three thousand six hundred. [18]Seventy thousand of them he assigned to bear burdens, eighty thousand to quarry in the hill country, and three thousand six hundred as overseers to make the people work.

The scale and magnificence of the Temple was clearly going to make huge demands on materials. We see from v. 2 that certain of these were obtained from within Solomon's territories, viz. stone from quarries in the mountains of Israel. Many of the richer materials, however, were obtained from beyond Israel's borders. We have seen how David had already amassed large quantities of materials for the building of the Temple (1 Chr. 22:2–4), including gold, silver, and bronze acquired as a result of his military campaigns (1 Chr. 18:7–11). The present chapter continues this theme. As usual, the Chronicler does not give us a bald account of how Solomon acquired his materials for the Temple. Rather, he uses the relationship with Huram (known in Kings as Hiram) to make points about Solomon's position in relation to other kings in the ancient world, and above all about Israel's God.

(i)

It is clear from v. 1 that the status of Solomon is closely linked with the recognition of the greatness of the Lord. This is the significance of the information that he planned to build not only a Temple but a palace too. Such a plan does not imply double-mindedness on Solomon's part but belongs to the theology of Chr. whereby his magnificence is a reflection of God's, even if the supreme reflection of God's glory is the Temple itself (v. 5).

As Solomon's greatness is used to point to that of the Lord, so his relationship with Huram is used to affirm the Lord's supremacy over other gods. The dealings between Solomon and Huram are presented in such a way as to leave no doubt that it is Solomon, and his God, who command in the situation. The clearest example of this is the confession by Huram of the creatorhood of God (v. 12), remarkable because it is an assertion of his universal dominion in the mouth of one who would have had gods of his own to think about.

Equally important, however, is the fact that Huram appears to play a subordinate role to Solomon. In v. 14 he refers to David as "my lord". 1 Chr. 14:1 showed that he had already sent cedar to David, and there is probably an implication of tribute there. There is a sense in which Solomon too appears to *command* the provision of timber. This becomes clearer when we notice that certain details in 1 Kings 5 have been omitted here. In that chapter, we find that Solomon actually made a treaty with Huram (v. 12), and also that he made payment to him in return for the timber (v. 11). Chr. does not tell us about the treaty, and stresses that the payments (of wheat, etc., 2 Chr. 2:10) were for the labour of those who cut the timber. These subtle differences are designed to suggest that Solomon's will was irresistible in the matter, even if the historical actuality was one of parity as represented in the treaty.

The fact that Solomon's relations with Lebanon are here in view, rather than with other of his smaller neighbours, further stresses his wide influence. Lebanon had for long supplied the empires of the east with timber for building. Her forests, and especially her cedars, were renowned for their abundance and luxuriance and were proverbial in Israel as symbols both of plenty and of pride (Isa. 2:13; Pss. 92:12; 104:16). For a building of splendour it was imperative to use what was universally recognized as best, and Solomon's ability to command it is a sign not only of his ascendancy over Huram, but of his eminence in the ancient world in general—and of course, of the supremacy of the Lord.

(ii)

In the course of his proclamation that the Lord is greater than all gods, Solomon testifies also to his transcendence. God is so great that no building, however magnificent, can contain him. Clearly this is a salutary thought for Solomon and Israel—and for the Chronicler's generation too—in the context of the mammoth national effort which was about to be put into the construction of the Temple. To the modern reader, for whom the fact that God and religion are spiritual is a commonplace, it may seem superfluous for Solomon to have to enter such a caveat as he begins his work. There was nothing superfluous about it, however, in the ancient world.

Temples were the order of the day in the religion of the ancient world. Cities in Canaan and Mesopotamia would have had one as a matter of course, and archaeologists have uncovered what remains of many of them. Israel was not unique, therefore, in having a Temple. (On the contrary, the Lord's initial reluctance to have a Temple built for him at all, 2 Sam. 7:5ff., is probably attributable to the fact that it typified Canaanite worship.) Solomon's letter to Huram shows that where Israel was unique was in her conception of what her Temple meant. Typically, temples were regarded as the dwelling-place of the god. Belief in his literal presence there was taken to such lengths that Canaanite and Babylonian rituals involved the provision of food and drink for the gods. Now, undoubtedly there were varying degrees of sophistication in the way in which worshippers thought of the nature of their gods. But it is against any notion of the Lord being limited to the house he was building, having a merely physical existence and dependent upon his worshippers for his well-being, that Solomon's letter guards. How should a mere building contain him whom heaven itself cannot contain! Israelites, it may be said, were by no means immune from debased conceptions of God along the lines of Canaan (cf. Jeremiah's criticism in Jer. 7:1–15). Even some of their rituals ran the risk of being interpreted in the sense of Canaanite rituals. There are, indeed, OT texts which speak in rather corporeal terms of God's acceptance of sacrifice (e.g. Gen. 8:21), and even of his presence in the sanctuary (Exod 25:22). So Israel must be educated about the God she worships— and no doubt the Chronicler, in recording Solomon's letter, is primarily concerned to make the point to his own contemporaries, even as he, like Solomon, endeavoured to promote the worship of God in a building.

(iii)

Finally on this point, let us notice once again the use of the idea of the *name* of God. It is in Deuteronomy that we first find this way of speaking abut his presence (Deut. 12:5), and it is a further safeguard against the belief that God was confined in the place of worship. The "name" at times seems to take on an existence of its own, as a kind of representative of God. It never actually becomes a separate entity, and indeed cannot, because in the OT a person's name and his personality, or very being, are far more intimately linked than in our own day. But the idea of God's name does suggest something of the elusiveness of God. Much of the OT's imagery surrounding his presence speaks of the fact that he is present and yet absent, or inaccessible, at one and the same time. Herein, perhaps, is the abiding truth which we may take from this chapter. God made himself available to Solomon and his Israel by permitting a building made with hands to symbolize his presence. Yet that concrete symbol could never reduce God to something which Solomon could manipulate to his own ends (again, a popular error of pagan religion). It ill behoves us moderns to scoff at these "primitive" delusions. The attempt to enlist God to the cause of this, that or the other cause or ideology is almost obsessional in parts of the modern western world, and, absurdly, suffers little from the fact that he is often thought to be on both sides at once. The use of religion for personal gain or advancement is nothing other than the sin of idolatry, against which the OT writers protest above all.

THE TEMPLE BUILT

2 Chronicles 3:1–4:22

¹Then Solomon began to build the house of the Lord in Jerusalem on Mount Moriah, where the Lord had appeared to David his father, at the place that David had appointed, on the threshing floor of Ornan the Jebusite. ²He began to build in the second month of the fourth year of his reign. ³These are Solomon's measurements for building the house of God: the length, in cubits of the old standard, was sixty cubits, and the breadth twenty cubits. ⁴The vestibule in front of the nave of the house was twenty cubits long, equal to the width of the house; and its height was a hundred and twenty cubits. He overlaid it on the inside with pure gold. ⁵The nave he lined with cypress, and covered it with fine gold, and made palms and chains on it. ⁶He adorned the house with settings of precious stones. The gold was gold of Parvaim. ⁷So he lined the house with gold—its beams, its thresholds, its walls, and its doors; and he carved cherubim on the walls.

⁸And he made the most holy place; its length, corresponding to the breadth of the house, was twenty cubits, and its breadth was twenty cubits; he overlaid it with six hundred talents of fine gold. ⁹The weight

of the nails was one shekel to fifty shekels of gold. And he overlaid the upper chambers with gold.

¹⁰In the most holy place he made two cherubim of wood and overlaid them with gold. ¹¹The wings of the cherubim together extended twenty cubits: one wing of the one, of five cubits, touched the wall of the house, and its other wing, of five cubits, touched the wing of the other cherub; ¹²and of this cherub, one wing, of five cubits, touched the wall of the house, and the other wing, also of five cubits, was joined to the wing of the first cherub. ¹³The wings of these cherubim extended twenty cubits; the cherubim stood on their feet, facing the nave. ¹⁴And he made the veil of blue and purple and crimson fabrics and fine linen, and worked cherubim on it.

¹⁵In front of the house he made two pillars thirty-five cubits high, with a capital of five cubits on the top of each. ¹⁶He made chains like a necklace and put them on the tops of the pillars; and he made a hundred pomegranates, and put them on the chains. ¹⁷He set up the pillars in front of the temple, one on the south, the other on the north; that on the south he called Jachin, and that on the north Boaz.

¹He made an altar of bronze, twenty cubits long, and twenty cubits wide, and ten cubits high. ²Then he made the molten sea; it was round, ten cubits from brim to brim, and five cubits high, and a line of thirty cubits measured its circumference. ³Under it were figures of gourds, for thirty cubits, compassing the sea round about; the gourds were in two rows, cast with it when it was cast. ⁴It stood upon twelve oxen, three facing north, three facing west, three facing south, and three facing east; the sea was set upon them, and all their hinder parts were inward. ⁵Its thickness was a handbreadth; and its brim was made like the brim of a cup, like the flower of a lily; it held over three thousand baths. ⁶He also made ten lavers in which to wash, and set five on the south side, and five on the north side. In these they were to rinse off what was used for the burnt offering, and the sea was for the priests to wash in.

⁷And he made ten golden lampstands as prescribed, and set them in the temple, five on the south side and five on the north. ⁸He also made ten tables, and placed them in the temple, five on the south side and five on the north. And he made a hundred basins of gold. ⁹He made the court of the priests, and the great court, and doors for the court, and overlaid their doors with bronze; ¹⁰and he set the sea at the southeast corner of the house.

¹¹Huram also made the pots, the shovels, and the basins. So Huram

finished the work that he did for King Solomon on the house of God; 12the two pillars, the bowls, and the two capitals on the top of the pillars; and the two networks to cover the two bowls of the capitals that were on the top of the pillars; 13and the four hundred pomegranates for the two networks, two rows of pomegranates for each network, to cover the two bowls of the capitals that were upon the pillars. 14He made the stands also, and the lavers upon the stands, 15and the one sea, and the twelve oxen underneath it. 16The pots, the shovels, the forks, and all the equipment for these Huram-abi made of burnished bronze for King Solomon for the house of the Lord. 17In the plain of the Jordan the king cast them, in the clay ground between Succoth and Zeredah. 18Solomon made all these things in great quantities, so that the weight of the bronze was not ascertained.

19So Solomon made all the things that were in the house of God: the golden altar, the tables for the bread of the Presence, 20the lampstands and their lamps of pure gold to burn before the inner sanctuary, as prescribed; 21the flowers, the lamps, and the tongs, of purest gold; 22the snuffers, basins, dishes for incense, and firepans, of pure gold; and the sockets of the temple, for the inner doors to the most holy place and for the doors of the nave of the temple were of gold.

At last the Temple is built. The account is an abridgment of that in 1 Kings chapters 6 and 7 which is about twice as long. We may deduce from this that it is not the Chronicler's main purpose to give a detailed description of the Temple and its construction. (As well as Kings, cf. Ezek. 40–43 for a more exhaustive portrayal of a temple.) Rather, the details are subordinate to the purpose of showing that Solomon did in fact carry out the work. His centrality in the account is perhaps designed to evoke that of Moses in the narrative of the construction of the tabernacle, Exod. 36:8–39:32. So we have a picture of the servant of God about his work, in the context of the forward movement of God's plans. These two chapters (together with ch. 5) are really the necessary prelude to the following (chs. 6, 7) which reflect upon the significance of the events described here. It is right, nevertheless, to consider briefly the significance of the Temple's symbolism.

(i)

To a great extent the detailed description of the building is meant to draw attention to its richness; hence the references to cypress wood overlaid with gold (3:5) and again, to the amount of materials used (3:8f.—here too the figures may be symbolic). But let us notice the way in which the Temple, in its design and decoration, speaks of God's presence. First, there is "the most holy place". Entering the Temple by the east, between the pillars called Jachin and Boaz (3:17), one finds oneself in the vestibule (3:4), whence one penetrates further into the nave (3:5), and finally stands before the "most holy place"—which might only be entered once a year by the High Priest. There is thus a gradation in the holiness of different parts of the Temple, designed to emphasize the unapproachability of God. The veil (3:14), mentioned only here in the OT but presumably similar to that in the later Herodian temple which was torn from top to bottom at the crucifixion (Matt. 27:51), is the final guardian of God's most intimate presence.

In addition to the design of the basic structure, the decorations too have their significance. In the "most holy place" we find figures of cherubim, and indeed pictures and carvings of these creatures appear on the veil and on the walls of the nave. As the holy place is a reflection of the heavenly dwelling-place of God, so these images of the creatures reflect the host that surrounds God in incessant adoration (cf. Isa. 6:2f.). Here is a picture of God's dominion. When Ezekiel had his vision in Babylon of God enthroned over that empire, cherubim were at the centre of it, representing the created order over which God is Lord. There (Ezek. ch. 1; cf. 10:15) they combined human and animal features in a way that seems grotesque (1:5–10), but which signified the whole range of the created order. Such is the symbolism of Solomon's Temple too, and the "oxen" of 4:4 (and also v. 3 where "gourds" is an unwarranted alteration of the Hebrew, which has "oxen") may have a similar function.

(ii)

Having said what sort of symbolism Solomon's Temple does manifest, let us notice what sort it does not. There is a tradition of interpretation of the temple and tabernacle imagery which seeks to find in it minute correspondences with the theology of the Person and work of Christ. Every detail, down to hangings, lampstands, tables, must have some distinctive theological significance. Such an approach is misguided. The Temple of the OT has a single and simple relationship to the work of Christ in the sense that Christ has brought God to dwell fully among humankind, in all his holiness, yet first and foremost approachable. It teaches us about the work of Christ almost in a negative way, by causing us to understand something of the immensity of what it is that the holy God should become "sin" (i.e. by dying on the cross, 2 Cor. 5:21) for the sake of humanity.

In Solomon's Temple certain things have symbolic value, but the symbolism is univocal and lies on the surface (as with the cherubim, which speak of the holiness and power of God, cf. above). The majority of things—Huram's pots, shovels, basins etc., 4:11ff.—have no particular symbolic value, but belong to the fact that that which represents God's presence and holiness in Israel before Christ is a material thing, a house built with hands, and its service must needs have a range of material accoutrements.

This prompts two final thoughts. (a) The theology of Christ's atonement should be sought in passages where it is taught (primarily in the New Testament, which draws, of course, on parts of the OT, such as Isa. 53, the sacrificial system in Lev. etc.) and not in the architecture of the Temple. (b) There is no such thing as "holy space"—or, to put it differently, "*un*holy space"—in the Christian era, even though many of our churches seem to be modelled on the Temple. Dual-purpose buildings—designed for acts of worship as well as the horseplay of the youth club—are fully in line with New Testament theology.

AN END, AND A BEGINNING

2 Chronicles 5:1–6:11

¹Thus all the work that Solomon did for the house of the Lord was finished. And Solomon brought in the things which David his father

had dedicated, and stored the silver, the gold, and all the vessels in the treasuries of the house of God.

²Then Solomon assembled the elders of Israel and all the heads of the tribes, the leaders of the fathers' houses of the people of Israel, in Jerusalem, to bring up the ark of the covenant of the Lord out of the city of David, which is Zion. ³And all the men of Israel assembled before the king at the feast which is in the seventh month. ⁴And all the elders of Israel came, and the Levites took up the ark. ⁵And they brought up the ark, the tent of meeting, and all the holy vessels that were in the tent; the priests and the Levites brought them up. ⁶And King Solomon and all the congregation of Israel, who had assembled before him, were before the ark, sacrificing so many sheep and oxen that they could not be counted or numbered. ⁷So the priests brought the ark of the covenant of the Lord to its place, in the inner sanctuary of the house, in the most holy place, underneath the wings of the cherubim. ⁸For the cherubim spread out their wings over the place of the ark, so that the cherubim made a covering above the ark and its poles. ⁹And the poles were so long that the ends of the poles were seen from the holy place before the inner sanctuary; but they could not be seen from outside; and they are there to this day. ¹⁰There was nothing in the ark except the two tables which Moses put there at Horeb, where the Lord made a covenant with the people of Israel, when they came out of Egypt. ¹¹Now when the priests came out of the holy place (for all the priests who were present had sanctified themselves, without regard to their divisions; ¹²and all the Levitical singers, Asaph, Heman, and Jeduthun, their sons and kinsmen, arrayed in fine linen, with cymbals, harps, and lyres, stood east of the altar with a hundred and twenty priests who were trumpeters; ¹³and it was the duty of the trumpeters and singers to make themselves heard in unison in praise and thanksgiving to the Lord), and when the song was raised, with trumpets and cymbals and other musical instruments, in praise to the Lord,

"For he is good,
    for his steadfast love endures for ever,"
the house, the house of the Lord, was filled with a cloud, ¹⁴so that the priests could not stand to minister because of the cloud; for the glory of the Lord filled the house of God.

¹Then Solomon said,
    "The Lord has said that he would dwell in thick darkness.

²I have built thee an exalted house,
    a place for thee to dwell in for ever."
³Then the king faced about, and blessed all the assembly of Israel, while all the assembly of Israel stood. ⁴And he said, "Blessed be the Lord, the God of Israel, who with his hand has fulfilled what he promised with his mouth to David my father, saying, ⁵'Since the day that I brought my people out of the land of Egypt, I chose no city in all the tribes of Israel in which to build a house, that my name might be there, and I chose no man as prince over my people Israel; ⁶but I have chosen Jerusalem that my name may be there and I have chosen David to be over my people Israel.' ⁷Now it was in the heart of David my father to build a house for the name of the Lord, the God of Israel. ⁸But the Lord said to David my father, 'Whereas it was in your heart to build a house for my name, you did well that it was in your heart; ⁹nevertheless you shall not build the house, but your son who shall be born to you shall build the house for my name.' ¹⁰Now the Lord has fulfilled his promise which he made; for I have risen in the place of David my father, and sit on the throne of Israel, as the Lord promised, and I have built the house for the name of the Lord, the God of Israel. ¹¹And there I have set the ark, in which is the covenant of the Lord which he made with the people of Israel."

Over this section of the Books of Chronicles hangs an atmosphere of fulfilment. The Temple has been built. Now as a final seal on the God-givenness of the place of worship, together with the peace, security and prosperity which are inseparable from its right use, the ark is taken on the final stage of its journey.

The account of the entry of the ark into the Temple illustrates well how tightly the Books of Chronicles are structured. No rambling, aimless history this. On the contrary, close affinities with 1 Chr. 15 and 16 make it clear that what is now reported is a completion of what was begun there. The structure of the two passages is similar. Each has an account of the actual transporting of the ark, emphasizing ritual correctness (1 Chr. 15:1–16:3; 2 Chr. 5:2–10); each reports an act of praise and celebration accompanying the ark's arrival (1 Chr. 16:4–36; 2 Chr. 5:11–14, with the refrain in 2 Chr. 5:13*b* echoing that in 1 Chr. 16:34); each is followed by a reflection, in different forms, upon God's plan that Solomon rather than David should be the builder of his house (1 Chr. 17:1–15; 2 Chr. 6:1–11). The closeness of the relationship between the two accounts is the Chronicler's way of stating finally that only Solomon could legitimately enshrine the ark in its final resting-place.

The sense of fulfilment is brought out further in some of the language used. The word translated "finished" (5:1) is *wattishlam*, which is linguistically akin to Solomon's name. Both words strongly suggest the idea of "peace" (*shalom*). The "finishing", therefore, is only an *end* in the sense of *purpose*. It opens on to something new, full of possibilities for good—for, as we have seen before, *shalom* suggests all the richness and delight that are part of God's deepest purposes for humanity in creation. Another word-play, in 6:10, suggests similar ideas. In the statements "the Lord has *fulfilled* his promise" and "I have *risen* in the place of David my father", the words in italics represent the same Hebrew verb (meaning "rise", or "stand"). Read superficially, this could look like conceit on Solomon's part. But such is far from the meaning of the passage. The point that is stressed through the repetition is that the Lord has now established circumstances within which his people can enjoy all that he desires to give them, at the same time worshipping him in truth. Even the psalm-fragment in 5:13, one of Chr.'s rare changes from 1 Kings 8, seems deliberately to point forward into a future that holds unlimited possibilities. Finally there is a reminiscence of Moses when, at the completion of the building of the tabernacle, he was unable to enter the Tent of Meeting because it was covered by a cloud, and the tabernacle itself was filled with the glory of the Lord (Exod. 40:34f.). As the ark now comes to its resting-place, the Temple is filled with a cloud and, like Moses, the priests cannot minister because of the presence of the Lord's glory. The point of this reminiscence of Moses is to suggest that in Solomon's day, as in his, the people of God are on the verge of something new and great.

Everything in this section, therefore, converges to make the point that the accession of Solomon heralds a new era for Israel. Now, as ever, the Chronicler is not interested in depicting the greatness of Solomon's reign for its own sake. The possibilities which Solomon brought to the Israel of his day are held out by him to his own later community. Indeed it is of the essence of his work that each new generation has the opportunity to secure "the good life" through obedience to God. It is for this reason that we can say that the present passage is a beginning as well as an end, for it not only signals a fulfilment of God's plans for Israel, but also becomes a reference point for the stories of subsequent kings. The issue with each of them is whether they were able to secure the blessings of God through obedience. And the Chronicler's purpose is to present the people of his time with that challenge.

And *our* time. The real significance of the ark for Chr., as is clear from 5:10, is that it stands for the Covenant made between God and Israel at Sinai and the standards which were required of Israel in the context of that relationship. It is in this way that Chr. can challenge the Church of our day. The Church knows the same covenant-making God that Israel did, though it looks back supremely to Calvary rather than to Sinai. Resembling Israel in so many ways, it does so perhaps chiefly in this, that it tends to presume upon God's commitment to it. While we think of the Church as "it", of course, the message remains comfortable, addressed to someone else. The Church is, however, "we", "us", "you and me". The possibilities before us for changing people, ourselves and others, into the kind of people fit for a kingdom of God are unlimited. If we love our Lord, we shall keep his commandments (John 14:15). The possibilities of knowing the blessing of God—understood in spiritual terms as the "peace that passes understanding" (Phil. 4:7) rather than a peace which has a primary political dimension—are also unlimited. (John 14 provides an interesting parallel to the present passage in its bringing together of the ideas of obedience and peace.)

Here, then, is one side of a paradox in biblical thought, which has at its other pole the knowledge that the purposes of God for humanity can only be finally achieved in a "new heaven and new earth" (Rev. 21:1). It is not necessary to resolve the paradox. But it is to the possibilities of experience and obedience in the present that the Chronicler chiefly addresses himself.

SOLOMON'S PRAYER—I

2 Chronicles 6:12–42

¹²Then Solomon stood before the altar of the Lord in the presence of all the assembly of Israel, and spread forth his hands. ¹³Solomon had made a bronze platform five cubits long, five cubits wide, and three cubits high, and had set it in the court; and he stood upon it. Then he knelt upon his knees in the presence of all the assembly of Israel, and spread forth his hands toward heaven; ¹⁴and said, "O Lord, God of Israel, there is no God like thee, in heaven or on earth, keeping covenant and showing steadfast love to thy servants who walk before thee with all their heart; ¹⁵who has kept with thy servant David my father what thou didst declare to him; yea, thou didst speak with thy mouth, and with thy hand hast fulfilled it this day. ¹⁶Now therefore, O Lord, God of Israel, keep with thy servant David my father what thou hast promised him, saying, 'There shall never fail you a man before me to sit upon the throne of Israel, if only your sons take heed to their way, to walk in my law as you have walked before me.' ¹⁷Now therefore, O Lord, God of Israel, let thy word be confirmed, which thou hast spoken to thy servant David.

¹⁸"But will God dwell indeed with man on the earth? Behold, heaven and the highest heaven cannot contain thee; how much less this house which I have built! ¹⁹Yet have regard to the prayer of thy servant and to his supplication, O Lord my God, hearkening to the cry and to the prayer which thy servant prays before thee; ²⁰that thy eyes may be open day and night toward this house, the place where thou hast promised to set thy name, that thou mayest hearken to the prayer which thy servant offers toward this place. ²¹And hearken thou to the supplications of thy servant and of thy people Israel, when they pray toward this place; yea, hear thou from heaven thy dwelling place; and when thou hearest, forgive.

²²"If a man sins against his neighbour and is made to take an oath, and comes and swears his oath before thy altar in this house, ²³then hear thou from heaven, and act, and judge thy servants, requiting the guilty by bringing his conduct upon his own head, and vindicating the righteous by rewarding him according to his righteousness.

²⁴"If thy people Israel are defeated before the enemy because they have sinned against thee, when they turn again and acknowledge thy name, and pray and make supplication to thee in this house, ²⁵then

hear thou from heaven, and forgive the sin of thy people Israel, and bring them again to the land which thou gavest to them and to their fathers.

26"When heaven is shut up and there is no rain because they have sinned against thee, if they pray toward this place, and acknowledge thy name, and turn from their sin, when thou dost afflict them, 27then hear thou in heaven, and forgive the sin of thy servants, thy people Israel, when thou dost teach them the good way in which they should walk; and grant rain upon thy land, which thou hast given to thy people as an inheritance.

28"If there is famine in the land, if there is pestilence or blight or mildew or locust or caterpillar; if their enemies besiege them in any of their cities; whatever plague, whatever sickness there is; 29whatever prayer, whatever supplication is made by any man or by all thy people Israel, each knowing his own affliction, and his own sorrow and stretching out his hands toward this house; 30then hear thou from heaven thy dwelling place, and forgive, and render to each whose heart thou knowest, according to all his ways (for thou, thou only, knowest the hearts of the children of men); 31that they may fear thee and walk in thy ways all the days that they live in the land which thou gavest to our fathers.

32"Likewise when a foreigner, who is not of thy people Israel, comes from a far country for the sake of thy great name, and thy mighty hand, and thy outstretched arm, when he comes and prays toward this house, 33hear thou from heaven thy dwelling place, and do according to all for which the foreigner calls to thee; in order that all the peoples of the earth may know thy name and fear thee, as do thy people Israel, and that they may know that this house which I have built is called by thy name.

34"If thy people go out to battle against their enemies, by whatever way thou shalt send them, and they pray to thee toward this city which thou hast chosen and the house which I have built for thy name, 35then hear thou from heaven their prayer and their supplication, and maintain their cause.

36"If they sin against thee—for there is no man who does not sin—and thou art angry with them, and dost give them to an enemy, so that they are carried away captive to a land far or near; 37yet if they lay it to heart in the land to which they have been carried captive, and repent, and make supplication to thee in the land of their captivity, saying, 'We have sinned, and have acted perversely and wickedly'; 38if they repent with all their mind and with all their heart in the land of their captivity, to which they were carried captive, and pray toward their land, which thou gavest to their fathers, the city which thou hast chosen, and the house which I have built for thy name, [39]then hear thou from heaven thy dwelling place their prayer and their supplications, and maintain their cause and forgive thy people who have sinned against thee. [40]Now, O my God, let thy eyes be open and thy ears attentive to a prayer of this place.

[41]"And now arise, O Lord God, and go to thy resting place,
    thou and the ark of thy might.
Let thy priests, O Lord God, be clothed with salvation,
    and let thy saints rejoice in thy goodness.
[42]O Lord God, do not turn away the face of thy anointed one!
    Remember thy steadfast love for David thy servant."

(i)

The ark having come to its final resting-place, the Temple is now used, in a powerful and exemplary way, for the purpose for which it is primarily intended—prayer. In one sense it is the figure of Solomon which bestrides this section like a colossus. And indeed, in his intercessory role and with quasi-priestly status, he reminds us once again of Moses. (cf. Moses' intercession for wayward Israel, Exod. 32.) Yet more important than the grandeur of the man is that which his very greatness lends to the act of praying. We have noticed prayers at crucial places before in Chr. (1 Chr. 17:16–27; 29:10–19). This of Solomon's is perhaps the central prayer in the two books, following as it does the most significant single event in them, and containing, moreover, the essence of Chr.'s theology of salvation.

The occurrence of a prayer at this point, therefore, is no accident. Two general things may be said about it.

(a) The subject of the prayer is, in a sense, prayer itself (vv. 19–21). It is for this reason that we called Solomon's prayer "exemplary". It envisages Israel, in future generations and as a matter of habit, seeking God in prayer in the Temple. Prayer is to be the essential instrument in the continuing relationship between God and his people. It is that which activates existing promises. Notice how Solomon's first petition (vv. 16f.) is that

God would keep promises that he has already made. Indeed Solomon can testify that he has actually begun to keep them (v. 15) and the circumstances in which he was speaking were perhaps as high a point as he could conceive in the keeping of them. Yet he is not content to leave it at that, but implores God to continue to keep his promises. This says much about the role of prayer in the relationship between God and man. If we feel that prayer is not worth while on the grounds that God is sovereign and will do what he pleases in any case, we fail to perceive that it belongs fundamentally to God's purposes for humanity that we should identify and come to desire the things which he desires for us. When Solomon pictures future generations at prayer it is again conceived as a laying claim to things promised long ago (vv. 26, 27).

A final observation related to the exemplary character of this prayer is its intensity. The prayer is not characterized by great variety of thought or even much logical progression. It concentrates upon one great theme (of which more anon). But it is this concentration which is arresting. The prayer expresses a longing that future generations should find God and his blessing, and that longing is expressed in Solomon's refusal to relinquish his theme, or to be content with a casual or vague expression of it. How much of ourselves—our emotional energy and simply our time—we are prepared to lay before God in prayer may be a measure of the extent to which we really desire the things we pray for.

(b) The second general point about prayer in this chapter is simply the fact that it is conceived as the real purpose for which the Temple was built. Notice the recurring phrase, "if they pray *toward this place/house*" (vv. 20, 24, 26, 29 etc.). It is assumed that those who wish to pray will seek the place of prayer. It would be misguided to see in this, however, an example of OT external-ism in religion, for it is the opposite that is intended. It is prayer, implicitly, rather than sacrifice, which is the supreme function of the Temple. And the spirituality of the activity commended is proved by the numerous references to the fact that the Temple itself is not the true dwelling-place of God, and indeed not even heaven can contain him. This fact is regularly alluded to more or less in the same breath as that in which the Israelite is depicted as praying "toward this house" (e.g. vv. 29, 30).

Man's relation to God here is, then, entirely spiritual. External institutions there may be, but they never have effected in themselves, nor ever can, a meaningful relationship between God and man. God "knows the hearts of the children of man", and seeks their genuine response to him in a desire for rectitude (v. 31).

SOLOMON'S PRAYER—II

2 Chronicles 6:12–42 (*cont'd*)

(ii)

So to the theology of the prayer. The basic premise is contained in v. 14 which depicts God as keeping covenant with those who "walk before thee with all their heart". The relationship is shown, here as elsewhere, to be entirely two-sided, and admitting of no half-measures. God's commitment has already been evidenced and is still desired. Verse 20 (cf. v. 40) expresses Solomon's desire that God's eyes should be open day and night to the Temple. The point is that he should be constantly attentive to the prayers of his people. (The idea of constancy is stressed by the form in which the phrase "may be open" is cast in the original, viz., a passive participle—"(be in a state of being) opened"— suggesting a habitual and unremitting readiness to hear.) Solomon knows that God is like this. And his granting of the Temple is a guarantee on his side, expressed in terms of his having set his name there (v. 20), that he will always be receptive. This constancy, however, is rightly met by a similar constancy on Israel's part. The full symbolic value of the Temple is as a focus of the reciprocal *seeking* of God and Israel (cf. on 1 Chr. 28:9).

The more specific theme of the prayer, however, is related to the eventuality of Israel sinning. Indeed the general picture of an Israel regularly faithful in prayer (v. 21) soon gives way to one of Israel at prayer in repentance for sin. Underlying Solomon's whole conception of the pattern of subsequent generations' life with God is an intimation, perhaps a foreboding, that it will be characterized by unfaithfulness rather than its opposite—an impression borne out by the account of those generations, to which most of the rest of 2 Chr. is devoted, and to which Solomon's prayer is closely related in the Chronicler's mind. Solomon rehearses again and again, therefore, a particular scenario: Israel sins, God removes the covenant blessings (resulting in defeat in battle and exile, v. 24, drought, v. 26, famine, plague etc., v. 28). Israel *turns again* (or repents) and *prays*—and to this Solomon adds his petition that God should forgive and restore to blessing. There is a regularity in this pattern, and indeed there even seems to be a rather mechanical inevitability about it contained in the recurring form of words: e.g. "When heaven is shut up... *because* they have sinned" (v. 26). Here again Solomon's prayer is closely related to the remainder of 2 Chr. We shall see how the fate of the kingdom under this or that king is regularly related to the king's righteousness or wickedness in a direct way. Is this the beginning of that Jewish legalism which forms a background to the pages of the New Testament?

In answer to this question it is important to realize that Chr. stands squarely within the framework of OT covenant-theology. (The present passage differs very little in detail from its counterpart in 1 Kings 8:22–53, and the proximity of the theology of Kings to that of Deuteronomy is widely acknowledged.) The basis of any relationship between God and Israel can only ultimately be God's *keeping covenant* and *showing steadfast love* (v. 14). God's action in establishing the relationship must precede any obedience on Israel's part. And when that obedience comes it is in the form, as we have noted, of a response which is profoundly personal, and which cannot therefore be constituted by a series of prescribed acts. We can take this thought a little further by a consideration of what is meant by the ideas of "judging" and "righteousness" in v. 23.

The OT's theology of judgment is perhaps best exemplified in the Psalms. What strikes the modern reader, for whom the idea of judgment is full of grim foreboding, is the way in which the Psalmists confidently and joyfully seek it (Ps. 7:6–8; Ps. 17:2, where RSV's "vindication" represents the same word—*mish-*

pat—that is usually translated "judgment"). This is because judgment has, for the saint of the OT, the idea of deliverance. The deliverance is often from enemies, though that is incidental to our point. What is essential to it is that the deliverance is based on a relationship which already exists between the saint and God—a relationship defined by God's covenant commitment. RSV's "vindication" in Ps. 17:2 is an attempt to catch this sense. The word *mishpat* can also sometimes be translated "right", or even "cause", as in vv. 35 and 39 of our passage. These last verses show that Solomon has this sort of judgment in mind in his prayer. God will hear the prayers of penitent Israel not because, by their praying, they merit his favour, but because he returns to his prior commitment to them.

Similar observations can be made about the idea of righteousness. Men of the OT can often be found protesting their righteousness (as in Pss. 7 and 17 which we have cited). Yet as we take into account the context of the OT as a whole, it becomes clear that they cannot mean by it that they possess some natural or inherent righteousness which makes them acceptable to God. Ps. 143 illustrates the point well. In v. 2 of that Psalm the Psalmist confesses—in a tone very similar to v. 36 of our present chapter— that "no man living is righteous before thee". Yet he can look to God to hear his *supplications* (a word that affords a further parallel to our chapter) on the basis of *God's* righteousness (v. 1). This idea of God's righteousness as a saving quality is highly illuminating for an understanding of the OT, and shows how close it is to the New Testament's understanding of God's dealings with humanity (Rom. 3:21f.). In Ps. 143 the Psalmist appeals to God on the basis not of his own merit, but rather on that of his covenant status, as is illustrated by his invocation of God's *faithfulness* alongside his righteousness (v. 1). Job also makes much of his *righteousness*, and indeed his *right (mishpat),* to come before God. But even he is well aware that in himself he is sinful (Job 14:16f.). His "right" too is based (implicitly) upon covenant. And this is the best way to understand not only Pss. 7 and 17, but also the righteousness which Solomon implores God to recognize in Israel when they return to him in prayer.

(iii)

Solomon's final words, in vv. 41, 42, are noteworthy because the account of the prayer deviates at this point from that in 1 Kings. As in 1 Chr. 28 (see commentary) we find a reference to Ps. 132, the psalm which speaks of God coming to his resting-place as the ark finds its home in the Temple. The function of the introduction of these verses at this point is to show that Solomon does not think, nor does the Chronicler, that God's promise has been finally fulfilled with the arrival of the ark. There remains a prayer that God would continue to remember his steadfast love to David, meaning that he should express it also to his descendants. The irony in the fact that the period of David and Solomon would never be equalled thereafter as a time of peace and righteousness is perhaps fully intended, and has been taken as a suggestion that the Chronicler's picture of the "rest" of God on Zion in Solomon's time has some eschatological significance (Williamson), i.e. that there remains a hope that God's rest with his people has some future reality unfulfilled in his own day.

"Thy priests" and "thy saints" (v. 41) are to be "clothed with salvation" and "rejoice in thy goodness" respectively. No hard and fast distinction is implied between "priests" and "saints" at this point. (Exod. 19:6 has described all Israel as a "kingdom of priests".) The point is rather that the whole nation should *exhibit* the salvation and goodness of God. This ties in with the emphasis in the prayer on the place of the foreigner (vv. 32ff.), and the thrust that we have seen and shall see (2 Chr. 9) relating to Israel's witness to the nations. A faithful people speaks naturally and inevitably about the excellence of its God (cf. 2 Cor. 5:14).

GOD'S RESPONSE—I

2 Chronicles 7:1–22

[1]When Solomon had ended his prayer, fire came down from heaven and consumed the burnt offering and the sacrifices, and the glory of the Lord filled the temple. [2]And the priests could not enter the house of the Lord, because the glory of the Lord filled the Lord's house. [3]When

all the children of Israel saw the fire come down and the glory of the Lord upon the temple, they bowed down with their faces to the earth on the pavement, and worshipped and gave thanks to the Lord, saying,
"For he is good,
    for his steadfast love endures for ever."
⁴Then the king and all the people offered sacrifice before the Lord. ⁵King Solomon offered as a sacrifice twenty-two thousand oxen and a hundred and twenty thousand sheep. So the king and all the people dedicated the house of God. ⁶The priests stood at their posts; the Levites also, with the instruments for music to the Lord which King David had made for giving thanks to the Lord—for his steadfast love endures for ever—whenever David offered praises by their ministry; opposite them the priests sounded trumpets; and all Israel stood.

⁷And Solomon consecrated the middle of the court that was before the house of the Lord; for there he offered the burnt offering and the fat of the peace offerings, because the bronze altar Solomon had made could not hold the burnt offering and the cereal offering and the fat.

⁸At that time Solomon held the feast for seven days, and all Israel with him, a very great congregation, from the entrance of Hamath to the Brook of Egypt. ⁹And on the eighth day they held a solemn assembly; for they had kept the dedication of the altar seven days and the feast seven days. ¹⁰On the twenty-third day of the seventh month he sent the people away to their homes, joyful and glad of heart for the goodness that the Lord had shown to David and to Solomon and to Israel his people.

¹¹Thus Solomon finished the house of the Lord and the king's house; all that Solomon had planned to do in the house of the Lord and in his own house he successfully accomplished. ¹²Then the Lord appeared to Solomon in the night and said to him: "I have heard your prayer, and have chosen this place for myself as a house of sacrifice. ¹³When I shut up the heavens so that there is no rain, or command the locust to devour the land, or send pestilence among my people, ¹⁴if my people who are called by my name humble themselves, and pray and seek my face, and turn from their wicked ways, then I will hear from heaven, and will forgive their sin and heal their land. ¹⁵Now my eyes will be open and my ears attentive to the prayer that is made in this place. ¹⁶For now I have chosen and consecrated this house that my name may be there for ever; my eyes and my heart will be there for all time. ¹⁷And as for you, if you walk before me, as David your father walked, doing according to all that I have commanded you and keeping my

statutes and my ordinances, [18]then I will establish your royal throne, as I covenanted with David your father, saying, 'There shall not fail you a man to rule Israel.'

[19]"But if you turn aside and forsake my statutes and my commandments which I have set before you, and go and serve other gods and worship them, [20]then I will pluck you up from the land which I have given you; and this house, which I have consecrated for my name, I will cast out of my sight, and will make it a proverb and a byword among all peoples. [21]And at this house, which is exalted, every one passing by will be astonished, and say, 'Why has the Lord done thus to this land and to this house?' [22]Then they will say, 'Because they forsook the Lord the God of their fathers who brought them out of the land of Egypt, and laid hold on other gods, and worshipped them and served them; therefore he has brought all this evil upon them.'"

(i)

Verses 1–10 describe the final public acts of the dedication ceremony, and provide a brief interlude before God replies privately to Solomon's prayer.

(vv. 1–3). The great ceremony now moves towards its conclusion. The descent of fire upon the burnt offering puts God's final seal of approval upon the newly-established arrangements for worship (as it had earlier identified the site on which the Temple should be built, 1 Chr. 21:26; cf. also Lev. 9:23f.). The glory of the Lord which, since 5:13, has excluded the priests from the interior of the building now also appears outside in the sight of all the people. God's affirmation that this is his chosen house of prayer and sacrifice is thus publicly witnessed and experienced, and the people's response in worship—taking upon their lips the by now familiar fragment of Ps. 106:1—shows that they have accepted the demonstration as a token of his commitment to them for the future.

(vv. 4–7). Chr. insists that it is the king and the people together who offer sacrifice and dedicate the Temple. While the king is thus singled out as leader the decision to enter into covenant with God is taken by the rank and file. Notice how Solomon's prayer (ch. 6) had spoken consistently in the plural, of *thy people* or *thy servants* (e.g. vv. 26f., 34), and how God's reply (below, v. 14) adopts the same mode of reference. Israel was not under the umbrella of its great leader to such an extent that individuals were absolved from the responsibility of making their own decisions before God.

The record of the sacrifices made shows that prayer has not completely displaced sacrifice, in Chr.'s view, from its place within the cult. Different kinds of sacrifices are mentioned, less out of a concern with the technical difference between them than to suggest comprehensiveness. (Broadly speaking, burnt offerings are whole meat-offerings, while peace offerings are those which are partly consumed by the fire and of which parts are reserved for the priests and Temple-staff to eat.) Verse 6 is a reference to the arrangements for the priestly service and the music made in 1 Chr. chs. 23–27. All these preparations have now been vindicated and we have a picture of Israel ready to embark upon a new life of service and worship.

(vv. 8–10). The date in v. 10 betrays the fact that the feast in question is that of Tabernacles (Lev. 23:24–36, where it is called Booths, RSV). The so-called "solemn assembly" formed part of that feast and was the climax of it. The actual dedication of the Temple evidently took place in a special week preceding the feast. All of Israel, therefore, was engaged in celebration for a two-week period, after which they departed for their homes full of gladness for the evidence they had seen of God's good favour towards them. (The expression, "From Hamath to the Brook of Egypt" stresses that all Israel was present, and is a reminiscence of 1 Chr. 13:5.)

We referred above to the intensity of Solomon's prayer. Let us notice here the intensity of Israel's celebration. It is a possible negative corollary of the Christian truth that God can be worshipped anywhere and anytime that our worship can become excessively individualistic, bland and monotonous. There is something in the human frame that revels in the great occasion. For Christians as for our Israelite forefathers it is vital to

join together to share our knowledge of and desire for
the great things that God has done. The writer to the Hebrews
knew of the danger of forgetting this (Heb. 10:25). Though we
are individually responsible before God, we find our full
identity only in community, and supremely in the community
of those who have faith in God. Isolation is destructive of faith,
and the faith of a community of God's people can well up
into the sort of joy Israel knew here and be a foretaste of
heaven itself.

GOD'S RESPONSE—II

2 Chronicles 7:1–22 (*cont'd*)

(ii)

(vv. 11–22). God now answers Solomon's prayer—privately—
with an undertaking to do all that he asks. The terms in which he
replies (especially vv. 13–15, which are not in 1 Kings 9) conform
very closely to those in which Solomon prayed. He will respond to
the people's repentance for sin by forgiving them and restoring
them to blessing, and he will be continually receptive to such
prayer. He also re-affirms his promise to the Davidic dynasty,
provided Solomon remains obedient.

The fact that God's words are here directed privately to Solomon emphasizes his immense responsibility. The terms in which
he confronts Solomon with the solemn choice between the way of
obedience and that of apostasy are those of the Covenant, normally addressed to Israel as a whole. Verses 19–22 in particular
recall the terms of the so-called "curses" of the Mosaic Covenant
(cf. Deut. 28:15–68, especially vv. 25, 37; 29:20ff.). These in
turn, incidentally, are paralleled in international treaties from the
ancient Near East, contracted between unequal partners, the
greater imposing conditions on the lesser, with dreadful "small
print". In a sense Solomon is in a unique position. For Chr. he is
something of a "test-case". If he is obedient the promises will be
established. The fact that the Chronicler still feels able to offer
the possibility of a continuation of the Davidic Covenant in his

own day shows that he regards Solomon as having passed that test. Yet the uniqueness of Solomon, and the success which Chr. attributes to him, need not deter us from letting some of the force of this challenge come to us. Christians are described as "a royal priesthood" (1 Pet. 2:9). Rank, in any real sense, has been abolished within the people of God. The significance of the response of a Solomon is not greater in God's eyes than that of the response of any modern individual. And given that each is called to his or her own sphere of service, more may hang upon the decision than that which affects us directly.

(iii)

Verse 14 deserves particular mention. The response which God desires from his people after they have sinned is here described as fourfold: "if my people *humble themselves . . . pray . . . seek my face . . . turn*". It is tempting to read quickly over these terms as if they all meant more or less the same thing. But there are both distinctions and sequence here. Other contexts (e.g. 12:6f) show that *humbling* implies a changed attitude with regard to oneself, a renunciation of some wrong course which had been determined upon and which involved an arrogant rejection of God. Let it not be thought that what God here requires of sinful man is any easy thing. The path of obedience is never the natural choice of any human being; and it is a great deal harder to choose it when there has been previous, perhaps public and openly self-reliant, commitment to some other path. A *prayerful* attitude is the opposite to that which asserts the self. It recognizes the right of God to dispose over and "judge" one's life. (The verb "to pray" is related to a verb meaning "judge" in Hebrew.) *Seeking God* describes the desire to determine what precisely God requires in terms of standards and of life-direction. And *turning* relates to the act of will which resolves to embark upon a life thus based. Each of the terms recurs at numerous points in the subsequent account of Israel's history. The Lord's reply thus refers forward in a specific way to that history, and the judgments made upon the kings there are based upon God's statement here. As we shall see when we come to examine the lives of the later kings, God does not simply make his statements about accountability and forgiveness in the abstract. He fills them in with examples drawn from the history of Israel (or better, Judah), in which he actually acted to forgive and restore.

AS HE MEANS TO GO ON

2 Chronicles 8:1–16

¹At the end of twenty years, in which Solomon had built the house of the Lord and his own house, ²Solomon rebuilt the cities which Huram had given to him, and settled the people of Israel in them.

³And Solomon went to Hamathzobah, and took it. ⁴He built Tadmor in the wilderness and all the store-cities which he built in Hamath. ⁵He also built Upper Beth-horon and Lower Beth-horon, fortified cities with walls, gates and bars, ⁶and Baalath, and all the store-cities that Solomon had, and all the cities for his chariots, and the cities for his horsemen, and whatever Solomon desired to build in Jerusalem, in Lebanon, and in all the land of his dominion. ⁷All the people who were left of the Hittites, the Amorites, the Perizzites, the Hivites, and the Jebusites, who were not of Israel, ⁸from their descendants who were left after them in the land, whom the people of Israel had not destroyed—these Solomon made a forced levy and so they are to this day. ⁹But of the people of Israel Solomon made no slaves for his work; they were soldiers, and his officers, the commanders of his chariots, and his horsemen. ¹⁰And these were the chief officers of King Solomon, two hundred and fifty, who exercised authority over the people.

¹¹Solomon brought Pharaoh's daughter up from the city of David to the house which he had built for her, for he said, "My wife shall not live in the house of David king of Israel, for the places to which the ark of the Lord has come are holy."

¹²Then Solomon offered up burnt offerings to the Lord upon the altar of the Lord which he had built before the vestibule, ¹³as the duty of each day required, offering according to the commandment of Moses for the sabbaths, the new moons, and the three annual feasts— the feast of unleavened bread, the feast of weeks, and the feast of tabernacles. ¹⁴According to the ordinance of David his father, he appointed the divisions of the priests for their service, and the Levites

for their offices of praise and ministry before the priests as the duty of each day required, and the gatekeepers in their divisions for the several gates; for so David the man of God had commanded. ¹⁵ And they did not turn aside from what the king had commanded the priests and Levites concerning any matter and concerning the treasuries.

¹⁶ Thus was accomplished all the work of Solomon from the day the foundation of the house of the Lord was laid until it was finished. So the house of the Lord was completed.

Verse 16 of this chapter represents an obvious rounding off of the long section dealing with Solomon's building of the Temple and institution of the worship. It is not easy to see a unity in the chapter, and tempting to regard it as a tidying-up operation recording a number of details which relate somehow to the completion of the Temple.

(vv. 2–10). These verses are linked to the temple-building theme at two points: first by the mention of Huram's cities, which leads into further information about Solomon's city-building activities in general, and secondly by the distinction between Israelites and non-Israelites in terms of the kinds of work to which they were put. (cf. on 2:17f., above.)

There are a number of points at which these verses, especially vv. 3–6, diverge from the corresponding passage in 1 Kings 9:10–19. Not the least of the differences is that, whereas Chr. tells of cities given by Huram to Solomon, Kings has it the other way round (v. 11)! A possible harmonization is based on the note in 1 Kings 9:12f. that Huram did not like the cities, and may therefore have given them back—or even held them as a kind of collateral (Myers) awaiting more satisfactory payment. There are also differences in the order and number of the places named. It may be that textual corruption is responsible for all the differences. In any case the record of Solomon's prosperity is just one further proof of the blessing of God upon him because of his faithful service.

(vv.11–16). The remaining verses show how Solomon went on after his initial labours. The note about his Egyptian wife (v. 11) might well have been disapproving (cf. 1 Kings 11:1f.). Chr. mentions the incident, however, only to illustrate the king's concern for the right handling of the ark. The corresponding passage in 1 Kings 9:24 furnishes no such explanation for Pharaoh's daughter going to "her own house". Chr. makes it explicit that it was because of Solomon's care that nothing, or no-one, unholy should be in the environs of the ark. His wife came into this category, apparently, by virtue of being a woman, since "women were more frequently unclean in the ritual sense (Lev. 15:19ff.) than men" (Myers).

Solomon's religious dutifulness is further illustrated by his attention to regular worship. Up to now the narrative about Solomon has been dominated by the great occasion. We said in relation to ch. 7 that great occasions could be helpful in Christian spirituality. Here we see the other side of the coin. No community can exist on great occasions alone. A nation can gear itself up for a coronation, a state-wedding or centenary celebrations. Such events have a vital significance in national life. But they cannot sustain its humdrum routine. Similarly the Temple was not built *for* the extraordinary occasion of its dedication. Rather it was to be the centre of the regular, routine worship of Israel. We now have a glimpse of Solomon making offerings "as the duty of each day required" (v. 13). Once again, everything is correct and meticulous. He undertakes for the three annual feasts (Exod. 23:14–17) and other regular cultic events. (A more extensive catalogue is found in Lev. 23.) The priests and Levites too do their work as prescribed by David (1 Chr. chs. 23–27), and again "as the duty of each day required" (v. 14).

If great occasions are important in Christian living they cannot fully sustain it. Indeed there seem to be those who develop a need, even craving, for the spectacular in worship—the "big name" conferences, the mass rally, the bizarre event. It is possible to slip into a lame-duck spirituality which cannot exist without artificial aids. This often happens in college or university days where so much that is "laid on" can simply be leant on—bringing anti-climax and disappointment when that context has to be left.

Christian living and spirituality are only real if they can survive in the long, quiet reaches of life. The Bible knows well the greatness of the "day of small things" (Zech. 4:10). It is the regular, unseen, perhaps solitary seeking of God that testifies to spiritual reality and that builds Christian character. The Chronicler only says that "the house of the Lord was completed" when he has shown us that Solomon has provided for, and exemplified, this its real and lasting use.

THE QUEEN OF SHEBA—I

2 Chronicles 8:17–9:31

[17]Then Solomon went to Eziongeber and Eloth on the shore of the sea, in the land of Edom. [18]And Huram sent him by his servants ships and servants familiar with the sea, and they went to Ophir together with the servants of Solomon, and fetched from there four hundred and fifty talents of gold and brought it to King Solomon.

[1]Now when the queen of Sheba heard of the fame of Solomon she came to Jerusalem to test him with hard questions, having a very great retinue and camels bearing spices and very much gold and precious stones. When she came to Solomon, she told him all that was on her mind. [2]And Solomon answered all her questions; there was nothing hidden from Solomon which he could not explain to her. [3]And when the queen of Sheba had seen the wisdom of Solomon, the house that he had built, [4]the food of his table, the seating of his officials, and the attendance of his servants, and their clothing, his cupbearers, and their clothing, and his burnt offerings which he offered at the house of the Lord, there was no more spirit in her.

[5]And she said to the king, "The report was true which I heard in my own land of your affairs and of your wisdom, [6]but I did not believe the reports until I came and my own eyes had seen it; and behold, half the greatness of your wisdom was not told me; you surpass the report which I heard. [7]Happy are your wives! Happy are these your servants, who continually stand before you and hear your wisdom! [8]Blessed be the Lord your God, who has delighted in you and set you on his throne as king for the Lord your God! Because your God loved Israel and would establish them for ever, he has made you king over them, that you may execute justice and righteousness." [9]Then she gave the king a

hundred and twenty talents of gold, and a very great quantity of spices, and precious stones: there were no spices such as those which the queen of Sheba gave to King Solomon.

¹⁰Moreover the servants of Huram and the servants of Solomon, who brought gold from Ophir, brought algum wood and precious stones. ¹¹And the king made of the algum wood steps for the house of the Lord and for the king's house, lyres also and harps for the singers; there never was seen the like of them before in the land of Judah.

¹²And King Solomon gave to the queen of Sheba all that she desired, whatever she asked besides what she had brought to the king. So she turned and went back to her own land, with her servants.

¹³Now the weight of gold that came to Solomon in one year was six hundred and sixty-six talents of gold, ¹⁴besides that which the traders and merchants brought; and all the kings of Arabia and the governors of the land brought gold and silver to Solomon. ¹⁵King Solomon made two hundred large shields of beaten gold; six hundred shekels of beaten gold went into each shield. ¹⁶And he made three hundred shields of beaten gold; three hundred shekels of gold went into each shield; and the king put them in the House of the Forest of Lebanon. ¹⁷The king also made a great ivory throne, and overlaid it with pure gold. ¹⁸The throne had six steps and a footstool of gold, which were attached to the throne, and on each side of the seat were arm rests and two lions standing beside the arm rests, ¹⁹while twelve lions stood there, one on each end of a step on the six steps. The like of it was never made in any kingdom. ²⁰All King Solomon's drinking vessels were of gold, and all the vessels of the House of the Forest of Lebanon were of pure gold; silver was not considered as anything in the days of Solomon. ²¹For the king's ships went to Tarshish with the servants of Huram; once every three years the ships of Tarshish used to come bringing gold, silver, ivory, apes, and peacocks.

²²Thus King Solomon excelled all the kings of the earth in riches and in wisdom. ²³And all the kings of the earth sought the presence of Solomon to hear his wisdom, which God had put into his mind. ²⁴Every one of them brought his present, articles of silver and of gold, garments, myrrh, spices, horses, and mules, so much year by year. ²⁵And Solomon had four thousand stalls for horses and chariots, and twelve thousand horsemen, whom he stationed in the chariot cities and with the king in Jerusalem. ²⁶And he ruled over all the kings from the Euphrates to the land of the Philistines, and to the border of Egypt. ²⁷And the king made silver as common in Jerusalem as stone, and

cedar as plentiful as the sycamore of the Shephelah. [28]And horses were imported for Solomon from Egypt and from all lands.

[29]Now the rest of the acts of Solomon, from first to last, are they not written in the history of Nathan the prophet, and in the prophecy of Ahijah the Shilonite, and in the visions of Iddo the seer concerning Jeroboam the son of Nebat? [30]Solomon reigned in Jerusalem over all Israel forty years. [31]And Solomon slept with his fathers, and was buried in the city of David his father; and Rehoboam his son reigned in his stead.

Sad to say, the visit of the Queen of Sheba to Solomon is *not* one of the Bible's great romances—or at least there is nothing in the text to indicate that it is. The story is, perhaps inevitably, "romantic", in the sense that it involves exotic characters. Solomon himself is exotic enough. The Queen of Sheba was probably exotic even to the people of ancient Israel. The vast wealth of both parties would be sufficient in itself to make the meeting gossip-column material in our own day. Yet here, as in other man-woman encounters that have romantic potential, the Bible is tantalizingly reticent. (This is true even of Ruth and Boaz, where the relationship in question has more to do with Israelite social structure than romance.) The truth is that the story of the Queen of Sheba merely furnishes further proof of some of the things which Chr. is concerned to say about Solomon.

The first thing to notice is that the queen's visit makes us think again of the qualities of Solomon which were outlined in 2 Chr. 1. That chapter spelt out the three "Ws"—wisdom, wealth and worship—which were to characterize his reign. It is these which form the substance of the story of the Queen of Sheba. The purpose of her visit is to see for herself whether the already legendary wisdom of Solomon is a reality. The quest is inextricably bound up with wealth, since, not only does she feel it necessary, according to the customs of the day, to approach the king of a foreign court with valuable gifts, but Solomon's wealth itself seems to be closely bound up with his wisdom. That wisdom is something that the queen "sees" (9:3), and she sees it in the form of "the house that he had built, the food of his table" etc., and of the worship of the Temple. (This too is not separable from the wealth theme, since much is made at certain points of the magnitude of the sacrifices Solomon offered.) Solomon's wisdom, then, is perceived by the queen in terms of his practical ability to act as a great king, to manifest the attributes of kingship in a conspicuous way. This perception tells us something of what the queen's real motivation was in coming to Solomon. The fact that the story is sandwiched between passages (8:17f., 9:13ff.), which tell of Solomon's success in the realm of international trade, suggests that the queen's visit is nothing other than a trade mission.

THE QUEEN OF SHEBA—II

2 Chronicles 8:17–9:31 (*cont'd*)

Sheba, or, as it is sometimes called, Saba, is well known in the OT as a rich and powerful trading nation. The great majority of references to it are in terms of its commercial success, for which it is almost a byword (cf. Isa. 60:6; Jer. 6:20; Job 6:19). The first two of the passages cited associated it particularly with gold and frankincense. Its prosperity, therefore, was based at least in part on trade in luxury merchandise, which was no doubt highly lucrative. Its position in southern Arabia probably meant that it was strategically placed for east-west trade (Africa and India), but it is clear from Ezek. 27:22, which is addressed to Tyre, that its interests extended northward, across and beyond the territories of Israel. There are indications that the 10th century B.C., the century of Solomon, was one of particular growth and prosperity for Sheba.

The rise of the united kingdom of David and Solomon, during which Israel was at the height of its international influence, impinged therefore upon the success of the Sabaeans both as an opportunity and a threat: an opportunity because Solomon was himself wealthy and must have offered the possibility of important outlets; and a threat because his use of ships from Ezion-Geber in the Red Sea and perhaps beyond (since it is not known where Ophir is located, 8:17f.) must have taken trade away from Arabian land-routes controlled by Sheba. In these circumstances the long and no doubt arduous journey undertaken by the queen—a fact which has sometimes been held to stand against the historicity of the story—is fully comprehensible. If possible, a modus vivendi must be achieved with the new and powerful entrepreneur in Israel.

Whatever may have been in the queen's mind as she made her way to Solomon, the Chronicler uses the incident to make the same sort of point that he made earlier in connection with Huram. Such is the greatness of Solomon that other nations are compelled to recognize the greatness of his God, and come bearing gifts. Like Huram (2 Chr. 2:11f.) the queen is moved to praise the Lord, and even to see something of his character as a just and righteous God who has loved Israel enough to wish to establish them for ever (v. 8). If she had come with preconceived notions about a great and wealthy king, as she no doubt knew other great and wealthy kings, and if she had thought that his celebrated wisdom could simply be that of the great of this world in large measure, she soon had cause to change her mind. The woman who had come to talk business in all the pomp of her great retinue (v. 1) was overwhelmed ("there was no more spirit in her") by the special kind of grandeur that was here; the wisdom she found she had not even half divined (v. 6), and she could only respond to it by glorifying God.

The Chronicler's message in all this may be seen on two levels. On one level he is teaching that Solomon's single-minded devotion to the fulfilment of God's purposes for him had resulted in his international recognition and hugely increasing wealth. The point was made in 2 Chronicles chapter 1. He does not wish to leave Solomon without ramming it home one more time. It is interesting that Psalm 72, which pictures the worldwide supremacy of the Israelite king, also touches on tribute from Sheba as a supreme demonstration of it (Ps. 72:10, 15).

On another level we may reflect upon the impact made upon the queen herself. There were others in the OT who came in contact with Israelite people and met their God in a decisive way (e.g. Naaman, 2 Kings 5:15–19; Ruth, Ruth 1:16f.). We cannot know how decisive was the Queen of Sheba's recognition of the greatness of Solomon's God, for once again the OT becomes reticent at the crucial point (v. 12). Any reflection upon Israel's general record as a missionary force must, of course, lead to gloomy conclusions. Her failure in this respect was, however, but part of her chronic propensity to apostasy. The impression made upon the Queen of Sheba shows the power that belongs to the children of God to bring God to those who are, figuratively speaking, "far off".

Verses 13–28 simply stress further the wealth and prestige of Solomon. Not only is Huram associated with the Queen of Sheba in his subordinate role to the Israelite king, but "all the kings of Arabia" (v. 14) brought him gold, many others are actually his vassals (v. 26), and "all the kings of the earth" (v. 23) sought his presence to hear his wisdom. Such is his wealth that things normally deemed precious become common (vv. 20, 27). But his wealth is inextricably linked with his wisdom to the end.

(For the House of the Forest of Lebanon, v. 16, see 1 Kings 7:2–5.)

A TURN OF AFFAIRS—I

2 Chronicles 10:1–11:4

¹Rehoboam went to Shechem, for all Israel had come to Shechem to make him king. ²And when Jeroboam the son of Nebat heard of it (for he was in Egypt, whither he had fled from King Solomon), then Jeroboam returned from Egypt. ³And they sent and called him; and Jeroboam and all Israel came and said to Rehoboam, ⁴"Your father made our yoke heavy. Now therefore lighten the hard service of your father and his heavy yoke upon us, and we will serve you." ⁵He said to them, "Come to me again in three days." So the people went away.

⁶Then King Rehoboam took counsel with the old men, who had stood before Solomon his father while he was yet alive, saying, "How do you advise me to answer this people?" ⁷And they said to him, "If you will be kind to this people and please them, and speak good words to them, then they will be your servants for ever." ⁸But he forsook the counsel which the old men gave him, and took counsel with the young men who had grown up with him and stood before him. ⁹And he said to

them, "What do you advise that we answer this people who have said to me, 'Lighten the yoke that your father put upon us'?" ¹⁰And the young men who had grown up with him said to him, "Thus shall you speak to the people who said to you, 'Your father made our yoke heavy, but do you lighten it for us'; thus shall you say to them, 'My little finger is thicker than my father's loins. ¹¹And now, whereas my father laid upon you a heavy yoke, I will add to your yoke. My father chastised you with whips, but I will chastise you with scorpions.'"

¹²So Jeroboam and all the people came to Rehoboam the third day, as the king said, "Come to me again the third day." ¹³And the king answered them harshly, and forsaking the counsel of the old men, ¹⁴King Rehoboam spoke to them according to the counsel of the young men, saying, "My father made your yoke heavy, but I will add to it; my father chastised you with whips, but I will chastise you with scorpions." ¹⁵So the king did not hearken to the people; for it was a turn of affairs brought about by God that the Lord might fulfil his word, which he spoke by Ahijah the Shilonite to Jeroboam the son of Nebat.

¹⁶And when all Israel saw that the king did not hearken to them, the people answered the king,

"What portion have we in David?

We have no inheritance in the son of Jesse.

Each of you to your tents, O Israel!

Look now to your own house, David."

So all Israel departed to their tents. ¹⁷But Rehoboam reigned over the people of Israel who dwelt in the cities of Judah. ¹⁸Then King Rehoboam sent Hadoram, who was taskmaster over the forced labour, and the people of Israel stoned him to death with stones. And King Rehoboam made haste to mount his chariot, to flee to Jerusalem. ¹⁹So Israel has been in rebellion against the house of David to this day.

¹When Rehoboam came to Jerusalem, he assembled the house of Judah, and Benjamin, a hundred and eighty thousand chosen warriors, to fight against Israel, to restore the kingdom to Rehoboam. ²But the word of the Lord came to Shemaiah the man of God: ³"Say to Rehoboam the son of Solomon king of Judah, and to all Israel in Judah and Benjamin, ⁴'Thus says the Lord, You shall not go up or fight against your brethren. Return every man to his home, for this thing is from me.'" So they hearkened to the word of the Lord, and returned and did not go against Jeroboam.

With the close of Solomon's reign we embark upon a new phase in Chr.'s account of Israel's history. That account can be broadly divided, as we have seen, into the pre-Davidic era, the time of David and Solomon, and the period of the divided monarchy up until the Babylonian exile. We now stand on the verge of this last phase.

Rehoboam, Solomon's first successor, is an important figure, partly because it is he who has the dubious honour of presiding over the division of the kingdom, and partly because he is in some ways typical of the kings who are yet to come, and of the way in which Chr. measures them against the major figures we have met so far.

The amount of space devoted by Chr. to the kings who followed Solomon is considerably less than that which is found in Kings. This is because of the single most important aspect of Chr.'s treatment by comparison with Kings, namely his omission of a systematic account of the history of the northern kingdom, to which he generally alludes only by way of illuminating the relationship of northerners to the legitimate Davidic institutions kept alive in the south.

The secession of the north (ten out of the twelve tribes) is obviously one of the most significant events in the history of Israel, heralding as it did a period of some two hundred years during which relations between the two kingdoms were never easy, and sometimes erupted into war (e.g. 1 Kings 15:7). Historically, it marked the end of a major aspect of the great achievements of David, namely his uniting of different elements within the pre-monarchical tribal league. This unity, together with the greatness it brought, would never be achieved again, the northern kingdom being destined to disappear, for ever, more than a century before the Babylonian exile of southern Judah. Of course, it is possible to see what happened under Rehoboam as nothing other than a return to natural political conditions which only the greatness of a David could obscure, and that artificially and temporarily. The appeal in 10:16 is directed to traditional "northern" sentiments. Nevertheless, in the Chronicler's view the relation of the north to the house of David must be described in terms of rebellion (10:19), a judgment which he applies to the entire history of the north.

A TURN OF AFFAIRS—II

2 Chronicles 10:1–11:4 (*cont'd*)

The section 10:1–11:4 describes how the division occurred, with the well-known story of Rehoboam's rejection of the sound advice of his elders in favour of that of his young contemporaries, regarding his treatment of the people. Their request, under Jeroboam, to "lighten the hard service of your father" (10:4) refers to the burden of taxes and forced labour which Solomon had introduced to finance and facilitate his immense building projects and grand life-style. (Chr. had hitherto played down this aspect of Solomon's rule, but cf. 1 Kings 4:22ff., 5:13ff. The request by the people under Jeroboam is not comprehensible unless Israelites themselves had somehow suffered from the heavy demands placed by Solomon upon those within his borders, even if in principle the oppressive measures were only directed against foreigners, as per 1 Kings 9:20–22, 2 Chr. 8:7–9.)

On the face of it, the people's request is justified. On no OT understanding of the role of kingship was it legitimate for the king to exploit the people for the purposes of self-aggrandizement. And indeed, in this chapter, no blame attaches to Jeroboam or the people for their decision to cut their links with the ruling house; nor is Jeroboam himself presented as having acted from self-aggrandizing motives. On the contrary, the chain of events leading to the secession is explicitly described as having been "brought about by God"—the phrase used lays some stress on his deliberate planning of it—in fulfilment of the prophecy of Ahijah (v. 15). This prophecy (recorded in 1 Kings 11:31ff.) is actually omitted in Chr., once again because of its policy of passing over anything which might bring Solomon's name into disrepute. The substance of Ahijah's prophecy was that the northern tribes would be torn from Solomon because of his idolatry. The ten tribes would be given to Jeroboam—who had hitherto been a loyal and able servant of Solomon (1 Kings 11:28), with apparently no thoughts of becoming king himself. While, therefore, the Chronicler has not referred to the original context of Ahijah's prophecy, he has retained the sense that the division has been brought about by God.

Because the original context of Ahijah's prophecy is not retained by him, it is not easy to decide what exactly the Chronicler has in mind in insisting on the fact that God ordained the division of the kingdom. In one important way Rehoboam's loss of ten of the twelve tribes corresponds very closely to the pattern of land-loss as the consequence of sin which the Chronicler has shown, ever since Saul, to be unalterable. This particular loss of land was the most serious and obvious in the whole monarchy period, apart from the disappearance of the north altogether in the seventh century B.C. and the Babylonian exile of Judah. Yet he does not make capital out of the event for his case. He does not attribute the loss of the north to the sin of Rehoboam.

Now indeed Rehoboam does not emerge from chapter 10 with a great deal of glory. It is clear that he had it within his grasp to hold the kingdom together, if only he had handled the approach of Jeroboam and the people better. But the narrative of his foolishness is devoid of the kind of language which the Chronicler reserves for explicit condemnation. That indeed *is* applied to Rehoboam, but not until 12:1. The Rehoboam of chapter 10 acts merely with the impetuosity of youth which lacks even the wisdom to make up for its deficiencies by seeking older counsel. There is nothing in chapter 10 to suggest that Rehoboam was malicious or cruel. He may have genuinely wanted to act responsibly. His fault at this stage is merely folly, a fact which is borne out by the description of him in 13:7 (where the terms are similar to those applied to Solomon when David judged him not yet ready to undertake for the arrangements for the Temple (1 Chr. 22:5; 29:1)), and by his misreading of the people's determination in the matter of the unfortunate Hadoram (10:18).

Rehoboam and Jeroboam have in common, therefore, that in relation to the decisive events which led to the split between north and south neither character has yet been fully drawn. Though each will be condemned, neither is blamed expressly for the division. As regards Rehoboam's loss of the north, it may be that Chr. refrains from relating this to his sin on the grounds that the north is still, after all, Israel, and as such must itself be judged by the same criteria as the south. The arena within which Rehoboam is to be judged is the territory which is left him following the division. This is emphasized by the command not to fight Jeroboam, "for this thing is from me" (11:4). Ultimately, therefore, Chr. is content to leave the reason for the division in the inscrutable mind of God.

It is not only at this point that the OT brings together the ideas of the unfathomability of God's mind and the need for wisdom. The Book of Proverbs, especially chapters 1–9, is full of fatherly exhortation to listen to instruction, on the grounds that "the fear of the Lord is the beginning of wisdom" (Prov. 1:7). The same book lays some stress on God's impenetrability to those who will not recognize their own limitations (e.g. 16:9, 25). Rehoboam did mature, to judge by chapter 11, as Solomon had matured before him. Neither the apparent inscrutability of God nor our present failures should lead us to despair of progress in the Christian life. But for those who seek wisdom it is open to all (Prov. 8:17).

THE PARTING OF THE WAYS

2 Chronicles 11:5–23

⁵Rehoboam dwelt in Jerusalem, and he built cities for defence in Judah. ⁶He built Bethlehem, Etam, Tekoa, ⁷Bethzur, Soco, Adullam, ⁸Gath, Mareshah, Ziph, ⁹Adoraim, Lachish, Azekah, ¹⁰Zorah, Aijalon, and Hebron, fortified cities which are in Judah and in Benjamin. ¹¹He made the fortresses strong, and put commanders in them, and stores of food, oil, and wine. ¹²And he put shields and spears in all the cities, and made them very strong. So he held Judah and Benjamin.

¹³And the priests and the Levites that were in all Israel resorted to him from all places where they lived. ¹⁴For the Levites left their common lands and their holdings and came to Judah and Jerusalem, because Jeroboam and his sons cast them out from serving as priests of

the Lord, [15]and he appointed his own priests for the high places, and for the satyrs, and for the calves which he had made. [16]And those who had set their hearts to seek the Lord God of Israel came after them from all the tribes of Israel to Jerusalem to sacrifice to the Lord, the God of their fathers. [17]They strengthened the kingdom of Judah, and for three years they made Rehoboam the son of Solomon secure, for they walked for three years in the way of David and Solomon.

[18]Rehoboam took as wife Mahalath the daughter of Jerimoth the son of David, and of Abihail the daughter of Eliab the son of Jesse; [19]and she bore him sons, Jeush, Shemariah, and Zaham. [20]After her he took Maacah the daughter of Absalom, who bore him Abijah, Attai, Ziza, and Shelomith. [21]Rehoboam loved Maacah the daughter of Absalom above all his wives and concubines (he took eighteen wives and sixty concubines, and had twenty-eight sons and sixty daughters); [22]and Rehoboam appointed Abijah the son of Maacah as chief prince among his brothers, for he intended to make him king. [23]And he dealt wisely, and distributed some of his sons through all the districts of Judah and Benjamin, in all the fortified cities; and he gave them abundant provisions, and procured wives for them.

We have seen that Rehoboam's foolishness in his handling of Jeroboam's reasonable approach did not constitute grounds for his condemnation. In fact the career of Rehoboam moves through three distinct stages, of which that ill-fated confrontation represents the first. The present verses bear upon the second, a period of piety and prosperity. This period is not recorded at all in Kings, where the reign of Rehoboam is remembered only for the secession of the north, and for the fact that in it "Judah did what was evil in the sight of the Lord" (1 Kings 14:22). The Chronicler is not unaware of this judgment, and it corresponds to the third part of his account of Rehoboam (chapter 12). But it is at the point of divergence from Kings, as so often, that he is most interesting. He has included the report of the period of Rehoboam's piety in pursuit of his careful policy of showing that, uniformly, piety is rewarded with blessing and apostasy with punishment. It is possible, therefore, that in the case of many kings he has provided a more fastidious and differentiated account than Kings—even though the reverse was the case with David and Solomon.

Having made the point, it must be admitted that he does not over-press the case for Rehoboam's piety. Much of the credit for the three-year period of stability which Judah enjoyed under him (v. 17) evidently goes to the priests and Levites who came to Judah from all parts of Israel, even giving up their possessions to do so (vv. 13f.), and indeed to other pious people also, who were determined to resist the path upon which Jeroboam was now embarked and who also came south—whether permanently or only periodically for purposes of worship is not clear (v. 16). Rehoboam at least maintained the legitimate institutions, in contrast to Jeroboam, who aped them and expelled the true priests (vv. 14f.). He also "dealt wisely" in his government (v. 23), which is more than our first encounter with him might have led us to expect. Perhaps his piety did not go much beyond this.

Verses 13–17 are important, however, because they show that henceforth both Rehoboam and Jeroboam are held responsible for the events recorded. Jeroboam emerges in his true colours when his refusal to submit to Rehoboam's oppressive measures gives way to a self-assertion which rejects also those things which were genuinely ordained by God. (See further on 13:8ff.) It is for this reason that the name of Jeroboam becomes more or less synonymous with idolatry in the Books of Kings. He shares some of the tragedy of Saul in that he had great potential but was ultimately incapable of channelling it. Jeroboam stands forever as a caution against the danger of becoming passionately angry about a rightly perceived evil, yet blinded by that passion to such an extent that all measures taken against it seem right. When this happens there is almost inevitably a failure, ironically, to distinguish between right and wrong. When in addition, and inevitably, one's own judgment becomes the ultimate arbiter, the consequences can be disastrous. Many a powerful personality, like Jeroboam, has begun with a genuine and righteous indignation, and finished by letting that indignation shift to match a popular prejudice or fear, and the passion become confused with self-glory.

Under Rehoboam, in contrast, Judah "walked . . . in the way of David and Solomon" (v. 17). The signs of God's blessing are primarily in the building operations by which Rehoboam fortified Judah—buildings being, since Solomon, more or less a stereotype for blessing in Chr. The king's numerous progeny are, similarly, a sign of blessing.

Finally, it should be noticed that Chr. does not "cut off the northerners without a penny". The term "Israel" is still applied to them (v. 13), implying that in principle the ten rebel tribes still had an interest in the Covenant. The term "all Israel in Judah and Benjamin" (11:3) suggests the same, since it resists any identification of Israel with those within the borders of the two tribes. On the contrary there is a *spiritual* understanding of Israel here, in the terms of v. 16: "those who had set their hearts to seek the Lord God of Israel". However much the Chronicler insists upon institutional correctness he never falls into the trap of equating it with reality in religion. That depends upon the orientation of the hearts of individuals. And this means that no institutional disruption, no severance of ties long held dear, no loss of identity with regard to a particular grouping can affect the standing before God of one who seeks him. That seeking is the mark of reality. It is not the "seeking" of those who have not found, and perhaps do not intend to find; but it is the seeking of those who have already found their God and who, because they have known him, must come back to him again and again. The Chronicler thus shares with the Psalmists the knowledge that true religion is characterized by a thirst (Ps. 42:1f.). Perhaps it is this knowlege that leads him to imply that the position of the northerners is not lost. Even those who now follow Jeroboam may yet return to the way of truth.

REHOBOAM'S DECLINE

2 Chronicles 12:1–16

> [1]When the rule of Rehoboam was established and was strong, he forsook the law of the Lord, and all Israel with him. [2]In the fifth year of King Rehoboam, because they had been unfaithful to the Lord, Shishak king of Egypt came up against Jerusalem [3]with twelve hun-

dred chariots and sixty thousand horsemen. And the people were without number who came with him from Egypt—Libyans, Sukkiim, and Ethiopians. ⁴And he took the fortified cities of Judah and came as far as Jerusalem. ⁵Then Shemaiah the prophet came to Rehoboam and to the princes of Judah, who had gathered at Jerusalem because of Shishak, and said to them, "Thus says the Lord, 'You abandoned me, so I have abandoned you to the hand of Shishak.'" ⁶Then the princes of Israel and the king humbled themselves and said, "The Lord is righteous." ⁷When the Lord saw that they humbled themselves, the word of the Lord came to Shemaiah: "They have humbled themselves; I will not destroy them, but I will grant them some deliverance, and my wrath shall not be poured out upon Jerusalem by the hand of Shishak. ⁸Nevertheless they shall be servants to him, that they may know my service and the service of the kingdoms of the countries."

⁹So Shishak king of Egypt came up against Jerusalem; he took away the treasures of the house of the Lord and the treasures of the king's house; he took away everything. He also took away the shields of gold which Solomon had made; ¹⁰and King Rehoboam made in their stead shields of bronze and committed them to the hands of the officers of the guard, who kept the door of the king's house. ¹¹And as often as the king went into the house of the Lord, the guard came and bore them, and brought them back to the guardroom. ¹²And when he humbled himself the wrath of the Lord turned from him, so as not to make a complete destruction; moreover, conditions were good in Judah.

¹³So King Rehoboam established himself in Jerusalem and reigned. Rehoboam was forty-one years old when he began to reign, and he reigned seventeen years in Jerusalem, the city which the Lord had chosen out of all the tribes of Israel to put his name there. His mother's name was Naamah the Ammonitess. ¹⁴And he did evil, for he did not set his heart to seek the Lord.

¹⁵Now the acts of Rehoboam, from first to last, are they not written in the chronicles of Shemaiah the prophet and of Iddo the seer? There were continual wars between Rehoboam and Jeroboam. ¹⁶And Rehoboam slept with his fathers, and was buried in the city of David; and Abijah his son reigned in his stead.

After three years of stability, Rehoboam led Judah into apostasy. There are conscious parallels with Saul. The "unfaithfulness" of v. 2 is the same term as that which was applied to Israel's first king (1 Chr. 10:13). Rehoboam, therefore, has entered upon what might be termed a "Saul" period in his reign, which contrasts with the early phase, in which he "walked . . . in the way of David and Solomon". And there is a contrast in the consequences also. While obedience had issued in prosperity and strength, disobedience results in forfeiture of the very fortifications which had marked Rehoboam's success and much of the land which they had been designed to protect (v. 4). In his loss he resembles Saul, as in his gain he had resembled Solomon. The principles, for Chr., do not change.

(a) Rehoboam's decline leads us to ask, first, what was the nature of his sin. 1 Kings 14:22–24 indicates that idolatry was involved. The Chronicler may assume that this was an obvious implication of his "forsaking the law of the Lord" (v. 1). He concentrates, however, on the idea of personal disloyalty to or defection from God. That abandonment of a personal commitment is essential to the idea of sin which is presented here is clear from v. 5—where the Lord declares, in a phrase whose point is unmissable, that he in turn has forsaken Rehoboam. This is typical, indeed, of how the OT, with its deeply covenantal theology, understands the nature of sin. Sin is not something abstract or theoretical. It is offence against God. The sinner, furthermore, is only able to perceive that he is such to the extent that he is within, or sees that he ought to be within, a relationship with God, who claims him utterly. We may compare the confession in Ps. 51:4. If, as the heading to the Psalm suggests, the sin involved is adultery, it may well seem that it had been perpetrated against other parties also. Yet sin takes its character as sin only from the fact that it is offence against God. It is because the modern world has largely rejected belief in the possibility of a personal relationship with God, and indeed in judgment, that it has difficulty in identifying *anything* as inherently wrong.

(b) Rehoboam makes amends, to a degree, by coming to his senses and repenting. He "humbles himself" (v. 6), a response which God had promised would meet with forgiveness (7:14). It may be that there had been a good deal of self-reliance in the king's sin. Verse 1 suggests that it was when he became strong that he forsook the Lord. Perhaps he had learned his lesson that there could be no strength which was not given by God. That lesson had been pointed enough. Rehoboam must be credited with *taking* the point. In repenting, therefore, he confesses that "The Lord is righteous", or perhaps "in the right" (v. 6). Here the character of repentance may be seen to correspond to that of sin. As sin is personal defection from the Lord—with the absurd and heinous implication that God has not the right to be Lord over the individual's life—so repentance involves the affirmation that he does after all have that right. He is God and thus no theoretical proposition; he is God and therefore entitled to be *my* Lord.

(c) As a result of Rehoboam's repentance the Lord grants him "some deliverance" (v. 7). The deliverance appears to amount to the sparing of Jerusalem, but it appears also that Rehoboam remained in vassal-status in relation to Shishak. Shishak is known from Egyptian records as Shoshenq I, who left his own account of this particular incursion into Palestine. Chr.'s account, fuller than that of 1 Kings 14:25–28, had been thought untrustworthy historically until it was found that some of his extra details, especially in relation to the Sukkiim (v. 3) had a plausible Egyptian background. This passage, then, is an important indicator that Chr. had access to at least some important historical sources in addition to earlier biblical material.

Of more interest to us than the historical details is the interpretation of them as a partial restoration of Rehoboam's fortunes. The phrase "some deliverance" does not disguise the fact that there is reservation in the favour which God now shows to the king. Other details point to a real impoverishment. Shishak's removal of the treasures of the Temple is a foreshadowing of that definitive plunder by Nebuchadnezzar over three centuries later. The replacement of the shields of gold by shields of bronze (vv. 9f.) speaks of the straits to which Rehoboam was reduced. The statement in v. 12, "conditions were good in Judah", is not as positive as RSV makes it appear. Better is something like: "There were [some] good things in Judah"—that is, there were some redeeming features. All this is mere mitigation of the fact that, taken on the whole, Rehoboam's reign was not a success in

terms of his devotion to God (cf. v. 14). A reign in which there
had been a limited measure of faithfulness is rewarded by a
limited measure of blessing. The rather enigmatic statement of
v. 8—"that they may know my service and the service of the
kingdoms of the countries"—implies a half-way house arrangement, whereby Rehoboam is denied the freedom which should
accompany an unadulterated service of God alone. There may be
a suggestion of comparison also. Let Rehoboam's Judah taste
servitude to Egypt, the better to appreciate and desire a true
servant-relationship to God.

(d) It is in place to enter a caveat at this point in relation to
Chr.'s whole presentation of the relation between human merit
and God's blessing. The case of Rehoboam has shown particularly clearly how much the Chronicler is concerned to show
that obedience and blessing, disobedience and impoverishment
are closely linked. If we take a sober look at Rehoboam's record
we may think that he had little to go on in seeking to show that he
had something to commend him. Yet he strives to make the
point, and this will be a pattern for his treatment of other kings
also.

The problem for the modern reader is that this presentation of
human experiences neither rings true, nor is it a view uniformly
taken by the Bible. The author of Job and Ps. 73, for example,
knew that there was not always a direct connection between
righteousness and blessing. And Jesus himself sided unam-
biguously with these (John 9:2f.).

How, then, can we take to ourselves this central thrust of the
Chronicler? Where he does agree with the unanimous voice of
the Bible is in insisting that the link between faithfulness and
blessing does ultimately exist. Job, Ps. 73, the New Testament
(even, in the end, Ecclesiastes, at 12:14) all assert this. Christian
readers know from the New Testament that the equations of
righteousness and blessing, sin and punishment are only finally
worked out beyond the present life in a great universal judgment.
The Chronicler did not know this. (Nor, by and large, did the
other OT authors—hence the perplexity of Job and of Ps. 73.)
And it is for this reason that for him the whole scenario must be

played out in the earthly life of each individual. We are able, from our position of advantage, to look beyond his narrow conception of the matter, so that we do not make the Pharisees' mistake (John 9:2) of attributing every misfortune to particular sin. But we should not try to avoid the principle that Chr. states again and again, that God does look for faithfulness in people, and that a reckoning is inevitable (cf. Rom. 2:6)—while bearing in mind the heart of that great epistle, that the only righteousness that can ever be acceptable to God is that of Jesus Christ, 3:21–26.

A TRIAL OF STRENGTH

2 Chronicles 13:1–14:1

[1]In the eighteenth year of King Jeroboam Abijah began to reign over Judah. [2]He reigned for three years in Jerusalem. His mother's name was Micaiah the daughter of Uriel of Gibeah.

Now there was war between Abijah and Jeroboam. [3]Abijah went out to battle having an army of valiant men of war, four hundred thousand picked men; and Jeroboam drew up his line of battle against him with eight hundred thousand picked mighty warriors. [4]Then Abijah stood up on Mount Zemaraim which is in the hill country of Ephraim, and said, "Hear me, O Jeroboam and all Israel! [5]Ought you not to know that the Lord God of Israel gave the kingship over Israel for ever to David and his sons by a covenant of salt? [6]Yet Jeroboam the son of Nebat, a servant of Solomon the son of David, rose up and rebelled against his lord; [7]and certain worthless scoundrels gathered about him and defied Rehoboam the son of Solomon, when Rehoboam was young and irresolute and could not withstand them.

[8]"And now you think to withstand the kingdom of the Lord in the hand of the sons of David, because you are a great multitude and have with you the golden calves which Jeroboam made you for gods. [9]Have you not driven out the priests of the Lord, the sons of Aaron, and the Levites, and made priests for yourselves like the peoples of other lands? Whoever comes to consecrate himself with a young bull or seven rams becomes a priest of what are no gods. [10]But as for us, the Lord is our God, and we have not forsaken him. We have priests ministering to the Lord who are sons of Aaron, and Levites for their service. [11]They offer to the Lord every morning and every evening

burnt offerings and incense of sweet spices, set out the showbread on the table of pure gold, and care for the golden lampstand that its lamps may burn every evening; for we keep the charge of the Lord our God, but you have forsaken him. [12]Behold, God is with us at our head, and his priests with their battle trumpets to sound the call to battle against you. O sons of Israel, do not fight against the Lord, the God of your fathers; for you cannot succeed."

[13]Jeroboam had sent an ambush around to come on them from behind; thus his troops were in front of Judah, and the ambush was behind them. [14]And when Judah looked, behold, the battle was before and behind them; and they cried to the Lord, and the priests blew the trumpets. [15]Then the men of Judah raised the battle shout. And when the men of Judah shouted, God defeated Jeroboam and all Israel before Abijah and Judah. [16]The men of Israel fled before Judah, and God gave them into their hand. [17]Abijah and his people slew them with a great slaughter; so there fell slain of Israel five hundred thousand picked men. [18]Thus the men of Israel were subdued at that time, and the men of Judah prevailed, because they relied upon the Lord, the God of their fathers. [19]And Abijah pursued Jeroboam and took cities from him, Bethel with its villages and Jeshanah with its villages and Ephron with its villages. [20]Jeroboam did not recover his power in the days of Abijah; and the Lord smote him, and he died. [21]But Abijah grew mighty. And he took fourteen wives, and had twenty-two sons and sixteen daughters. [22]The rest of the acts of Abijah, his ways and his sayings, are written in the story of the prophet Iddo.

[1]So Abijah slept with his fathers, and they buried him in the city of David; and Asa his son reigned in his stead. In his days the land had rest for ten years.

Rehoboam's son Abijah gains more extended treatment in Chr. than he does in 1 Kings 15:1–8 (where he is called Abijam). The author of Kings does little more than record that Abijah was unfaithful. The Chronicler presents him in a very different light, depicting him as a champion of orthodox Yahwism. It may be that he had access to information about Abijah that the author of Kings did not have. (Such information would have included at least the note in v. 19.) We have seen time and again how he can be selective in his portrayal of individuals in order to lend support to his major contentions, though this is not to say that he does utter violence to historical actuality. In any case his treatment of

Abijah is less a character-portrait than a record of a particular confrontation with Jeroboam and the northerners designed to illuminate the true condition of the latter.

(a) The confrontation between north and south is the first that Chr. records, since Rehoboam was expressly forbidden to take up arms against Jeroboam (11:4—though 12:15 shows that his early restraint did not last). This becomes, therefore, a sort of test-case or trial of strength. Can the rebellion of the north be sustained? Or will the Lord vindicate the two tribes which have clung to the house of David, with whom his Covenant still stands, v. 5? (The term "covenant of salt" is obscure in its origins and precise connotations, but evidently means the covenant is eternal.) The battle-lines are drawn, v. 3. But Abijah begins with an appeal and a challenge. His address to Israel (which increasingly seeks to bypass Jeroboam, as in vv. 6f.) is based upon the twin facts that God's kingdom is rightly in the hands of the "sons of David" (v. 8), and that the cult of the Jerusalem Temple—to which so much of the narrative of David was devoted—is alone legitimate. The appeal takes on a scathing tone in v. 9, when Abijah tries to press home the folly of the attempt to construct one's own way of worshipping God when God himself has made it clear how it ought to be done. More important than the replacement of the true instrument of worship is the fact that it brings with it the worship of false gods. Jeroboam, in seeking to create his own duplication of the worship of Jerusalem, had set up golden calves in Bethel and Dan (cf. 11:15; 1 Kings 12:28f.). These were reminiscent of the golden calf which Aaron, under pressure from an impatient people, had made in the wilderness (Exod. 32) and which the Lord had roundly condemned as idolatrous (32:8). It may be that there were enlightened Israelites who did not actually identify the calves with God. Yet the making of images was foreign to the spirit of true Yahwism, and forbidden by God (Exod. 20:4f.) who, in his wisdom, knew the tendency of the human heart to worship the creature rather than the creator. We see the modern form of this tendency in the idolization of certain kinds of people (the young, the beautiful and the rich) and their life-style.

(b) Abijah's appeal is further based upon his conviction that Israel *ought to know* that they were in the wrong (v. 5). It had indeed been given to them to know, because of the public nature of all the ceremonies by which the kingship of David had been transmitted to Solomon and the Temple-worship established under him (see, e.g. 6:3–12, and note "in the presence of all the assembly of Israel", v. 12). It is typical of OT covenant-theology that the knowledge of God which it affords carries with it a special responsibility to obey him. This is not to say that other people are not also under obligation to God. The prophetic oracles against the nations (e.g. Amos 1:1–2:3) show that they are. But those who have known God by reason of his special revelation and commitment to them are bound to him particularly, as Amos 2:3 testifies: "You only [Israel] have I known of all the families of the earth; *therefore* I will punish you for all your iniquities." Today this word comes most strongly, perhaps, to those who used to have a lively faith and active discipleship, but who have let their lives become mere service of themselves. Such, however, have still the opportunity to repent and return to God. Hence Abijah's final appeal to the northerners not to "fight against the Lord, the God of your fathers" (v. 12).

(c) The confrontation has much to do with the question as to the real source of strength. To Jeroboam belongs the bigger army (v. 3). As Abijah puts it, he plans to "withstand" the kingdom of the Lord. The verb is properly "strengthen oneself", and is related to the "strength" of Rehoboam (12:1) which, apparently, led to his fall. Jeroboam's "withstanding" God implies a belief in the sufficiency of his own strength. The victory of Abijah gives the lie, in line with one of the OT's favourite themes (cf. David and Goliath), to the belief that the stronger party must come out on top. Abijah explicitly throws down the gauntlet to this kind of thinking when he draws attention to Jeroboam's greater numbers (v. 8). He subsequently finds himself, the battle engaged, in an impossible position (vv. 13f.). Yet it is the weaker party that emerges on top. The verb "prevailed", v. 18, has connotations of strength. The weaker has proved strong, because of his reliance on God. Jeroboam never recovers his strength thereafter (v. 20), while Abijah grows mighty (v. 21). It is hard to avoid the thought that, in biblical theology, weakness is a positive advantage, because it is a prerequisite of reliance (cf. 2 Cor. 12:10).

The word translated "subdued" (v. 18) is an important final comment on Jeroboam's ill-fated attempt to resist God. It is the same word that is elsewhere rendered "humbled" (7:14; 12:6). That is, it refers to that submission to God which constitutes the first step in repentance following rebellion against him. This, of course, is precisely what Jeroboam has not done. The force of the use of the word here, however, is to show, with some irony, that he who will not humble *himself* before God will yet be humbled *by* God, and with none of the ensuing advantages. Self-affirmation against God *is* an option for his creatures. But it is inevitably temporary, and must bring final and great cost.

(d) As a footnote to Judah's reliance on God, it is worth pausing for a moment over their battle-shout, v. 15. This is raised at the moment when they realize the extremity in which they are placed. And it is followed by the defeat of the enemy. We are told nothing of the manner of their defeat (as we are on other occasions of miraculous deliverance, e.g. 2 Kings 7:5f.). The narrative simply implies that it was by means of the Lord's swift and dramatic action. The battle-shout was an act of faith that this would ensue (cf. the shouting which attended the capture of Jericho, centuries earlier, Josh. 6:20). The faith of the men of Judah was, therefore, no mere theoretical faith. They were prepared to take the step that would at once identify them as men of faith, and put their God to the test. Here is a discipleship that is prepared to let major decisions hang utterly upon the reality of God and his power to vindicate, and as such is worthy of imitation.

ASA IN STRENGTH—I

2 Chronicles 14:2–15:19

> ²And Asa did what was good and right in the eyes of the Lord his God. ³He took away the foreign altars and the high places, and broke down

the pillars and hewed down the Asherim, ⁴and commanded Judah to seek the Lord, the God of their fathers, and to keep the law and the commandment. ⁵He also took out of all the cities of Judah the high places and the incense altars. And the kingdom had rest under him. ⁶He built fortified cities in Judah, for the land had rest. He had no war in those years, for the Lord gave him peace. ⁷And he said to Judah, "Let us build these cities, and surround them with walls and towers, gates and bars; the land is still ours, because we have sought the Lord our God; we have sought him, and he has given us peace on every side." So they built and prospered. ⁸And Asa had an army of three hundred thousand from Judah, armed with bucklers and spears, and two hundred and eighty thousand men from Benjamin, that carried shields and drew bows; all these were mighty men of valour.

⁹Zerah the Ethiopian came out against them with an army of a million men and three hundred chariots, and came as far as Mareshah. ¹⁰And Asa went out to meet him, and they drew up their lines of battle in the valley of Zephathah at Mareshah. ¹¹And Asa cried to the Lord his God, "O Lord, there is none like thee to help, between the mighty and the weak. Help us, O Lord our God, for we rely on thee, and in thy name we have come against this multitude. O Lord, thou art our God; let not man prevail against thee." ¹²So the Lord defeated the Ethiopians before Asa and before Judah, and the Ethiopians fled. ¹³Asa and the people that were with him pursued them as far as Gerar, and the Ethiopians fell until none remained alive; for they were broken before the Lord and his army. The men of Judah carried away very much booty. ¹⁴And they smote all the cities round about Gerar, for the fear of the Lord was upon them. They plundered all the cities, for there was much plunder in them. ¹⁵And they smote the tents of those who had cattle, and carried away sheep in abundance and camels. Then they returned to Jerusalem.

¹The Spirit of God came upon Azariah the son of Oded, ²and he went out to meet Asa, and said to him, "Here me, Asa, and all Judah and Benjamin: The Lord is with you, while you are with him. If you seek him, he will be found by you, but if you forsake him, he will forsake you. ³For a long time Israel was without the true God, and without a teaching priest, and without law; ⁴but when in their distress they turned to the Lord, the God of Israel, and sought him, he was found by them. ⁵In those times there was no peace to him who went out or to him who came in, for great disturbances afflicted all the inhabitants of the lands. ⁶They were broken in pieces, nation against nation

and city against city, for God troubled them with every sort of distress. [7]But you, take courage! Do not let your hands be weak, for your work shall be rewarded."

[8]When Asa heard these words, the prophecy of Azariah the son of Oded, he took courage, and put away the abominable idols from all the land of Judah and Benjamin and from the cities which he had taken in the hill country of Ephraim, and he repaired the altar of the Lord that was in front of the vestibule of the house of the Lord. [9]And he gathered all Judah and Benjamin, and those from Ephraim, Manasseh, and Simeon who were sojourning with them, for great numbers had deserted to him from Israel when they saw that the Lord his God was with him. [10]They were gathered at Jerusalem in the third month of the fifteenth year of the reign of Asa. [11]They sacrificed to the Lord on that day, from the spoil which they had brought, seven hundred oxen and seven thousand sheep. [12]And they entered into a covenant to seek the Lord, the God of their fathers, with all their heart and with all their soul; [13]and that whoever would not seek the Lord, the God of Israel, should be put to death, whether young or old, man or woman. [14]They took oath to the Lord with a loud voice, and with shouting, and with trumpets, and with horns. [15]And all Judah rejoiced over the oath; for they had sworn with all their heart, and had sought him with their whole desire, and he was found by them, and the Lord gave them rest round about.

[16]Even Maacah, his mother, King Asa removed from being queen mother because she had made an abominable image for Asherah. Asa cut down her image, crushed it, and burned it at the brook Kidron. [17]But the high places were not taken out of Israel. Nevertheless the heart of Asa was blameless all his days. [18]And he brought into the house of God the votive gifts of his father and his own votive gifts, silver, and gold, and vessels. [19]And there was no more war until the thirty-fifth year of the reign of Asa.

The story of Asa, soon told in Kings (1 Kings 15:8–24), occupies three chapters in Chr. (14–16). Kings remembers Asa as one of the few faithful rulers of Judah, centring its judgment upon his measures against idolatrous worship (1 Kings 15:11ff.). Once again, we find a more differentiated picture in Chr. Two items which Kings had noticed but refrained from commenting on become significant in Chr.'s treatment, viz. Asa's wars with the northern king Baasha, which involved him in an alliance with

Ben-hadad of Syria, and the illness which afflicted him in his declining years. Chr. also relates the invasion of "Zerah the Ethiopian", which is not recorded in Kings. All these things have their place in Chr.'s assessment of Asa. That assessment identifies a period of faithfulness (chapters 14 and 15) and one of unfaithfulness (chapter 16). We begin with the former.

(i)

As the account of Asa's reign opens, Chr. makes the general statement that he "did what was good and right in the eyes of the Lord his God" (14:2). This reflects that zeal against idolatry which had occupied the attention of the writers of Kings. Asa's determination to extirpate false worship had apparently total success in Judah (14:3), but could not extend to all Israel (15:17). But it did involve a stern measure against his mother, whom he removed from her place of honour as queen mother, and whose idol he destroyed (15:16). This detail speaks much for the reality of Asa's concern for right worship of God, for discipleship is always most difficult and demanding when it involves standing against members of one's own family. In this respect Asa stands in striking contrast to the infamous northern King Ahab, with his spineless subordination to his wife Jezebel (1 Kings 21:5ff.). The theme of subjecting family consideration to the call of discipleship is important to Jesus' teaching too (e.g. Luke 14:26).

(ii)

The career of Asa affords Chr. further opportunity for reflection on God's response to human obedience and disobedience. We have two clear examples of what we might call a "mirror-image" theology. The first is in 14:7, where, instead of reading "we have sought him" twice, we should probably read the second occurrence of the phrase as "he has sought us". This brings it close to 1 Chr. 28:9, where we saw that God actively seeks the response and faithfulness of his people. Asa uses this truth as a basis for exhortation. When he says "we have sought the Lord" it is not a matter for self-congratulation or complacency. He sees that Judah's continued possession of the land is indeed due to their past faithfulness. But that becomes a ground for *continued* faithfulness: "Let us build these cities". And when they do, they prosper more. As in Christian discipleship, the vital decision is not the one that was made yesterday or last year or ten years ago, but that which is made today. It was a decision "here and now" for the people of the Chronicler's day also, who must have thought they had a slender hold on the land, and who could not rest on the laurels of past generations. We can, of course, rejoice in our experience of God's blessing hitherto, and are always drawing upon the accumulated knowledge of our ongoing relationship with him. But God seeks an active, renewed commitment from each of his people every day.

ASA IN STRENGTH—II

2 Chronicles 14:2–15:19 (*cont'd*)

(iii)

The second example of "mirror-image theology" comes in 15:1–7, where the prophet Azariah addresses Asa and all Judah, following their remarkable victory over Zerah. Three statements (in v. 2) emphasize the complementarity of God's faithfulness to Judah and Judah's to God, viz. (a) "The Lord is with you while [= as long as] you are with him"; (b) "if you seek him he will be found by you"—not as the mute object of a search, but as one who *would* be found; and (c) "but if you forsake him, he will forsake you". Verses 3–7 then expand upon these statements by reference to Israel's experience in her early nationhood under the judges. Verse 4 is reminiscent of a phrase which recurs frequently in the Book of Judges (e.g. 3:9, 15) when Israel cried to God for deliverance from the hand of the oppressor. (The Book of Judges, like Chronicles, shows how closely faithfulness and unfaithfulness are related to peace and disruption respectively.) Verses 5f. describe the absence of peace, and insist that God is its author, just as he is of peace itself. The first half of v. 5 stands in stark contrast to Ps. 121:8, in which the Psalmist affirms that "the

Lord will keep your going out and your coming in from this time forth and for evermore." Here is a going out and coming in that knows nothing of the peace and "help" that are the subject of the Psalm. The way of God-rejection brings dis-ease to all of life.

The verses (3–7) are finely balanced however. Verses 3f. contain in themselves the possibilities both of desertion of God, including contempt for his word, and of seeking him again. What is striking here is the readiness with which God responds to a cry of distress. It was characteristic of Israel's Judges period, and is still characteristic of humanity in general, that repentance was wrung from a people at the end of its tether. One of the most encouraging aspects of the Chronicler's theology is his insistence upon the openness of God to receive back his wayward children, even after great apostasy. And he is no less willing if any should return to him only because they have exhausted all other possibilities. This puts an important new perspective on the fact that God is often portrayed in Chr. as being the author of distress in the lives of the people presented to us. God knows the reluctance of the human heart to respond to him and is gracious enough to accept response that is motivated by the most basic human fears. It is in moments of distress that we perceive most acutely our own frailty, and the extent of our need of God.

Verses 5–7 recapitulate vv. 3f., in that they move from the adversities of God's people to another portrayal of blessedness. This time, however, the blessedness is not that which has been experienced in the past, but that which is now set before Asa and Judah as a possibility for the future. The past dealings of God with Israel become a model for present decision. God will keep faith now, again, with those who, like their forefathers, seek their well-being only in him, and in his service.

(iv)

The exhortation of Azariah is followed (vv. 8–15) by an account of Asa's removal of the paraphernalia of idolatry from Judah and of a renewal of the people's Covenant with God. How Azariah's prophecy and the subsequent measures relate chronologically to the reforms and achievements mentioned in chapter 14 is not entirely clear. It is possible that 14:1–8 actually refer to the same reform that is taken up again in chapter 15, the former standing as a preliminary assessment of Asa's good deeds. Azariah's prophecy may, then, have in fact preceded the reform. And indeed Asa's building programme and his defeat of Zerah the Ethiopian may have followed it. The Chronicler is hardly a stickler for chronology, however, and it is more important to observe the relationship between actions and events and God's response to them.

It should not bother us too much, therefore, that Azariah's exhortation comes after Asa's faithfulness, and indeed his reward for it, has been reported. The themes of fortification (14:5f.) and victory (8ff.) are familiar to us by now as marks of God's approval and reward. It is worth pausing over the scale of Zerah's army. If it really was a million strong it was fantastically large for its day. The phrase translated "a million", however, may be better translated "a thousand units" (see Introduction), which would make it impossible to be precise about the size of the army. Nevertheless, Chr. evidently intends to stress that it was large. The issue, yet again, is the source of real strength, as appears from Asa's prayer: "O Lord, thou art our God; let not man prevail against thee" (14:11). It is one thing to assent to the proposition that God is greater than man; it is quite another to believe it when one is facing threat from a human agency, especially when that agency is many times more powerful than oneself. Events like this one are recorded in the Bible precisely to encourage faith that can hold in the face of such odds. "There is none like thee to help," he prays, *"between the mighty and the weak"* (v. 11). This last phrase is difficult to interpret. The likeliest explanation is that the relative strength of forces becomes an irrelevancy when God has an interest in the outcome of the conflict. There is no ally, or adversary, like God. And he who is on the Lord's side must prevail. Defeat of the enemy, in our day and terms, will not be of the military sort. Our victories will often be inward, such that others will not witness them at all. Yet God still controls our circumstances, and there will be the visible victories also, when we have invested in what we know to be right.

(v)

The Covenant entered into, 15:12–15, commits Judah to "seek the Lord" (v. 12), that catchword for faithfulness. The absoluteness of the commitment appears from the language of both v. 12*b* and 15*a* ("with all their heart and with all their soul"). This absoluteness refers to the commitment of each individual. But there is an absoluteness too that relates to the commitment of Israel as a totality. Those who refused to seek the Lord were to be put to death (v. 13). The thinking behind this uncompromising justice is that the people as a whole are responsible for keeping covenant commitment. When in Exod. 24 Moses, on behalf of Israel, entered into covenant with God for the first time, he sprinkled sacrificial blood on those of the people who were present (in a representative capacity) and called it "the blood of the covenant which the Lord has made with you" (24:8). The likeliest significance of this ritual is that by it the people, in committing themselves to that first Covenant, acknowledged the justice of the penalty of death for breaking it. This amounts to an expression not only of each individual's commitment, but also of the corporate responsibility to exact the maximum penalty of covenant-breakers, with the purpose of keeping the Covenant intact. The same logic underlies Asa's covenant renewal. Entering into a relationship with God was a solemn matter and, according to the standards of the day, must be shown to be so.

The New Testament also knows of an exclusion from the Christian community for a flagrant disregard of God's standards that is incompatible with real Christian commitment (1 Cor. 5:1–6). The aim in that case, it should be noted, is the ultimate salvation of the offender. There are vast differences, therefore, between the practices of Israel and of the Church, that are rooted in the different characters of the two. Yet both Old and New Testaments agree upon the solemnity of a commitment to God. Such a commitment cannot, by its nature, be taken lightly. It is the making over of life itself, as God, in Jesus Christ, made over his for us.

ASA IN WEAKNESS

2 Chronicles 16:1–14

¹In the thirty-sixth year of the reign of Asa, Baasha king of Israel went up against Judah, and built Ramah, that he might permit no one to go out or come in to Asa king of Judah. ²Then Asa took silver and gold from the treasures of the house of the Lord and the king's house, and sent them to Ben-hadad king of Syria, who dwelt in Damascus, saying, ³"Let there be a league between me and you, as between my father and your father; behold, I am sending to you silver and gold; go, break your league with Baasha king of Israel, that he may withdraw from me." ⁴And Ben-hadad hearkened to King Asa, and sent the commanders of his armies against the cities of Israel, and they conquered Ijon, Dan, Abel-maim, and all the store-cities of Naphtali. ⁵And when Baasha heard of it, he stopped building Ramah, and let his work cease. ⁶Then King Asa took all Judah, and they carried away the stones of Ramah and its timber, with which Baasha had been building, and with them he built Geba and Mizpah.

⁷At that time Hanani the seer came to Asa king of Judah, and said to him, "Because you relied on the king of Syria, and did not rely on the Lord your God, the army of the king of Syria has escaped you. ⁸Were not the Ethiopians and the Libyans a huge army with exceedingly many chariots and horsemen? Yet because you relied on the Lord, he gave them into your hand. ⁹For the eyes of the Lord run to and fro throughout the whole earth, to show his might in behalf of those whose heart is blameless toward him. You have done foolishly in this; for from now on you will have wars." ¹⁰Then Asa was angry with the seer, and put him in the stocks, in prison, for he was in a rage with him because of this. And Asa inflicted cruelties upon some of the people at the same time.

¹¹The acts of Asa, from first to last, are written in the Book of the Kings of Judah and Israel. ¹²In the thirty-ninth year of his reign Asa was diseased in his feet, and his disease became severe; yet even in his disease he did not seek the Lord, but sought help from physicians. ¹³And Asa slept with his fathers, dying in the forty-first year of his reign. ¹⁴They buried him in the tomb which he had hewn out for himself in the city of David. They laid him on a bier which had been filled with various kinds of spices prepared by the perfumer's art; and they made a very great fire in his honour.

(i)

Chapter 16 tells of Asa's defection from the faithfulness that the previous two chapters have celebrated. Instead of putting his trust in God (14:11) he now relies upon Ben-hadad, king of Syria, to protect him from the attack of Baasha, king of Israel, even going to the extent of using treasures consecrated to God as payment for his services (vv. 2f). Ben-hadad proved, to be sure, an effective ally (v. 4), though the fragility of his friendship, and thus the extent of Asa's folly, is already hinted at in the fact that his mercenary reduction of Israel involved the breach of a "league" (or, perhaps better, treaty—the word is the same as that for "covenant") into which he had previously entered (and for which Baasha too may have paid dearly).

The issue, however, goes beyond the question whether Asa's political strategy was rewarded with short-term success. Chr. broaches here a theme which is of the utmost importance to the OT prophets. (It is no coincidence that it is spelled out in this passage too by a prophet.) The most celebrated instance of a prophet warning a king not to trust in political alliances occurs in Isa. 7, where Isaiah warns Ahaz not to trust Assyria (in the passage which contains the famous "Immanuel" prophecy, v. 14). There Ahaz, with a hypocritical show of piety (v. 12), opts to throw in his lot with the visible and apparently invincible might of empire. (Chr.'s account of Ahaz's reign comes at 2 Chr. ch. 28.) And here Asa prefers to rely on Syria rather than on God. In his treatment of the prophet Hanani and others (v. 10), which is a symptom of his rejection of God's word, he further aligns himself with kings who had no time for God's word (cf. Johoiakim's treatment of the prophet Uriah, Jer. 26: 20–23).

Asa, then, has done a complete volte-face from his earlier faithfulness. It is as if we meet two altogether different Asas. He appeared first in the strength of God-reliance, now in the weakness of self-reliance. That it is the same Asa emerges, however, from the hint of a guilty conscience, the sense of better things in the past, that produced his anger (v. 10). We have seen this anger before in Chr., in David's reaction to the fate of Uzzah (1 Chr. 13:11). It is the anger that recognizes the justice of the accusation. In Asa's case it issues, not in repentance (as it did with David) but in a rage of self-assertion. Human beings, regrettably, are not so made that an exposure to the truth will inevitably bring them to accept its implications and change their lives accordingly. It can, on the contrary, and quite irrationally, harden them in their opposition to it. Yet, as the whole tenor of Chr. implies, there is no immutable law which decrees that we *must* be subject to rebellious passions. Asa's refusal at the last hurdle is wholly culpable, and receives no mitigation from the Chronicler. Even in the extremity he seeks no help from the Lord (v. 12), in direct refusal of the offer that was made in the sermon of Azariah (15:4). Despite early trust in God, attended by evidence that such trust was well placed, Asa's end is sombre, lacking the knowledge that there is a God who can help in every kind of trouble. Had Asa treasured the moments in his life when he had clearly seen God's hand at work, his dying hours would have been greatly comforted.

(ii)

Hanani does not fail to draw out the special irony of Asa's failure. There are occasions in the Bible when a person's handling of some small matter is taken as an indication of his capacity to handle a large one (e.g. Matt. 25:21, 23; Jer. 12:5). Asa, however, having passed the sternest of tests first (by withstanding Zerah), fails a comparatively trivial one. Hanani refers expressly to the greatness of the army of the Ethiopians and Libyans in order to lend the greater point to the absurdity of Asa's final failure of nerve.

Yet though there is irony here, there is great psychological truth. There is that in us which runs to accept great challenges, because they flatter us and will bring us celebrity, while we jib at those tasks where there seems to be little to gain and everything to lose. Naaman almost squandered his opportunity to be healed for such ignoble reasons, until his servants took courage and pointed out his folly (2 Kings 5:13f.). Many who have been faithful in great things have found it hard to keep faith in smaller matters. Perhaps a major sacrifice has been made in a choice that has been perceived to be a matter of principle, or ethics, or indeed a special call. Yet the major decision has been followed by a host of little compromises, felt to be somehow covered by the first act of commitment, yet in reality rooted in a refusal to let that sacrifice lead to its real conclusion under God. Perhaps some have embarked upon a path of discipleship in their youth which has involved a choice of career, and find themselves in middle life in positions of disadvantage by comparison with their contemporaries, who have become richer and more powerful. And their faith barely matches the open stance they have taken up.

To such come the words of Hanani in v. 9. The Lord has not ceased to be active on behalf of any of his people. His power embraces the whole earth avidly and infallibly, achieving the good of those who persist in seeking him. The theme of perseverance is close to the hearts of biblical writers. (cf. the idea of conquest in the Book of Revelation, e.g. 21:7, and the warnings about apostasy in the Letter to the Hebrews, e.g. 6:1–8). It is tragic and unnecessary once to have known God, yet finally to come to self-obsession and self-reliance. It is never too late to return to God.

JEHOSHAPHAT

2 Chronicles 17:1–19

[1]Jehoshaphat his son reigned in his stead, and strengthened himself against Israel. [2]He placed forces in all the fortified cities of Judah, and set garrisons in the land of Judah, and in the cities of Ephraim which Asa his father had taken. [3]The Lord was with Jehoshaphat, because he walked in the earlier ways of his father; he did not seek the Baals, [4]but sought the God of his father and walked in his commandments, and not according to the ways of Israel. [5]Therefore the Lord established the kingdom in his hand; and all Judah brought tribute to Jehoshaphat; and he had great riches and honour. [6]His heart was courageous in the ways of the Lord; and furthermore he took the high places and the Asherim out of Judah.

⁷In the third year of his reign he sent his princes, Ben-hail, Obadiah, Zechariah, Nethanel, and Micaiah, to teach in the cities of Judah; ⁸and with them the Levites, Shemaiah, Nethaniah, Zebadiah, Asahel, Shemiramoth, Jehonathan, Adonijah, Tobijah, and Tobadonijah; and with these Levites, the priests Elishama and Jehoram. ⁹And they taught in Judah, having the book of the law of the Lord with them; they went about through all the cities of Judah and taught among the people.

¹⁰And the fear of the Lord fell upon all the kingdoms of the lands that were round about Judah, and they made no war against Jehoshaphat. ¹¹Some of the Philistines brought Jehoshaphat presents, and silver for tribute; and the Arabs also brought him seven thousand seven hundred rams and seven thousand seven hundred he-goats. ¹²And Jehoshaphat grew steadily greater. He built in Judah fortresses and store-cities, ¹³and he had great stores in the cities of Judah. He had soldiers, mighty men of valour, in Jerusalem. ¹⁴This was the muster of them by fathers' houses: Of Judah, the commanders of thousands: Adnah the commander, with three hundred thousand mighty men of valour, ¹⁵and next to him Jehohanan the commander, with two hundred and eighty thousand, ¹⁶and next to him Amasiah the son of Zichri, a volunteer for the service of the Lord, with two hundred thousand mighty men of valour. ¹⁷Of Benjamin: Eliada, a mighty man of valour, with two hundred thousand men armed with bow and shield, ¹⁸and next to him Jehozabad with a hundred and eighty thousand armed for war. ¹⁹These were in the service of the king, besides those whom the king had placed in the fortified cities throughout all Judah.

Chr. now devotes four chapters to King Jehoshaphat, which makes him one of the most significant figures in 2 Chr. The account of religious reforms and two major wars represents a significant expansion over Kings, where the story of Jehoshaphat is very much subordinate to that of his northern contemporary Ahab, and where he is mentioned in his own right it is only to record the judgment that he was righteous, 1 Kings 22:43. Relations with Ahab continue to play an important role in Chr.'s account, but the weight of Chr.'s interest rests on Jehoshaphat.

Chapter 17 represents a general introduction to his reign, describing him, in terms which are by now familiar to us, as one who was faithful to God. He "sought the God of his father" and not the Baals (vv. 3f.); he followed God's commandments and not the ways of the idolatrous north (v. 4); his heart was courageous (literally "lifted up") in the ways of the Lord, rather than "lifted up" in pride and self-reliance (v. 6). In all this he resembled his father Asa in his earlier righteousness (v. 3). Because of his righteousness he is rewarded in ways which are also by now familiar, namely with wealth (v. 5), the tribute of foreign nations (v. 11, that of the Philistines recalling especially that this is a king in the mould of David and not of Saul), and the prosperity and military power which are the emblems of a strong kingdom (vv. 12ff.). This general picture of Jehoshaphat is, then, rather stylized. It serves primarily as a backcloth to the incidents in his reign which are to follow, and to which we shall come in due course.

Before leaving chapter 17, however, it is worth noting that the general portrayal of Jehoshaphat differs from portraits of other righteous kings in two ways.

(i) He appears to surpass Rehoboam, Abijah, and Asa (at their best) in his zeal for the law. Not content with ensuring that offical religious practices are correct and pure by eradicating idolatry (which had presumably crept back in in Asa's declining years), v. 6, he undertakes the major task of spreading an understanding of the inherited faith among the common people. This is the first time in Chr. that such a ministry is expressly referred to. It is, of course, clear in the cases of David and Solomon and subsequent reformers that their measures were intended to have an impact on all the people. Yet their sphere of action tended to be the great religious occasion, their prayers and pronouncements mediated to the populace, we suppose, by representatives (cf. e.g. 1 Chr. 28:1). Jehoshaphat evidently has a pastor's instinct. He knows that you cannot affect people's hearts by imposing change from the top. No amount of desecration of the trappings of Baalism, no decree however stern that henceforth Yahweh will be worshipped, can prevent the hankering of people in Judah after the foreign gods which had been an irresistible temptation to them ever since their possession of the land centuries before Jehoshaphat. We shall read in due course of the greatest reformer of all in Judah, Josiah (chs. 34f.), whose reform, however, could not prevent his contemporary the prophet Jeremiah from delivering the most savage attack in the OT upon Judah's chronic apostasy. Josiah's reform did not reach the hearts of the people. Jehoshaphat comes closer perhaps than any other king in Judah or Israel to the ideal of the leader who is subject to the law himself and who desires to make it the ruling principle in his land.

Very significant is the fact that it is his *princes* who are charged with the task of teaching, although of course they are accompanied by priests and Levites who may be regarded as the technical experts. But the role of the princes, who were not in any sense dynastic, but rather officials appointed by Jehoshaphat himself, shows that this king was prepared to organize his whole kingdom for the purpose of propagating the law. So often the leaders in Israel were castigated by the prophets for arrogating to themselves power which should have been used for this very purpose. And indeed the acquisition of the authority which is necessary to the exercise of responsibility can so easily have a corrupting effect upon weak human beings. Here, however, is a picture of power used selflessly and utterly responsibly. It behoves every Christian to ask himself whether he turns such influence as he has to his own advantage or to the good of others—supremely to the cause of propagating the truth about God in Jesus Christ.

(ii) The second way in which the portrayal of Jehoshaphat differs from that of other kings is in the pointed contrasts which are drawn between him and his northern neighbour. The first thing that we read about him is that "he strengthened himself against Israel" (v. 1). He does this particularly in cities which Asa had taken from Israel in the territory of Ephraim (v. 2). It is as if that strengthening, which we have met before as the gift of God for the protection of a kingdom that is faithful, is directed, in Jehoshaphat's case, particularly against Israel. His faithfulness—especially in that "he did not seek the Baals" (v. 3) and in his exemplary kingship—seems to be defined as a maintenance of what is right in contrast to his apostate northern brethren. The pressure to conform to northern idolatry was always present, stronger no doubt than pressure from beyond Israel's borders because of the ties of kinship with the north. Again we have occasion to note that pressure to depart from the path of discipleship can be strongest from those closest to us, especially if they share a background of faith and maintain some nominal commitment. The general judgment on Jehoshaphat's reign is that he resisted such influence. Yet there is irony in this assessment, in the light of what happens next.

THE LIE—I

2 Chronicles 18:1–34

¹Now Jehoshaphat had great riches and honour; and he made a marriage alliance with Ahab. ²After some years he went down to Ahab in Samaria. And Ahab killed an abundance of sheep and oxen for him and for the people who were with him, and induced him to go up against Ramoth-gilead. ³Ahab king of Israel said to Jehoshaphat king of Judah, "Will you go with me to Ramoth-gilead?" He answered him, "I am as you are, my people as your people. We will be with you in the war."

⁴And Jehoshaphat said to the king of Israel, "Inquire first for the word of the Lord." ⁵Then the king of Israel gathered the prophets together, four hundred men, and said to them, "Shall we go to battle against Ramoth-gilead, or shall I forbear?" And they said, "Go up; for God will give it into the hand of the king." ⁶But Jehoshaphat said, "Is there not here another prophet of the Lord of whom we may inquire?" ⁷And the king of Israel said to Jehoshaphat, "There is yet one man by whom we may inquire of the Lord, Micaiah the son of Imlah; but I hate him, for he never prophesies good concerning me, but always evil." And Jehoshaphat said, "Let not the king say so." ⁸Then the king of Israel summoned an officer and said, "Bring quickly Micaiah the son of Imlah." ⁹Now the king of Israel and Jehoshaphat the king of Judah were sitting on their thrones, arrayed in their robes; and they were sitting at the threshing floor at the entrance of the gate of Samaria; and all the prophets were prophesying before them. ¹⁰And Zedekiah the son of Chenaanah made for himself horns of iron, and said, "Thus says the Lord, 'With these you shall push the Syrians until they are destroyed.'" ¹¹And all the prophets prophesied so, and said, "Go up to

Ramoth-gilead and triumph; the Lord will give it into the hand of the king."

¹²And the messenger who went to summon Micaiah said to him, "Behold, the words of the prophets with one accord are favourable to the king; let your word be like the word of one of them, and speak favourably." ¹³But Micaiah said, "As the Lord lives, what my God says, that I will speak." ¹⁴And when he had come to the king, the king said to him, "Micaiah, shall we go to Ramoth-gilead to battle, or shall I forbear?" And he answered, "Go up and triumph; they will be given into your hand." ¹⁵But the king said to him, "How many times shall I adjure you that you speak to me nothing but the truth in the name of the Lord?" ¹⁶And he said, "I saw all Israel scattered upon the mountains, as sheep that have no shepherd; and the Lord said, 'These have no master; let each return to his home in peace.'" ¹⁷And the king of Israel said to Jehoshaphat, "Did I not tell you that he would not prophesy good concerning me, but evil?" ¹⁸And Micaiah said, "Therefore hear the word of the Lord: I saw the Lord sitting on his throne, and all the host of heaven standing on his right hand and on his left; ¹⁹and the Lord said, 'Who will entice Ahab the king of Israel, that he may go up and fall at Ramoth-gilead?' And one said one thing, and another said another. ²⁰Then a spirit came forward and stood before the Lord, saying, 'I will entice him.' And the Lord said to him, 'By what means?' ²¹And he said, 'I will go forth, and will be a lying spirit in the mouth of all his prophets.' And he said, 'You are to entice him, and you shall succeed; go forth and do so.' ²²Now therefore behold, the Lord has put a lying spirit in the mouth of these your prophets; the Lord has spoken evil concerning you."

²³Then Zedekiah the son of Chenaanah came near and struck Micaiah on the cheek, and said, "Which way did the Spirit of the Lord go from me to speak to you?" ²⁴And Micaiah said, "Behold, you shall see on that day when you go into an inner chamber to hide yourself." ²⁵And the king of Israel said, "Seize Micaiah, and take him back to Amon the governor of the city and to Joash the king's son; ²⁶and say, 'Thus says the king, Put this fellow in prison, and feed him with scant fare of bread and water, until I return in peace.'" ²⁷And Micaiah said, "If you return in peace, the Lord has not spoken by me." And he said, "Hear, all you peoples!"

²⁸So the king of Israel and Jehoshaphat the king of Judah went up to Ramoth-gilead. ²⁹And the king of Israel said to Jehoshaphat, "I will disguise myself and go into battle, but you wear your robes." And the

king of Israel disguised himself; and they went into battle. ³⁰Now the king of Syria had commanded the captains of his chariots, "Fight with neither small nor great, but only with the king of Israel." ³¹And when the captains of the chariots saw Jehoshaphat, they said, "It is the king of Israel." So they turned to fight against him; and Jehoshaphat cried out, and the Lord helped him. God drew them away from him, ³²for when the captains of the chariots saw that it was not the king of Israel, they turned back from pursuing him. ³³But a certain man drew his bow at a venture, and struck the king of Israel between the scale armour and the breastplate; therefore he said to the driver of his chariot, "Turn about, and carry me out of the battle, for I am wounded." ³⁴And the battle grew hot that day, and the king of Israel propped himself up in his chariot facing the Syrians until evening; then at sunset he died.

(i)

Having passed the general judgment that Jehoshaphat was right- eous, Chr. now relates one great lapse. (2 Kings 3 records an- other, not mentioned here.) His marriage-alliance with Ahab may have seemed innocent enough, but such alliances com- monly had political implications in the ancient Near East, as at other times and in other places, and as the events of the chapter show. Furthermore, the marriage-partner thus procured for Jehoshaphat's son Jehoram was the dreadful Athaliah, a true daughter of Jezebel, as we shall see (22:10–23:21).

The marriage arrangement merely serves as a preparation for the specific error of Jehoshaphat which is now related, namely his military alliance with Ahab in Israel's ongoing war with Syria. True, we are told that Ahab *enticed* Jehoshaphat, with a show of wealth in a celebration designed to flatter him. Yet this is not said by way of mitigation of Jehoshaphat's guilt. Compliance with Ahab's suggestions carried with it compromise in a fundamental way. It may be that Jehoshaphat did not fully perceive his action as a betrayal of principle. His statement in v. 3 may arise from a sense, in itself laudable, that Israel is still ideally united and ought to act concertedly against an attack on the historic promised land. Yet the alliance inevitably involved identification with the out- rages of Jezebel's Israel in a way which made it impossible for

Jehoshaphat to maintain his integrity. (The full story of Ahab and Jezebel is told in 1 Kings chs. 17–22; 2 Kings 9:30–37.)

(ii)

The action in chapter 18 centres on the issue of seeking God's word for the campaign. The story has often been felt to be one of the most problematic in the OT because of the implication that God himself perpetrates a deception by his authorization of the "spirit" (v. 20) to be "a *lying* spirit in the mouth of all [Ahab's] prophets" (v. 21).

The issue of trustworthiness of the prophetic word arises at the outset, however. Jehoshaphat very properly insists on hearing what the prophets, as the mouthpieces of God, have to say about the campaign (v. 4 lending support to the view that his guilt in the matter involves a large amount of well-intentioned naïvety). Our first hint that all is not well comes when he appears dissatisfied with the initial prophetic encouragement, and asks the question which forces Ahab to produce Micaiah (vv. 6ff.). Ahab's reluctance to hear Micaiah (v. 7) is, at one level, one of the most amusing passages in the Bible. At another, it betrays his character utterly, forms the centre of the present action, and provides the key to its mysteries.

To try to understand this chapter by beginning with the question: how can God perpetrate a falsehood? is to fail to appreciate that the issue of falsehood is raised long before v. 19. The whole reign of Ahab and the constitution of Israel is a falsehood. To say this is by no means an attempt to dodge the issue, but can be confirmed by precise analogies within the OT. The prophet Jeremiah used the term here translated "lying" (*sheqer*) not only to mean a straightforward lie (Jer. 37:14) but also, and more regularly, to depict the state of apostasy into which the Judah of his day had sunk. (Jer. 9:3–6 is a sustained meditation upon falsehood as that which characterizes his people.)

For Jeremiah, as for the Chronicler, a king who is intent on his own grandeur rather than that of God, prophets who use their position merely to bolster the status quo and give the king the answers he wants to hear, a people that are exploited by the leaders whose calling it is to serve them and give them justice, constitute a state of deep-seated falsehood. That falsehood is heinous supremely in the fact that the people involved is Israel, and bears the name of enjoying a covenant relationship with God. An Israel that has no interest in God or his commandments is no "true" Israel, and, in this context, cannot in any "true" way claim the blessing and protection of God upon its efforts to preserve a territory which it has a right to hold only in obedience. For this reason Micaiah *could* not prophesy good concerning Ahab—since "good" is so much a product of covenant-faithfulness. Jehoshaphat, too, implies that Ahab is no true king—wittingly or unwittingly—when he says: "Let not the king say so" (v. 7), which may well bear the sense, "A king *should* not say so!" These judgments upon Ahab become explicit in v. 16, when Micaiah says that Israel is without a shepherd (a term often used for kings and other leaders in Israel), and reports God's judgment that Ahab has no real entitlement to kingship, nor any authority to undertake a "holy" war.

THE LIE—II

2 Chronicles 18:1–34 (*cont'd*)

(iii)

Having recognized that the constitution of Israel under Ahab was a lie, we go on to observe that such a state of affairs could only be maintained by means of a *wilful* suppression of the truth. This affected both Ahab and his "official" prophets. Ahab *knew* that Micaiah would tell him he had no sanction from God, not only for this battle, but for anything—the paths of the two had clearly crossed before! He knew it, not because Micaiah was simply an awkward customer who was determined to give him no satisfaction, but because his conscience told him that he was fundamentally in rebellion against God.

The prophets, too, had an interest in maintaining their view of things to the exclusion of dissentient voices. The words of the messenger, v. 12, are not merely an account of the action so far for Micaiah's benefit, coupled with a pious wish that the official prophets might be right. They are tantamount to a threat. The prophets' "trade union" put pressure on Micaiah—via another member of Ahab's establishment—to toe the party line. A little later (v. 23) the anger of the prophetic hierarchy is expressed through the piqued Zedekiah-ben-Chenaanah, drawing a word of ominous condemnation from Micaiah (v. 24).

In the confrontation between Micaiah and the false prophets we have a further anticipation of Jeremiah, who first denounces then runs into open conflict with prophets whose whole aim is to bolster up the status quo (Jer. 23:9–40; 28; 29:15–23). The fate of Hananiah-ben-Azzur in that conflict (Jer. 28:15–17) shows how precarious is the position of Zedekiah (v. 24—for whose implications cf. Isa. 2:19, 21). The last exchange between Ahab and Micaiah (vv. 25–27), in which the prophet is confined to prison and, as he goes, pronounces the impossibility of Ahab knowing peace, represents Ahab's final, enraged attempt to suppress the truth. (On the suppression of the truth as a work of men in rebellion against God see further Rom. 1:18, and the wider context there.)

It comes as a shock to us to see the official prophets cast in this role as obstructors of the truth. In fact those prophets of Israel who have been remembered because their pronouncements have been canonized in scripture probably had to exercise their ministries as often as not in the teeth of opposition from those who bore the *name* of prophet. So discredited were the official prophets in the eyes of Amos that he made it clear that he was not one of them (Amos 7:14). And their record stands as a warning to the Church. Too often it too has abandoned its prophetic role for the softer option of providing a respectable religious sanction for the policies of government, however unpleasant. Individual Christians too need to be aware of the temptation to reconcile proclamation of the gospel with a concern for personal advancement. Rather let us say with Micaiah: "As the Lord lives, what my God says, that will I speak"—come what may!

(iv)

We are now in a position to return to the despatch of a "lying spirit" from the council of heaven. God's action becomes readily comprehensible when we see it (a) as a response in kind to Israel in general and Ahab in particular. The "lying spirit" or, more literally, the "spirit of falsehood" corresponds exactly to the "spirit of falsehood" prevailing in Israel, and represents God's refusal to reward it with "peace" (v. 27), of which a necessary precondition is truth. (b) Nevertheless, it is important to realize that the "spirit of falsehood" sent by God *actually deceives no-one*. It is sent, as we have seen, to those who recognize the truth and suppress it. When Micaiah first addresses Ahab with the ironic words of v. 14 (i.e. in the terms which the "spirit of falsehood" has suggested), Ahab sees through it at once and demands—irony of ironies—the truth (v. 15)! When Ahab goes to battle he has heard and recognized the truth, and does not pretend otherwise. His lament of v. 17 is not an accusation of the prophet, but a grim knowledge that he would never enjoy blessing from God. He goes to his destiny against Syria because—*in spite* of the word of God—he is determined to be godless.

(v)

Verses 28–34 describe Ahab's sad but inevitable end. Throughout the story there has been considerable emphasis upon the hand of God controlling events. One function of the "lying spirit" was to affirm that even in the prophets' ignominious betrayal of their office God had been "working his purposes out" (as the hymn puts it). This by no means diminishes the guilt of those prophets. It simply shows that God operates within all circumstances to achieve his own ends. This theme is now continued in the story of the demise of Ahab. Ahab thought that he would ensure his own safety by going into battle in disguise, while letting Jehoshaphat appear in full royal battle-dress (Jehoshaphat's naïvety appears to reach fresh heights here!) The story is told so as to obtain maximum effect for the point. The odds are piled against Jehoshaphat because of the king of Syria's battle-instructions (v. 30). But God "drew [the Syrians] away from him" (v. 31), when Jehoshaphat called upon him. Appropriately, the same verb is used for God's "drawing away" the Syrians as was used for Ahab's "inducing" Jehoshaphat, v. 2. God thus reclaims his servant from the snares of apostasy by his careful management of the situation. Perhaps too the extremity of Jehoshaphat's situation showed where his heart truly lay, viz. in dependence upon God. Here, no more than with the false prophets, should we suppose that God's sovereignty has extinguished human responsibility.

In contrast to the salvation of Jehoshaphat is the perdition of Ahab. Some Syrian (the Hebrew is no more precise) fired an arrow at random, and, as we might say, Ahab's name was written on it. Thus Ahab's defiance of God was met by his judgment, from which there is no escape.

JEHOSHAPHAT REBUKED

2 Chronicles 19:1–11

¹Jehoshaphat the king of Judah returned in safety to his house in Jerusalem. ²But Jehu the son of Hanani the seer went out to meet him, and said to King Jehoshaphat, "Should you help the wicked and love those who hate the Lord? Because of this, wrath has gone out against you from the Lord. ³Nevertheless some good is found in you, for you destroyed the Asherahs out of the land, and have set your heart to seek God."

⁴Jehoshaphat dwelt at Jerusalem; and he went out again among the people, from Beer-sheba to the hill country of Ephraim, and brought them back to the Lord, the God of their fathers. ⁵He appointed judges in the land in all the fortified cities of Judah, city by city, ⁶and said to the judges, "Consider what you do, for you judge not for man but for the Lord; he is with you in giving judgment. ⁷Now then, let the fear of the Lord be upon you; take heed what you do, for there is no perversion of justice with the Lord our God, or partiality, or taking bribes."

⁸Moreover in Jerusalem Jehoshaphat appointed certain Levites and priests and heads of families of Israel, to give judgment for the Lord and to decide disputed cases. They had their seat at Jerusalem. ⁹And he charged them: "Thus you shall do in the fear of the Lord, in

faithfulness, and with your whole heart: [10]whenever a case comes to you from your brethren who live in their cities, concerning bloodshed, law or commandment, statutes or ordinances, then you shall instruct them, that they may not incur guilt before the Lord and wrath may not come upon you and your brethren. Thus you shall do, and you will not incur guilt. [11]And behold, Amariah the chief priest is over you in all matters of the Lord; and Zebadiah the son of Ishmael, the governor of the house of Judah, in all the king's matters; and the Levites will serve you as officers. Deal courageously, and may the Lord be with the upright!"

(i)

Jehoshaphat now has to face the music for his aberration in the matter of his alliance with Ahab. The accusation of infidelity is pronounced by Jehu the seer (to be distinguished from Jehu the son of Nimshi who would later become king in the north, 1 Kings 19:16). It places Jehoshaphat close to Rehoboam in giving him modified approval. As "some deliverance" was granted to the latter (12:7), so now "some good" is found in Jehoshaphat (v. 3). The terms used in Jehoshaphat's case are actually somewhat more positive (literally: "good things have been found in you"), suggesting that Jehoshaphat is viewed more favourably than Rehoboam. But the principle is the same. Jehoshaphat has stained an otherwise glittering record with an act of great folly.

He is now faced with the full implications of the choice he had made in going with Ahab. It was a case of "loving those who hate the Lord" (v. 2). The phrase implies not so much emotional attachment, in this case, as deliberate choice. The ideas of "loving" and "hating" are used elsewhere in the Bible simply to convey preference (Matt. 6:24; Luke 14:26). Passages like these seem to us to be overstatements and we naturally seek to diminish their harsh impact. Yet the terms are chosen advisedly, in order to show the full implications of choices. We have seen already how much Jehoshaphat underestimated the extent to which he was maintaining the cause of false religion. Here the point specifically relates to the sphere of activity, or the social ambience, which one naturally chooses. A Christian's attachment to God is necessarily expressed in the kind of atmosphere in which he prefers to live and move and have his being. Company, pursuits, ambitions will all bear upon them the mark of a love of God. This is by no means to put an embargo upon normal social intercourse with those who are not basically like-minded. It has to do with the sort of life-pattern which one chooses to construct. The task of construction is no easy one, and the temptation is to model oneself upon the "architects" about us. This was Jehoshaphat's fault, and his error calls us to consistency in exhibiting the characteristics which are truly Christian. (See further Rom. 12:1f.; Gal. 5:16–26.)

(ii)

It is instructive that we next find Jehoshaphat once more about the kind of business in which we found him engaged in 17:7ff. Verse 4 tells us that he went out *again* among the people, indicating that he now picks up the pastoral work which he saw as part of his role where he had left it in order to take up arms. This tells us two important things.

(a) It shows, first of all, that Jehoshaphat bore well the rebuke delivered by Jehu. He did not know how the wrath that had "gone out against [him] from the Lord" (v. 2) would strike (see 20:35ff.), but he responded to the chastisement not with bitterness but with the repentance that proves itself to be true by issuing in a changed or renewed life-style.

(b) It shows, secondly, the Lord's readiness to restore to his services those who have abandoned it. We read that Jehoshaphat "brought back [the people] to the Lord" (v. 4). It may well be that the king's alliance with Ahab had given encouragement to those within Judah who sought to promote Baal-worship, and that ground gained in his earlier teaching campaign had since been lost. This is one possible explanation of the need to "bring the people back". Yet it would be equally possible to take the phrase to mean no more than that he caused the people to repent, since the verb to "bring back" is simply the causative form of a verb which typically bears that meaning. Jehoshaphat, therefore, is instrumental in a genuine turning to the Lord on the part of his people. One of the greatest sadnesses of Christians who have been in positions of responsibility within the Church, but who have become burdened by guilt because of some sin, is a sense that they are no more qualified to serve. The author of the greatest penitential Psalm feared as much. Yet in the throes of his prayer for restoration he gains the assurance that he *shall* again "teach transgressors thy ways" (Ps. 51:13). The experience of Jehoshaphat proves the point.

(iii)

Jehoshaphat's bringing of God's law to the people not only consisted of teaching them to follow it, but also of ensuring that they enjoyed the protection which it was intended to afford. The mere possession of the law in Israel by no means guaranteed for all the benefits that it envisaged. Indeed some would *boast* of its possession while living lives that flouted it (Jer. 8:8). And the disadvantaged in the land were constantly open to its abuses. (Many of the prophets' denunciations are probably directed against oppression which is *technically* within the law but which offends against its spirit, e.g. Isa. 5:8, which may refer to the legitimate practice of taking debtors' possessions in pledge. The law itself was never bad. It is self-interested exploitation of it that is criticized in the OT as in the New.)

Jehoshaphat, therefore, takes measures (v. 5) to carry on the business of applying the law to the creation of an equitable society which Moses had begun when he appointed the first judges to decide in legal disputes (Exod. 18:13ff.). Essential to proper "judging" was the desire to do it scrupulously "for the Lord". Any judicial system has inherent in it the possibility of encouraging corruption; and the ancient sin of "man-pleasing" (Eph. 6:6) had crude materialistic overtones in the OT, as its numerous condemnations of the practice show (Exod. 23:6; Prov. 17:23). Jehoshaphat's charge to his judges to be fair (v. 7) has more than a hint that all their actions are under the scrutiny of God and subject to his final judgment. The same thought is salutary for all of us who are tempted to let self-interest infiltrate in any sense our Christian service. Jehoshaphat's concern for the people seems to be influenced by his own experience with Ahab. As he has repented so he brings the people to repent. As he has heard a prophetic voice proclaim that his kingship will somehow know loss because of the wrath of God (v. 2) he now acts to ensure that the people themselves will avoid wrath (v. 10). His ministry is to bring them to take God utterly seriously, as he has come to do.

TRIUMPH—WITH RESERVATIONS—I

2 Chronicles 20:1–37

¹After this the Moabites and Ammonites, and with them some of the Meunites, came against Jehoshaphat for battle. ²Some men came and told Jehoshaphat, "A great multitude is coming against you from Edom, from beyond the sea; and, behold, they are in Hazazon-tamar" (that is, Engedi). ³Then Jehoshaphat feared, and set himself to seek the Lord, and proclaimed a fast throughout all Judah. ⁴And Judah assembled to seek help from the Lord; from all the cities of Judah they came to seek the Lord.

⁵And Jehoshaphat stood in the assembly of Judah and Jerusalem, in the house of the Lord, before the new court, ⁶and said, "O Lord, God of our fathers, art thou not God in heaven? Dost thou not rule over all the kingdoms of the nations? In thy hand are power and might, so that none is able to withstand thee. ⁷Didst thou not, O our God, drive out the inhabitants of this land before thy people Israel, and give it for ever to the descendants of Abraham thy friend? ⁸And they have dwelt in it, and have built thee in it a sanctuary for thy name, saying, ⁹'If evil comes upon us, the sword, judgment, or pestilence, or famine, we will stand before this house, and before thee, for thy name is in this house, and cry to thee in our affliction, and thou wilt hear and save.' ¹⁰And now behold, the men of Ammon and Moab and Mount Seir, whom thou wouldest not let Israel invade when they came from the land of Egypt, and whom they avoided and did not destroy— ¹¹behold, they reward us by coming to drive us out of thy possession, which thou hast given us to inherit. ¹²O our God, wilt thou not execute judgment upon them? For we are powerless against this great multitude that is coming against us. We do not know what to do, but our eyes are upon thee."

¹³Meanwhile all the men of Judah stood before the Lord, with their little ones, their wives, and their children. ¹⁴And the Spirit of the Lord came upon Jahaziel the son of Zechariah, son of Benaiah, son of Je-iel,

son of Mattaniah, a Levite of the sons of Asaph, in the midst of the assembly. ¹⁵And he said, "Hearken, all Judah and inhabitants of Jerusalem, and King Jehoshaphat: Thus says the Lord to you, 'Fear not, and be not dismayed at this great multitude; for the battle is not yours but God's. ¹⁶Tomorrow go down against them; behold, they will come up by the ascent of Ziz; you will find them at the end of the valley, east of the wilderness of Jeruel. ¹⁷You will not need to fight in this battle; take your position, stand still, and see the victory of the Lord on your behalf, O Judah and Jerusalem.' Fear not, and be not dismayed; tomorrow go out against them, and the Lord will be with you."

¹⁸Then Jehoshaphat bowed his head with his face to the ground, and all Judah and the inhabitants of Jerusalem fell down before the Lord, worshipping the Lord. ¹⁹And the Levites, of the Kohathites and the Korahites, stood up to praise the Lord, the God of Israel, with a very loud voice.

²⁰And they rose early in the morning and went out into the wilderness of Tekoa; and as they went out, Jehoshaphat stood and said, "Hear me, Judah and inhabitants of Jerusalem! Believe in the Lord your God, and you will be established; believe his prophets, and you will succeed." ²¹And when he had taken counsel with the people, he appointed those who were to sing to the Lord and praise him in holy array, as they went before the army, and say,

"Give thanks to the Lord,
    for his steadfast love endures for ever."

²²And when they began to sing and praise, the Lord set an ambush against the men of Ammon, Moab, and Mount Seir, who had come against Judah, so that they were routed. ²³For the men of Ammon and Moab rose against the inhabitants of Mount Seir, destroying them utterly, and when they had made an end of the inhabitants of Seir, they all helped to destroy one another.

²⁴When Judah came to the watchtower of the wilderness, they looked toward the multitude; and behold, they were dead bodies lying on the ground; none had escaped. ²⁵When Jehoshaphat and his people came to take the spoil from them, they found cattle in great numbers, goods, clothing, and precious things, which they took for themselves until they could carry no more. They were three days in taking the spoil, it was so much. ²⁶On the fourth day they assembled in the Valley of Beracah, for there they blessed the Lord; therefore the name of that place has been called the Valley of Beracah to this day. ²⁷Then they returned, every man of Judah and Jerusalem, and Jehoshaphat at their

head, returning to Jerusalem with joy, for the Lord had made them rejoice over their enemies. 28They came to Jerusalem, with harps and lyres and trumpets, to the house of the Lord. 29And the fear of God came on all the kingdoms of the countries when they heard that the Lord had fought against the enemies of Israel. 30So the realm of Jehoshaphat was quiet, for his God gave him rest round about.

31Thus Jehoshaphat reigned over Judah. He was thirty-five years old when he began to reign, and he reigned twenty-five years in Jerusalem. His mother's name was Azubah the daughter of Shilhi. 32He walked in the way of Asa his father and did not turn aside from it; he did what was right in the sight of the Lord. 33The high places, however, were not taken away; the people had not yet set their hearts upon the God of their fathers.

34Now the rest of the acts of Jehoshaphat, from first to last, are written in the chronicles of Jehu the son of Hanani, which are recorded in the Book of the Kings of Israel.

35After this Jehoshaphat king of Judah joined with Ahaziah king of Israel, who did wickedly. 36He joined him in building ships to go to Tarshish, and they built the ships in Eziongeber. 37Then Eliezer the son of Dodavahu of Mareshah prophesied against Jehoshaphat, saying, "Because you have joined with Ahaziah, the Lord will destroy what you have made." And the ships were wrecked and were not able to go to Tarshish.

vv. 1–3. The account of Jehoshaphat's reign now comes to its climax, with the greatest external threat to him, and his deliverance from it. The advance of the Moabites and Ammonites, together with the more obscure Meunites, represents the resurgence of traditional enemies of Israel in a fearsome new alliance. The odds are against Jehoshaphat, as they had been against his father Asa on another occasion (14:9ff.), and he is driven to seek the Lord. The Chronicler's purpose in this chapter, apart from the concern to relate history, was probably to contrast Jehoshaphat's going into battle in a right relation to God with his waywardness in joining himself to Ahab (chapter 18). The basic theme is typical of Chr., viz. the need to humble oneself before God in the face of huge odds, together with the resultant victory. The chapter falls into four distinct parts.

TRIUMPH—WITH RESERVATIONS—II

2 Chronicles 20:1–37 (*cont'd*)

(a) *Jehoshaphat's prayer* (vv. 5–12)

The key to the prayer is in the expressions of helplessness in v. 12: "we are powerless against this great multitude . . . We do not know what to do". Chr. has always insisted that kings only succeed when they humble themselves before God. Yet there is perhaps a subtle change in tone here. The Davidic model of war laid some stress on the might of the warrior. There is nothing of this here, but rather a sense that God's people must stand back and wait for him to act. For this reason Jehoshaphat appeals to the Lord in terms that recall his former dispossession of other nations in order to give the land to Israel, basing himself also (v. 9) upon an assurance once given to Solomon following that king's prayer at the dedication of the Temple (2 Chr. 7:14). There is a conviction in the prayer of God's power to change any situation utterly, without any need of human co-operation. This is still the essence of Christian prayer. Many in our age know full well the desolation and despair of the cry, "We do not know what to do". When people's temporal hopes are gone—and dreams of perfect happiness on earth inevitably prove illusory—the best secular answer is an acquiescent, perhaps bitter, resignation. Where there is faith in God, in glorious contrast, the "we do not know what to do" merely leads into "but our eyes are upon thee." There is no excuse for Christian hopelessness. The Christian's response in the blackest hour must be: "My eyes are upon thee."

(b) *The oracle and response* (vv. 13–21)

The oracle of Jahaziel the Levite also stresses that this victory will, in a special way, be God's alone (v. 15*b*). Verse 17 makes clear that Jehoshaphat and his army will have the role of onlooker on this occasion. The present battle is thus distinguished from the great majority of encounters which Chr. relates, in which God empowers the armies of Judah to win. The theology associated with those occasions was expressed as early as 1 Chr. 12 in the theme of "help". We noticed in that place that the idea of God helping his people to victory differed from and complemented the other important biblical picture of divine victory which stressed God's action alone, and which we now find here. The Davidic pattern is not reversed by the pronouncement of Jahaziel. Rather, there is a recognition here of the danger which dogs those who "succeed" in any sense in God's service, the danger of forgetting that God's work is, in the last analysis, wholly his own. God chooses, in this instance, therefore, to make a demonstration of that independent and total power. The result is, for Jehoshaphat and Judah, both humbling—as is shown by their falling down to worship this mighty God (vv. 18f.)—and faith-restoring.

The Jehoshaphat of v. 20 is one who has come from his initial fear (v. 3) to a new confidence that God is for him. His exhortation to Judah, "Believe in the Lord your God and you will be established" (v. 20), is similar to the prophet Isaiah's appeal to Ahaz (Isa. 7:9). The thought may be paraphrased. *Trust* in the Lord your God, and you will find him *trustworthy*. There is in the exhortation a call to commitment. The trustworthiness of the Lord cannot be known until one begins to make decisions on the basis of his promises, staking wealth and welfare on the outcome—just as it is impossible to know certainly that a chair will bear one's weight without actually sitting on it. It is perverse to blame God for circumstances if there has been no prior life-commitment to him.

(c) *The victory* (vv. 22–30)

The battle takes its promised course. It is the Lord who sets the ambush (v. 22), meaning, as is indicated by the following verse, that he sets Judah's enemies against each other. Several features of the battle have parallels in other OT battles in which stress is laid on God's independent action—e.g. the people's singing, reminiscent of the shouting at the fall of Jericho (Josh. 6:20); cf. enemies set against each other, Judg. 7:22; slaughter and the taking of spoil, 2 Kings 7:3–16; 19:35.

The result of the battle is a restoration of Judah under

Jehoshaphat to a state of blessing (the meaning of Beracah, v. 26), characterized by riches, possession of her land, the inspiration of fear in her enemies, and joyful worship in the Temple, which reminds of Israel's prosperity at her zenith, under Solomon.

(d) *Final comments on Jehoshaphat* (vv. 31–37)
Verses 31–34 furnish a standard summarizing reflection on Jehoshaphat's reign, and judge him to have been basically righteous. The final note casts a shadow, however, possibly taking up the word of condemnation spoken in 19:2, and which has not otherwise found an explanation. The effect of the final verses is to show that, however much a person's life might be characterized by obedience to God, the possibility of lapse and compromise is forever present. The statement about the high places (v. 33), in contrast to that in 17:6, may show that Jehoshaphat's reforms were not final—as no reform can be—and that a relaxed attitude on his part at the end of his reign allowed idolatry to obtain a foothold once more. The statement in v. 33*b* clearly implies an inconstancy on the part of the people which would point in this direction.

Jehoshaphat's dealings with Ahaziah (vv. 35–37) recall his earlier readiness to be allied with Ahab. The Chronicler presents Jehoshaphat as being rather more open to Ahaziah's overtures than does the author of Kings (1 Kings 22:48f.). The full story of their relationship hardly emerges from the two rather compressed accounts. What is clear is that Chr. makes an explicit link between the foundering of Jehoshaphat's ships, before they had earned him a penny, and this further unholy alliance. And so a reign that was in many ways glorious, ends on this sad and unsatisfying note.

AS THE HOUSE OF AHAB—I JEHORAM

2 Chronicles 21:1–20

¹Jehoshaphat slept with his fathers, and was buried with his fathers in the city of David; and Jehoram his son reigned in his stead. ²He had

brothers, the sons of Jehoshaphat: Azariah, Jehiel, Zechariah, Azariah, Michael, and Shephatiah; all these were the sons of Jehoshaphat king of Judah. ³Their father gave them great gifts, of silver, gold, and valuable possessions, together with fortified cities in Judah; but he gave the kingdom to Jehoram, because he was the first-born. ⁴When Jehoram had ascended the throne of his father and was established, he slew all his brothers with the sword, and also some of the princes of Israel. ⁵Jehoram was thirty-two years old when he became king, and he reigned eight years in Jerusalem. ⁶And he walked in the way of the kings of Israel, as the house of Ahab had done; for the daughter of Ahab was his wife. And he did what was evil in the sight of the Lord. ⁷Yet the Lord would not destroy the house of David, because of the covenant which he had made with David, and since he had promised to give a lamp to him and to his sons for ever.

⁸In his days Edom revolted from the rule of Judah, and set up a king of their own. ⁹Then Jehoram passed over with his commanders and all his chariots, and he rose by night and smote the Edomites who had surrounded him and his chariot commanders. ¹⁰So Edom revolted from the rule of Judah to this day. At that time Libnah also revolted from his rule, because he had forsaken the Lord, the God of his fathers.

¹¹Moreover he made high places in the hill country of Judah, and led the inhabitants of Jerusalem into unfaithfulness, and made Judah go astray. ¹²And a letter came to him from Elijah the prophet, saying, "Thus says the Lord, the God of David your father, 'Because you have not walked in the ways of Jehoshaphat your father, or in the ways of Asa king of Judah, ¹³but have walked in the way of the kings of Israel, and have led Judah and the inhabitants of Jerusalem into unfaithful-ness, as the house of Ahab led Israel into unfaithfulness, and also you have killed your brothers, of your father's house, who were better than yourself; ¹⁴behold, the Lord will bring a great plague on your people, your children, your wives, and all your possessions, ¹⁵and you yourself will have a severe sickness with a disease of your bowels, until your bowels come out because of the disease, day by day.' "

¹⁶And the Lord stirred up against Jehoram the anger of the Phi-listines and of the Arabs who are near the Ethiopians; ¹⁷and they came up against Judah, and invaded it, and carried away all the possessions they found that belonged to the king's house, and also his sons and his wives, so that no son was left to him except Jehoahaz, his youngest son.

¹⁸And after all this the Lord smote him in his bowels with an incurable disease. ¹⁹In course of time, at the end of two years, his

bowels came out because of the disease, and he died in great agony. His people made no fire in his honour, like the fires made for his fathers. ²⁰He was thirty-two years old when he began to reign, and he reigned eight years in Jerusalem; and he departed with no one's regret. They buried him in the city of David, but not in the tombs of the kings.

There now follow the reigns of two kings, Jehoram and Ahaziah, which are in stark contrast to those of Asa and Jehoshaphat (as is made explicit in 21:12). Each in turn is compared, rather, with Ahab (21:6; 22:3), that paradigm of perversity in exercising royal authority.

(a) *Jehoram's sin*

The essence of Ahab's wickedness lay in the fact that he had turned the possession of kingship to his own advantage, notably in the Naboth episode (1 Kings 21). Jehoram quickly shows, in the massacre of his brothers, that he is no more predisposed to a proper discharge of his divinely ordained duties. Rather he is motivated by a jealous protection of his own interests, and perhaps by covetousness of that wealth which his father's will had denied him (v. 3). Jehoram's sin is based, therefore, on the illusion that life and security can be achieved by human means and without regard for morality or compassion. Ironically, Jehoram's efforts to safeguard his royal position put at risk the very continuance of the dynasty, the massacre being the first in a sequence of events which will result in its near extinction. But his false calculation comes more immediately to his own door. Far from increasing the extent of his power by the grabbing of his brothers' cities, he sees it diminished by the loss of Edom and Libnah (vv. 8–10); far from securing advantage for his own children by the slaughter of his brothers, he sees them suffer a similar fate (vv. 14, 17); far from securing life for himself, he suffers premature and agonizing death (vv. 18f.). He dies unmourned, and without the honours that normally attended the funeral of a king (vv. 19f.).

It cannot be said too often that the tracing of cause and effect which so typifies Chr. does not imply that all suffering is the result of specific sin. The central point here relates rather to the folly and wickedness of usurping the place of God. Jehoram did not merely aim to exercise authority. He sought to control destinies. The same urge is not absent from the twentieth century. It is indulged wherever there is systematic suppression of, or discrimination against, classes of people for the preservation of group-interests. It is indulged most hideously in the realm of genetic manipulation and convenience-abortions. In every area of life (government, science, arts, etc.) men and women are under the necessity of distinguishing between an authority derived from God and the sovereign province of God himself. There is infallibly a moral dimension in the perception of the distinctions.

A word is in place about Elijah. It is not untypical in Chr. that words of accusation against kings should be spoken by prophets. Elijah stands out here simply because he is among the more distinguished of that group of people. There is a slight problem in that a plain reading of 2 Kings 2–3 would suggest that Elijah was by now dead. (2 Kings 3:11 shows that Elisha, Elijah's successor, had begun his ministry already in Jehoshaphat's reign.) It may be, of course, that Elisha was recognized as a prophet before taking Elijah's mantle, and there is therefore some uncertainty about the chronology here. But the Chronicler may well intend us to understand that Elijah's letter came from heaven. The appropriateness of Jehoram's condemnation coming from Elijah rather than another prophet lies in the fact that he was the great antagonist of Ahab (1 Kings 17–18), with whom Jehoram is now compared.

(b) *God's grace*
The threat to the Davidic dynasty which Jehoram's disobedience poses reminds us of Saul, whose family died out with him (1 Chr. 10:6). The punishment of Jehoram is thus put on a par with that of Saul. Yet the dynasty will in fact continue, by a slender thread, because of God's promise to David (21:7). The classic obedience of David and Solomon had in fact secured the continuation of the dynasty even through a period which bore all the marks of Saul.

The measure of Jehoram's sin, therefore, becomes a measure of God's disposition to make ever new beginnings. Chr.'s insistence on this as a reason for the dynasty continuing, in an age when in fact no king sat upon the throne, betrays a conviction that that disposition of God to put human sin behind and to persevere with humanity through a son of David had yet to reach its full expression. In Jesus Christ the eternal Covenant with David has been vindicated, nor can it ever be frustrated by human frailty—though the divine imperative lies still upon the participants in it.

AS THE HOUSE OF AHAB—II AHAZIAH

2 Chronicles 22:1–9

¹And the inhabitants of Jerusalem made Ahaziah his youngest son king in his stead; for the band of men that came with the Arabs to the camp had slain all the older sons. So Ahaziah the son of Jehoram king of Judah reigned. ²Ahaziah was forty-two years old when he began to reign, and he reigned one year in Jerusalem. His mother's name was Athaliah, the granddaughter of Omri. ³He also walked in the ways of the house of Ahab, for his mother was his counsellor in doing wickedly. ⁴He did what was evil in the sight of the Lord, as the house of Ahab had done; for after the death of his father they were his counsellors, to his undoing. ⁵He even followed their counsel, and went with Jehoram the son of Ahab king of Israel to make war against Hazael king of Syria at Ramoth-gilead. And the Syrians wounded Joram, ⁶and he returned to be healed in Jezreel of the wounds which he had received at Ramah, when he fought against Hazael king of Syria. And Ahaziah the son of Jehoram king of Judah went down to see Joram the son of Ahab in Jezreel, because he was sick.

⁷But it was ordained by God that the downfall of Ahaziah should come about through his going to visit Joram. For when he came there he went out with Jehoram to meet Jehu the son of Nimshi, whom the Lord had anointed to destroy the house of Ahab. ⁸And when Jehu was executing judgment upon the house of Ahab, he met the princes of Judah and the sons of Ahaziah's brothers, who attended Ahaziah, and he killed them. ⁹He searched for Ahaziah, and he was captured while hiding in Samaria, and he was brought to Jehu and put to death. They

buried him, for they said, "He is the grandson of Jehoshaphat, who sought the Lord with all his heart." And the house of Ahaziah had no one able to rule the kingdom.

Ahaziah is a man in the mould of Jehoram, linked strongly to the house of Ahab by his descent, through Athaliah, from Omri, Ahab's father. The influence of Athaliah on the young king (the report that he was forty-two at his accession must be due to scribal error, since his father was only forty when he died) casts her in a role very similar to that of Jezebel in relation to Ahab (v. 3).

Ahaziah, however, is judged for his own sin, like his father before him. Once again it is clear that his downfall was purposely and ineluctably brought about by God (22:7). Verses 7–9 represent a compression of events reported more fully in 2 Kings 9 (with 10:12–14). Ahaziah's alliance with the spirit of Ahab in the north is not unprecedented, for the great Jehoshaphat had himself succumbed to such a temptation (see on 2 Chr. 18). While that alliance, however, was not a true indication of Jehoshaphat's character, Ahaziah is evidently thoroughly at one with Jehoram, Ahab's son, in disposition and aspirations. (Jehoram is sometimes called Joram to distinguish him from Ahaziah's father, the son of Jehoshaphat). In the Kings account which Chr. presupposes, Ahaziah is implicated by association in the dreadful judgment which Jehu is commissioned by God to bring upon Ahab's house (2 Kings 9:7). Chr. makes this even more explicit (v. 7). Ahaziah's end is no more glorious than his father Jehoram's, for he is not granted royal burial either. With his demise there is no obvious ruler in Judah (v. 9). The dynasty is at its lowest ebb. And the stage is set for the entry of a monster.

COUPS D'ETAT—I

2 Chronicles 22:10–23:21

[10]Now when Athaliah the mother of Ahaziah saw that her son was dead, she arose and destroyed all the royal family of the house of Judah. [11]But Jehoshabeath, the daughter of the king, took Joash the son of Ahaziah, and stole him away from among the king's sons who

were about to be slain, and she put him and his nurse in a bedchamber. Thus Jehoshabeath, the daughter of King Jehoram and wife of Jehoiada the priest, because she was a sister of Ahaziah, hid him from Athaliah, so that she did not slay him; ¹²and he remained with them six years, hid in the house of God, while Athaliah reigned over the land.

¹But in the seventh year Jehoiada took courage, and entered into a compact with the commanders of hundreds, Azariah the son of Jeroham, Ishmael the son of Jehohanan, Azariah the son of Obed, Maaseiah the son of Adaiah, and Elishaphat the son of Zichri. ²And they went about through Judah and gathered the Levites from all the cities of Judah, and the heads of fathers' houses of Israel, and they came to Jerusalem. ³And all the assembly made a covenant with the king in the house of God. And Jehoiada said to them, "Behold, the king's son! Let him reign, as the Lord spoke concerning the sons of David. ⁴This is the thing that you shall do: of you priests and Levites who come off duty on the sabbath, one third shall be gatekeepers, ⁵and one third shall be at the king's house and one third at the Gate of the Foundation; and all the people shall be in the courts of the house of the Lord. ⁶Let no one enter the house of the Lord except the priests and ministering Levites; they may enter, for they are holy, but all the people shall keep the charge of the Lord. ⁷The Levites shall surround the king, each with his weapons in his hand; and whoever enters the house shall be slain. Be with the king when he comes in, and when he goes out."

⁸The Levites and all Judah did according to all that Jehoiada the priest commanded. They each brought his men, who were to go off duty on the sabbath, with those who were to come on duty on the sabbath; for Jehoiada the priest did not dismiss the divisions. ⁹And Jehoiada the priest delivered to the captains the spears and the large and small shields that had been King David's, which were in the house of God; ¹⁰and he set all the people as a guard for the king, every man with his weapon in his hand, from the south side of the house to the north side of the house, around the altar and the house. ¹¹Then he brought out the king's son, and put the crown upon him, and gave him the testimony; and they proclaimed him king, and Jehoiada and his sons anointed him, and they said, "Long live the king."

¹²When Athaliah heard the noise of the people running and praising the king, she went into the house of the Lord to the people; ¹³and when she looked, there was the king standing by his pillar at the entrance, and the captains and the trumpeters beside the king, and all the people

of the land rejoicing and blowing trumpets, and the singers with their musical instruments leading in the celebration. And Athaliah rent her clothes, and cried, "Treason! Treason!" [14]Then Jehoiada the priest brought out the captains who were set over the army, saying to them, "Bring her out between the ranks; any one who follows her is to be slain with the sword." For the priest said, "Do not slay her in the house of the Lord." [15]So they laid hands on her; and she went into the entrance of the horse gate of the king's house, and they slew her there.

[16]And Jehoiada made a covenant between himself and all the people and the king that they should be the Lord's people. [17]Then all the people went to the house of Baal, and tore it down; his altars and his images they broke in pieces, and they slew Mattan the priest of Baal before the altars. [18]And Jehoiada posted watchmen for the house of the Lord under the direction of the Levitical priests and the Levites whom David had organized to be in charge of the house of the Lord, to offer burnt offerings to the Lord, as it is written in the law of Moses, with rejoicing and with singing, according to the order of David. [19]He stationed the gatekeepers at the gates of the house of the Lord so that no one should enter who was in any way unclean. [20]And he took the captains, the nobles, the governors of the people, and all the people of the land; and they brought the king down from the house of the Lord, marching through the upper gate to the king's house. And they set the king upon the royal throne. [21]So all the people of the land rejoiced; and the city was quiet, after Athaliah had been slain with the sword.

The events that follow the death of Ahaziah are striking because of their uniqueness in several respects: there is a break in the succession of Davidic kings in Judah, a queen rules, and a high-priest has decisive influence in the land.

Athaliah, of whom we know nothing other than what we learn here and in 2 Kings 11, evidently had all the ruthlessness of the house of Ahab, and perhaps some of the grandeur of its founder Omri (with whom she is expressly linked, 22:2). Perhaps our horror at her crimes is rightly tinged with admiration for one who, without any legitimate right and despite all the impediments of her womanhood, took and held the reins of power for as long as she did (six years). (cf. the play *Athalie* by Racine, in which she becomes a kind of heroine because of her Promethean qualities.)

Her story is briefly told. The death of her son Ahaziah threatens her with the loss of the pre-eminence she has enjoyed as queen mother, and she therefore perpetrates the hideous massacre which is designed to remove all pretenders to the throne save herself. This would have included, naturally, her own grandchildren, though it may have gone wider than Ahaziah's offspring. She reigns until destroyed in a counter-coup mounted by the forces of legitimacy under Jehoiada the high-priest. The overthrow of Athaliah is achieved by the restoration of the legitimate line in Joash, who was a small child at the time of his father's death (cf. 24:1), and who was hidden and educated in the Temple precincts during Athaliah's reign (cf. 2 Kings 11:3—Chr. omits this information, although his account of the coup assumes that Joash is in the Temple).

COUPS D'ETAT—II

2 Chronicles 22:10–23:21 (*cont'd*)

The Chronicler introduces, as always, certain of his own emphases into the telling of the story. Athaliah's reign is seen as the low point of a period of religious and moral backruptcy in Judah, which had begun with Jehoram and Ahaziah, and had resulted in material and territorial loss for the kingdom. It is a low point, not only because rule by women was evidently regarded as a curse in Israel (Isa. 3:12), but because under Athaliah there is no son of David on the throne. Athaliah's northern links symbolize an invasion of the spirit of false religion, and of chaos—for in the north the dynastic principle quickly gave way to power-grabbing like that of Athaliah (cf. 2 Kings 15). Politically, this would have minimized the differences between north and south. Theologically, it threatened the Lord's guarantee that Judah should continue as a state at all. The situation has much in common with that into which Saul led Israel, dominated and threatened with extinction by the Philistines (1 Chr. 10).

Having suggested that analogy, the Chronicler goes on to show that the accession of Joash has much in common with that of

David. He has already hinted that no full end is to be made of the Davidic dynasty even in this dark period, cf. 21:7. The dramatic rescue of the child Joash becomes evidence for this, and his reception as king, therefore, bears the marks of David's own acclamation. Indeed, 23:3 contains a reference to the Davidic promise. But the most significant point of similarity lies in his stress on the fact that all Judah, led by the Levites and the "heads of fathers' houses" (i.e. heads of extended families), took part in the ceremony, and that it was these (v. 16, note "all the people") who renewed the Covenant, with the king, to be the Lord's people.

In addition to the representatives of the assembly in and around the Temple, the Chronicler is concerned to show that not only the monarchy but also the worship of the Temple is being restored. Athaliah's sacrileges, reported in 24:7, must have disrupted this. We can certainly suppose that she had no interest in maintaining the correct procedures and distinctions as instituted by David (1 Chr. 23–26). Chr.'s account of the coup, which is centred in the Temple, is shot through with a concern to respect its sanctity. Only the priests and those Levites who are on duty may be within it (v. 6). Verse 8 even shows a concern to maintain the proper priestly courses of duty as laid down in 1 Chr. 23–24. And v. 19 reflects the horror of anything ritually unclean crossing the threshold of the Lord's house.

The restoration of Joash, therefore, amounts to a thoroughgoing reform. This is no mere dispute between rival claimants. At stake is the promise to David. And it is fitting that, the true line restored, all the trappings of false worship should be destroyed, along with her under whose patronage it had flourished (v. 17). The story of Athaliah is a story not only of the zeal of the righteous Jehoiada, but of God's determination to keep his promise. However low his people might sink, and however much the signs of his presence have been withdrawn, there is in every generation the opportunity to return to him and enjoy a full and fulfilling relationship with him.

Two further points may be made.

(i) There is something exemplary about both Jehoiada and his wife Jehoshabeath, in their different ways. The former represents that boldness and courage which carries people along by its forceful demonstration of what is right. The true "prophetic" spirit is that which perceives the truth and will stand for it at personal risk and with the zeal of the crusader. It is always lampooned, and regarded, even by those who broadly sympathize, as "extremist". But it is immensely powerful. Whenever the Church has prospered there have been figures like Jehoiada.

The heroism of Jehoshabeath is of a quieter kind, though no less real, nor any less necessary to the goal that was achieved. (And it should be noticed that she was a daughter of Jehoram.) The complementary roles of Jehoiada and his wife well illustrate the mutual dependence of those with different gifts and tasks within the Church.

(ii) The story of Athaliah, like that of Jehoram and Ahaziah, is a testimony to the ephemeral and ultimately illusory character of brute power exercised in a self-serving way. The judgment on Athaliah is poetic, executed by the parties which she had treated so shamefully. There is a particular irony in her cry of "Treason! Treason!" (v. 13), for it condemns not Jehoiada and the king's guard, but herself. So much are the enemies of truth hardened in their perceptions! Her cry is the frantic desperation of the cornered animal that knows it cannot escape death. By Athaliah's own standards there *can* be no treason, since, for her, power is rightly held by those who can hold it (the morality, incidentally, of the most respectable modern diplomacy). Perhaps we can credit her, after her first savage reaction, with a dignified acceptance of her fall. Older commentators translated the first phrase of v. 15 "They made way for her". This would be consistent with the ensuing statement "she went" (rather than "they brought her"), suggesting that she went proudly to meet her death. Such a pride, however, while it is regarded as noble by worldly standards, invites a shudder when seen for what it is, a defiance of the judgment of God.

JOASH DID NOT REMEMBER—I

2 Chronicles 24:1–27

¹Joash was seven years old when he began to reign, and he reigned forty years in Jerusalem; his mother's name was Zibiah of Beer-sheba. ²And Joash did what was right in the eyes of the Lord all the days of Jehoiada the priest. ³Jehoiada got for him two wives, and he had sons and daughters.

⁴After this Joash decided to restore the house of the Lord. ⁵And he gathered the priests and the Levites, and said to them, "Go out to the cities of Judah, and gather from all Israel money to repair the house of your God from year to year; and see that you hasten the matter." But the Levites did not hasten it. ⁶So the king summoned Jehoiada the chief, and said to him, "Why have you not required the Levites to bring in from Judah and Jerusalem the tax levied by Moses, the servant of the Lord, on the congreation of Israel for the tent of testimony?" ⁷For the sons of Athaliah, that wicked woman, had broken into the house of God; and had also used all the dedicated things of the house of the Lord for the Baals.

⁸So the king commanded, and they made a chest, and set it outside the gate of the house of the Lord. ⁹And proclamation was made throughout Judah and Jerusalem, to bring in for the Lord the tax that Moses the servant of God laid upon Israel in the wilderness. ¹⁰And all the princes and all the people rejoiced and brought their tax and dropped it into the chest until they had finished. ¹¹And whenever the chest was brought to the king's officers by the Levites, when they saw that there was much money in it, the king's secretary and the officer of the chief priest would come and empty the chest and take it and return it to its place. Thus they did day after day, and collected money in abundance. ¹²And the king and Jehoiada gave it to those who had charge of the work of the house of the Lord, and they hired masons and carpenters to restore the house of the Lord, and also workers in iron and bronze to repair the house of the Lord. ¹³So those who were engaged in the work laboured, and the repairing went forward in their hands, and they restored the house of God to its proper condition and strengthened it. ¹⁴And when they had finished, they brought the rest of the money before the king and Jehoiada, and with it were made utensils for the house of the Lord, both for the service and for the burnt offerings, and dishes for incense, and vessels of gold and silver. And

they offered burnt offerings in the house of the Lord continually all the days of Jehoiada.

15 But Jehoiada grew old and full of days, and died; he was a hundred and thirty years old at his death. 16 And they buried him in the city of David among the kings, because he had done good in Israel, and toward God and his house.

17 Now after the death of Jehoiada the princes of Judah came and did obeisance to the king; then the king hearkened to them. 18 And they forsook the house of the Lord, the God of their fathers, and served the Asherim and the idols. And wrath came upon Judah and Jerusalem for this their guilt. 19 Yet he sent prophets among them to bring them back to the Lord; these testified against them, but they would not give heed.

20 Then the Spirit of God took possession of Zechariah the son of Jehoiada the priest; and he stood above the people, and said to them, "Thus says God, 'Why do you transgress the commandments of the Lord, so that you cannot prosper? Because you have forsaken the Lord, he has forsaken you.'" 21 But they conspired against him, and by command of the king they stoned him with stones in the court of the house of the Lord. 22 Thus Joash the king did not remember the kindness which Jehoiada, Zechariah's father, had shown him, but killed his son. And when he was dying, he said, "May the Lord see and avenge!"

23 At the end of the year the army of the Syrians came up against Joash. They came to Judah and Jerusalem, and destroyed all the princes of the people from among the people, and sent all their spoil to the king of Damascus. 24 Though the army of the Syrians had come with few men, the Lord delivered into their hand a very great army, because they had forsaken the Lord, the God of their fathers. Thus they executed judgment on Joash.

25 When they had departed from him, leaving him severely wounded, his servants conspired against him because of the blood of the son of Jehoiada the priest, and slew him on his bed. So he died; and they buried him in the city of David, but they did not bury him in the tombs of the kings. 26 Those who conspired against him were Zabad the son of Shimeath the Ammonitess, and Jehozabad the son of Shimrith the Moabitess. 27 Accounts of his sons, and of the many oracles against him, and of the rebuilding of the house of God are written in the Commentary on the Book of the Kings. And Amaziah his son reigned in his stead.

Chr.'s account of the reign of Joash falls into two parts: the reform which he initiated (vv. 1–14), and his subsequent apostasy (vv. 15–27). The parallel account in Kings sees Joash only in a good light (2 Kings 12). Chr., therefore, once again presents a more differentiated picture, stressing the possibility of a righteous person going into serious decline.

JOASH DID NOT REMEMBER—II

2 Chronicles 24:1–27 (*cont'd*)

(a) *Joash's Reform*. Joash, though clearly under the influence of Jehoiada during his lifetime (v. 2), decides himself to undo the damage done to the Temple by "the sons of Athaliah" (v. 7. This must be a figurative reference to the queen's adherents, since she had destroyed her own family in order to retain power, 22:10.) Throughout Chr. a king's attitude to the Temple and its worship has been a measure of his righteousness. Joash's measures, with his reference to "the tax levied by Moses" (cf. Exod. 30:11–16) and his enlisting of the Levites, is therefore exemplary. The reform of Joash was, in fact, one of the significant landmarks in the development of the upkeep of the Temple. This is not principally because of the apparent extent of the repairs, which was considerable (vv. 12f.). It can be imagined how much routine repair would have been necessary on a building as large, opulent—and by now as old!—as Solomon's Temple. The importance of the change lies in the shifting of financial responsibility for the upkeep from king to people. The account of it is not intended to diminish Joash's real concern for it, however. Quite possibly his own resources did not stretch to doing the job properly. And clearly the responsibility was not imposed upon a grudging people (v. 10); rather was the king's zeal welcomed, showing how, in his righteous period, the people recognized that the way of blessing was that of obedience.

Some details in the account require mention. The Levites do not emerge in an entirely good light, because of their apparent reluctance to put the king's measures into effect (v. 5). No reason is given for their tardiness, but 2 Kings 12:4–8 implies that they were not being entirely honest with money received. Perhaps some of the influence of Athaliah had affected even the guardians of the Temple.

There is apparent conflict between v. 14, which says that some of the money collected from the people was used to make "utensils for the house of the Lord", and 2 Kings 12:13f., which states expressly that such use was not made of the money. The Chronicler, who must have had 2 Kings 12 before him, can hardly have perpetrated so plain a contradiction. He may have felt that his phrase "And when they had finished . . ." explained the matter, suggesting that while money was not applied to utensils during the time of the repairs, it *was* so applied when the repairs were completed.

(b) *Joash's apostasy*. The turning-point in Joash's reign comes with the death of Jehoiada, who is accorded honour normally reserved for kings (vv. 15f.). That this should be a traumatic experience for Joash, to whom the priest had been father and mentor since infancy and who was perhaps effective regent even into the king's maturity, is fully understandable. Joash's immediate betrayal of all that Jehoiada had instilled in him, however, shows a fatal weakness of character. Just as he had been receptive to the good counsels of the priest, so he now yields entirely to pressure from what must have been a powerful Baal-party among the leaders of the people (v. 17), men who must have enjoyed favour and prestige under Athaliah. In this respect Joash shares a characteristic with Rehoboam who lost most of his kingdom because of his susceptibility to the wrong influence (2 Chr. 10). Yet his change of heart seems far more savage and violent than Rehoboam's, because of his former advantages and commitment, and especially because of his murder of the prophet Zechariah, Jehoiada's son (v. 21). This element of ingratitude, central to Chr.'s final condemnation of Joash, supplies a variation on the theme of apostasy which we have met in other kings (e.g. Rehoboam, Asa). Joash's murderous response to love (the word "kindness" is the same as that which is often used for the love or grace of God) exposes apostasy in its most abominable form. It has a reverberation in the parable of the vineyard (Mark 12:1–12), where the murdered son represents Christ himself. The New Testament further recalls this incident when Jesus refers to it to castigate Israel for its crimes (Luke 11:49–51). cf. also, again, Heb. 6:4–6.

(c) *Joash's punishment.* Zechariah's dying words (v. 22) have been compared unfavourably, rightly, with those of Christ (Luke 23:34), and indeed of the apostle Stephen (Acts 7:60). Yet there is no intention here to present the prophet in a poor light (nor does the New Testament, as we have just noticed). His words, rather, are used by Chr. to announce the fate of Joash. There is a terrible irony in them. In his earlier zeal (v. 6) Joash had taken Jehoiada to task for not *requiring* (Heb. *darash*) the Levites to collect the taxes which he had levied. Zechariah uses the same word, translated in RSV as "avenge", to condemn Joash. It is the same word, indeed, which at an earlier point (1 Chr. 28:9) denoted the Lord's appeal for a loving response from the heart of Solomon. Here, as there, the idea of a mutual *"seeking"* is paralleled by one of a mutual *forsaking* (v. 20), which the fate of Joash now dreadfully exemplifies. In the absence of a "seeking" response, the Lord's "seeking" takes on a terrible quality. We are far from human vengefulness here, though there will always be attempts to reduce the God of Israel to that level. The proper human response to the idea of God's vengeance is adoration. Heb. 12:28f. furnish a strangely apt comment on the final state of Joash, and an exhortation to God's people in every age.

The king's discomfiture ensues, first in a raid by the Syrians (which may be a different occasion from that which is recorded in 2 Kings 12:17f.), in which he himself suffers badly, and finally in his assassination by servants who had evidently been outraged by his murder of Zechariah. Though he started well he is not even honoured, in the end, by burial "in the tombs of the kings" (v. 25).

AMAZIAH WOULD NOT LISTEN—I

2 Chronicles 25:1-28

¹Amaziah was twenty-five years old when he began to reign, and he reigned twenty-nine years in Jerusalem. His mother's name was Jehoaddan of Jerusalem. ²And he did what was right in the eyes of the Lord, yet not with a blameless heart. ³And as soon as the royal power was firmly in his hand he killed his servants who had slain the king his father. ⁴But he did not put their children to death, according to what is written in the law, in the book of Moses, where the Lord commanded, "The fathers shall not be put to death for the children, or the children be put to death for the fathers; but every man shall die for his own sin."

⁵Then Amaziah assembled the men of Judah, and set them by fathers' houses under commanders of thousands and of hundreds for all Judah and Benjamin. He mustered those twenty years old and upward, and found that they were three hundred thousand picked men, fit for war, able to handle spear and shield. ⁶He hired also a hundred thousand mighty men of valour from Israel for a hundred talents of silver. ⁷But a man of God came to him and said, "O king, do not let the army of Israel go with you, for the Lord is not with Israel, with all these Ephraimites. ⁸But if you suppose that in this way you will be strong for war, God will cast you down before the enemy; for God has power to help or to cast down." ⁹And Amaziah said to the man of God, "But what shall we do about the hundred talents which I have given to the army of Israel?" The man of God answered, "The Lord is able to give you much more than this." ¹⁰Then Amaziah discharged the army that had come to him from Ephraim, to go home again. And they became very angry with Judah, and returned home in fierce anger. ¹¹But Amaziah took courage, and led out his people, and went to the Valley of Salt and smote ten thousand men of Seir. ¹²The men of Judah captured another ten thousand alive, and took them to the top of a rock and threw them down from the top of the rock; and they were all dashed to pieces. ¹³But the men of the army whom Amaziah sent back, not letting them go with him to battle, fell upon the cities of Judah, from Samaria to Beth-horon, and killed three thousand people in them, and took much spoil.

¹⁴After Amaziah came from the slaughter of the Edomites, he brought the gods of the men of Seir, and set them up as his gods, and worshipped them, making offerings to them. ¹⁵Therefore the Lord was

angry with Amaziah and sent to him a prophet, who said to him, "Why have you resorted to the gods of a people, which did not deliver their own people from your hand?" ¹⁶But as he was speaking the king said to him, "Have we made you a royal counsellor? Stop! Why should you be put to death?" So the prophet stopped, but said, "I know that God has determined to destroy you, because you have done this and have not listened to my counsel."

¹⁷Then Amaziah king of Judah took counsel and sent to Joash the son of Jehoahaz, son of Jehu, king of Israel, saying, "Come, let us look one another in the face." ¹⁸And Joash the king of Israel sent word to Amaziah king of Judah, "A thistle on Lebanon sent to a cedar on Lebanon, saying, 'Give your daughter to my son for a wife'; and a wild beast of Lebanon passed by and trampled down the thistle. ¹⁹You say, 'See, I have smitten Edom,' and your heart has lifted you up in boastfulness. But now stay at home; why should you provoke trouble so that you fall, you and Judah with you?"

²⁰But Amaziah would not listen; for it was of God, in order that he might give them into the hand of their enemies, because they had sought the gods of Edom. ²¹So Joash king of Israel went up; and he and Amaziah king of Judah faced one another in battle at Beth-shemesh, which belongs to Judah. ²²And Judah was defeated by Israel, and every man fled to his home. ²³And Joash king of Israel captured Amaziah king of Judah, the son of Joash, son of Ahaziah, at Beth-shemesh, and brought him to Jerusalem, and broke down the wall of Jerusalem for four hundred cubits, from the Ephraim Gate to the Corner Gate. ²⁴And he seized all the gold and silver, and all the vessels that were found in the house of God, and Obed-edom with them; he seized also the treasuries of the king's house, and hostages, and he returned to Samaria.

²⁵Amaziah the son of Joash king of Judah lived fifteen years after the death of Joash the son of Jehoahaz, king of Israel. ²⁶Now the rest of the deeds of Amaziah, from first to last, are they not written in the Book of the Kings of Judah and Israel? ²⁷From the time when he turned away from the Lord they made a conspiracy against him in Jerusalem, and he fled to Lachish. But they sent after him to Lachish, and slew him there. ²⁸And they brought him upon horses; and he was buried with his fathers in the city of David.

Amaziah continues a succession of kings who have been judged partly favourably and partly unfavourably. Amaziah's career in-

cludes a spell of faithfulness to God which results in a successful
Edomite campaign, but settles into disobedience which issues in
defeat and humiliation. As so often, Chr. has material which is
absent in Kings. Here it consists principally of Amaziah's enlisting of Israelite mercenaries (vv. 6–10) and his worship of Edomite
gods (vv. 14–16).

AMAZIAH WOULD NOT LISTEN—II

2 Chronicles 25:1–28 (*cont'd*)

(a) *Amaziah's half-heartedness*
It is not so clear as in the case of some others just where the
division between Amaziah's obedient period and his disobedient
period falls. There is probably something stylized about the
Chronicler's treatment in general of the ruined careers of the
kings, with its clean breaks between phases of their reigns. But
here he has not even attempted to make such a break. Amaziah is
depicted as fundamentally half-hearted, and his mediocrity is
announced at the outset (v. 2: "yet not with a blameless heart").

His first recorded action, the execution of his father's mur-
derers, is told without censure. Indeed he is implicitly congratu-
lated for his restraint, which is in obedience to the law of Deut.
24:16. (There is no need to see a tension between this law and the
principle enunciated in Exod. 20:5f. That this is so is illustrated
by the inclusion of the reference to Deut. 24:16 in 2 Kings 14:6,
the parallel passage, even though the Books of Kings stand as a
monument to the theology of Exod. 20:5f., cf. 2 Kings 23:25f.
The difference between Exod. 20:4ff. and Deut. 24:16 is that the
former speaks of God's own application of his justice and love in
history, according to his mysterious ways, while the latter legislates for human judicial processes.)

Amaziah's next action is to prepare for war against Edom. This
he does by organizing his own army (v. 5), and enlisting mercenaries from Israel (whether these were part of an Israelite standing
army or free-lancers is not clear). Although in the course of his
preparations Amaziah proves receptive to a prophetic word

(vv. 7–10) and his campaign is successful (vv. 11f.) his resort to Israelite help suggests a basic double-mindedness. The unnamed "man of God" (v. 7) has to remind him that the Lord alone is the source of help for his people (cf. again 1 Chr. 12). As Israel was currently in rebellion against God, to appeal to her was tantamount to an act of rebellion also. (This theme will come to a head in relation to Ahaz, chapter 28.)

Amaziah takes the lesson, but his mind goes first to the large sum which he must forfeit by dismissing the mercenaries. The unspiritual mind is reluctant to relinquish short-term advantage. In reply, the prophet says: "The Lord is able to give you much more than this." The words are more than a statement; they are a challenge to faith and discipleship. The call to self-denial is a commonplace one within biblical spirituality (e.g. Luke 9:57–62). But it is not made because to possess nothing has any value in itself. Much of the OT (including the Books of Chronicles) shows that the reverse is the case. The call to self-denial is really a call to *rely* on nothing except the resources of the Lord, as the present passage makes clear. It is impossible to make real sacrifices in the cause of Christian discipleship, or, having made them, to retain one's peace of mind, unless there is implicit faith in the capacity of God to provide. Those who know his provision know it because they have experienced the slenderness of their own resources, and have found that it is rich. (cf. Mark 10:28–31.)

(b) *His final rejection of God*

Having defeated the Edomites with the help of the Lord (as is implied by the exchange in vv. 7–10), Amaziah now resorts, not only with ingratitude, but with a conspicuous irrationality—as a prophet points out (v. 15)—to the gods of the subjugated people. We have noticed on other occasions that where there is a rebellious will, appeals to the mind cut little ice. As always, the offending leader is given a chance to repent through the ministrations of a prophet (cf. 24:20f.—it was a dangerous profession). But it is Amaziah's characteristic failing that he was desperately reluctant to recognize and heed sound advice. This is apparent in his encounters both with the prophet and with Joash, king of Israel.

The prophet's logic was irresistible (v. 15). Amaziah, however, stopped him in his tracks (v. 16). There follows a play on words designed to show the measure of his folly. The prophet, though threatened, risks going on to pronounce God's verdict, "because you . . . have not listened to my *counsel*" (=God's counsel). The following verse takes up the motif of counsel using a form of the same word which shows that, in reality, Amaziah was himself the author of its content. Verse 17 might read: "Amaziah . . . had himself advised . . ." By choosing whom he would listen to, and perhaps hinting at what he wished to hear, he could be sure to obtain the right answer. His determination to go his own way, therefore, is bolstered both by a falsely-based confidence in his own judgment and by the delusion that he had taken adequate measures in his decision-making. His villainy is therefore less "honest" than that of, say, Athaliah, and is tinged with self-righteous fancies.

The same self-deluding confidence is evident in his ill-fated sortie against Israel (which may have been prompted by the rampage of the mercenaries, after their dismissal had denied them the possibility of booty in the Edomite war). Joash's parable (v. 18) pointedly puts Amaziah's military power in perspective. His squaring up to Israel is as foolish as if a thistle should think itself the equal of a mighty cedar. Once again, having been given good advice, ". . . Amaziah would not listen" (v. 20). The word "listen" has connotations which make the phrase suggest not only rejection of Joash's advice but disobedience to God. The consequences are predictable: humiliating defeat, and loss of national wealth (vv. 21–24).

Amaziah's fate is less severe than that of other rebellious kings. He outlives the king of Israel who defeated him and, though finally murdered, is granted honourable burial. (These details, which show that retribution was not immediate, together with the description of the Israelite rampage, v. 13, which does not follow neatly from Amaziah's positive response to the first prophecy, show that the Chronicler has respected his historical material, and not tailored it to his theological ends.)

PRESUMPTION

2 Chronicles 26:1–23

¹And all the people of Judah took Uzziah, who was sixteen years old, and made him king instead of his father Amaziah. ²He built Eloth and restored it to Judah, after the king slept with his fathers. ³Uzziah was sixteen years old when he began to reign, and he reigned fifty-two years in Jerusalem. His mother's name was Jecoliah of Jerusalem. ⁴And he did what was right in the eyes of the Lord, according to all that his father Amaziah had done. ⁵He set himself to seek God in the days of Zechariah, who instructed him in the fear of God; and as long as he sought the Lord, God made him prosper.

⁶He went out and made war against the Philistines, and broke down the wall of Gath and the wall of Jabneh and the wall of Ashdod; and he built cities in the territory of Ashdod and elsewhere among the Philistines. ⁷God helped him against the Philistines, and against the Arabs that dwelt in Gurbaal, and against the Meunites. ⁸The Ammonites paid tribute to Uzziah, and his fame spread even to the border of Egypt, for he became very strong. ⁹Moreover Uzziah built towers in Jerusalem at the Corner Gate and at the Valley Gate and at the Angle, and fortified them. ¹⁰And he built towers in the wilderness, and hewed out many cisterns, for he had large herds, both in the Shephelah and in the plain, and he had farmers and vinedressers in the hills and in the fertile lands, for he loved the soil. ¹¹Moreover Uzziah had an army of soldiers, fit for war, in divisions according to the numbers in the muster made by Jeiel the secretary and Maaseiah the officer, under the direction of Hananiah, one of the king's commanders. ¹²The whole number of the heads of fathers' houses of mighty men of valour was two thousand six hundred. ¹³Under their command was an army of three hundred and seven thousand five hundred, who could make war with mighty power to help the king against the enemy. ¹⁴And Uzziah prepared for all the army shields, spears, helmets, coats of mail, bows, and stones for slinging. ¹⁵In Jerusalem he made engines, invented by skilful men, to be on the towers and the corners, to shoot arrows and great stones. And his fame spread far, for he was marvellously helped, till he was strong.

¹⁶But when he was strong he grew proud, to his destruction. For he was false to the Lord his God, and entered the temple of the Lord to burn incense on the altar of incense. ¹⁷But Azariah the priest went in

after him, with eighty priests of the Lord who were men of valour; [18]and they withstood King Uzziah, and said to him, "It is not for you, Uzziah, to burn incense to the Lord, but for the priests the sons of Aaron, who are consecrated to burn incense. Go out of the sanctuary; for you have done wrong, and it will bring you no honour from the Lord God." [19]Then Uzziah was angry. Now he had a censer in his hand to burn incense, and when he became angry with the priests leprosy broke out on his forehead, in the presence of the priests in the house of the Lord, by the altar of incense. [20]And Azariah the chief priest, and all the priests, looked at him, and behold, he was leprous in his forehead! And they thrust him out quickly, and he himself hastened to go out, because the Lord had smitted him. [21]And King Uzziah was a leper to the day of his death, and being a leper dwelt in a separate house, for he was excluded from the house of the Lord. And Jotham his son was over the king's household, governing the people of the land.

[22]Now the rest of the acts of Uzziah, from first to last, Isaiah the prophet the son of Amoz wrote. [23]And Uzziah slept with his fathers, and they buried him with his fathers in the burial field which belonged to the kings, for they said, "He is a leper." And Jotham his son reigned in his stead.

With Uzziah (known in Kings as Azariah) we come to the last of those kings who are judged to have been partly faithful and partly unfaithful. Little is known about him apart from Chr.'s account, for that in Kings is very short (2 Kings 14:21f.; 15:1–7). Perhaps he is best remembered, ironically, for his death!—which is used to date the call of the prophet Isaiah (Isa. 6:1). His reign must have been an important one, however. It lasted fifty-two years (c. 791–739 B.C., including a period of co-regency with his father Amaziah), and was apparently a time of relative stability and prosperity for Judah, as for Israel. This is suggested by the comments of some of the prophets, whose classical period was the eighth century, even if their attacks on the people's obsession with wealth and self reveal the fact in a negative way (cf. Isa. 3:18–26; Amos 6:1–8).

In his long and prosperous reign it is no surprise that Uzziah should have undertaken the sort of operations that are described in vv. 6–15. He evidently regained territory that had been lost because of Amaziah's folly, as well as rebuilding Jerusalem following its reduction by Joash. It seems that the depredations of the Israelites had resulted in a weakness which had been exploited by the Philistines, and perhaps also by the Edomites, in revenge for their earlier defeat at Amaziah's hands (25:11ff.). It was probably from these that Uzziah now recaptured Eloth (modern Eilat).

Chr.'s description of Uzziah's strength shows that it derives from his righteousness and God's help (vv. 4f., 7, 15. The Zechariah of v. 5 is not otherwise known; the name was evidently a common one. Uzziah's relationship with him is reminiscent of Joash's with Jehoiada, though presumably without the overtones of guardianship.) The themes of strength, fame and tribute (v. 8), capacity for war yet enjoyment of peace, remind of the reigns of both David and Solomon. The allusion to his love of farming (v. 10) is an unusual touch, which brings us closer to the man's personality than Chr.'s stylized descriptions generally do. Uzziah in his greatness was clearly a lover of peace, and understood it in its full sense of freedom to enjoy the richness of God's provision.

As with Rehoboam (2 Chr. 12:1) it is strength itself which is the undoing of Uzziah. Strength is one of Chr.'s great themes. It can, however, be differently evaluated, according to whence it is derived. Uzziah comes to believe that his strength is his own. His pride leads to a cultic offence of the utmost gravity. (Verse 16*a* might better read "he grew proud, *so that he acted corruptly*", showing that the offence is a result of his pride. Pride does not in itself, therefore, constitute the offence entirely.) Seeing himself supreme in the political sphere he now wishes to arrogate to himself supremacy in an area which is properly closed to him. The offence was hardly the entry of the Temple itself, since other kings did that (Solomon, Joash), but the burning of incense. Exod. 30:7ff. show that this—like other sacrifices—was the province of the priests. Uzziah's act was, therefore, a deliberate challenge to their authority, and tantamount to defiance of the holiness of God himself. There is thus a dimension to it that is more than mere disobedience. The fate of Korah's rebels (Num. 16) is an indicator of the seriousness of trespass in this area. Kings

were, apparently, particularly susceptible to this sort of temptation (e.g. Saul, 1 Sam. 13:8ff.; Jeroboam I, 1 Kings 13). Uzziah
illustrates well the nature of such temptation—it is another facet
of the urge to turn legitimate, delegated authority into a power
that is absolute and self-glorifying (see on Jehoram and
Athaliah).

The priests' confrontation with Uzziah, therefore, is no petty
demarcation dispute. Their command that he leave the Temple
has, rather, the ring of a sentence. The prediction that "it will
bring you no honour from the Lord God" (v. 18) is an ironic
understatement in view of what follows, since honour, or eminence, is exactly what Uzziah coveted.

The king's anger (v. 19) is difficult to evaluate. We have met it
before at moments when its subject recognized a rightful accusation (e.g. 1 Chr. 13:11). In view of Uzziah's previous piety and of
his willingness to be escorted from the Temple following his
affliction with "leprosy" (v. 20), we may surmise that Uzziah's
sentiments were indeed along these lines. On the other hand it
may be that the anger in this case represents a heightening of
defiance, which might explain why it was in the moment of his
anger that he was afflicted (v. 19). It may have been the affliction
itself which brought him to see the awfulness of his situation.

The disease with which the king was stricken may not have
been leprosy as it is known today. The Hebrew term probably
covers a variety of unpleasant skin conditions. Anything to which
it did apply, however, rendered the sufferer "unclean" in ritual
terms, and he was therefore disqualified from taking part in the
Temple worship (Lev. 13–14). Uzziah's leprous condition, therefore, compounds the defilement which he has committed, and is
the last straw for the priests, who bundle him out. His acquies-
cence may suggest that his pride has given way to a proper fear of
God once more. He lives out his days in sad isolation, unable
even to exercise his royal duties, which had been his privilege,
and which he is now seen to have squandered in his lust for more.

On the whole, the feeling with which Chr. leaves us about
Uzziah's reign is one in which piety dominated. (This accords
with the picture in Kings.) No losses of territory are recorded,

and he is buried in a field that belonged to the kings (though not apparently in the *tombs* of the kings, because of his leprosy). Yet his lapse from the path of obedience is given a prominent position because of its egregious character.

A SUCCESS

2 Chronicles 27:1–9

¹Jotham was twenty-five years old when he began to reign, and he reigned sixteen years in Jerusalem. His mother's name was Jerushah the daughter of Zadok. ²And he did what was right in the eyes of the Lord according to all that his father Uzziah had done—only he did not invade the temple of the Lord. But the people still followed corrupt practices. ³He built the upper gate of the house of the Lord, and did much building on the wall of Ophel. ⁴Moreover he built cities in the hill country of Judah, and forts and towers on the wooded hills. ⁵He fought with the king of the Ammonites and prevailed against them. And the Ammonites gave him that year a hundred talents of silver, and ten thousand cors of wheat and ten thousand of barley. The Ammonites paid him the same amount in the second and the third years. ⁶So Jotham became mighty, because he ordered his ways before the Lord his God. ⁷Now the rest of the acts of Jotham, and all his wars, and his ways, behold, they are written in the Book of the Kings of Israel and Judah. ⁸He was twenty-five years old when he began to reign, and he reigned sixteen years in Jerusalem. ⁹And Jotham slept with his fathers, and they buried him in the city of David; and Ahaz his son reigned in his stead.

The account of the reign of Jotham is hardly more than a footnote to that of Uzziah. The approval extended to him is without qualification, the first time this has happened since Abijah (2 Chr. 13). Chr. has expanded the even briefer account in 2 Kings 15:32–36 to show that Jotham had military success and international influence because of his piety.

The portrayal of Jotham is designed to contrast sharply with that of Uzziah. Verse 2 aligns him broadly with his father's righteousness, carefully making the exception that the son committed no sacrilege. (The meaning of "only he did not enter the

Temple" must be that he did not do so with the same intent as Uzziah, since entry of the Temple as such can scarcely have been prohibited him. The proximity of this account to that of Uzziah makes such an interpretation probable.)

A second point of contrast is in v. 6, where Jotham's strength is attributed to his careful obedience to God. The meaning is that obedience became the basis for his whole life. His strength therefore did not become a snare to him.

It is instructive to notice (v. 2) that the people in general do not follow Jotham in his faithfulness. Chr. is clearly not under the delusion, therefore, that righteousness on a king's part automatically procured an ideal state of affairs in the nation, even if its somewhat schematized narrative tends to give that impression. Nor, conversely, does his wickedness necessarily drag all his subjects down with him, as appears from the indignant, if misguided, assassination of Joash (2 Chr. 24:25). We are compelled, of course, to acknowledge a *general* tendency for the people to follow the tone set by the king—this is why, after all, so much importance is attached to his behaviour. The note about the people's sin seems to be included here, however, to exonerate Jotham from blame for wickedness that occurred during his reign. Jotham's irreproachable reign contrasts not only with that of his predecessor, but also with that of his successor, and much more starkly.

A DISASTER

2 Chronicles 28:1–27

¹Ahaz was twenty years old when he began to reign, and he reigned sixteen years in Jerusalem. And he did not do what was right in the eyes of the Lord, like his father David, ²but walked in the ways of the kings of Israel. He even made molten images for the Baals; ³and he burned incense in the valley of the son of Hinnom, and burned his sons as an offering, according to the abominable practices of the nations whom the Lord drove out before the people of Israel. ⁴And he sacrificed and burned incense on the high places, and on the hills, and under every green tree.

⁵Therefore the Lord his God gave him into the hand of the king of Syria, who defeated him and took captive a great number of his people and brought them to Damascus. He was also given into the hand of the king of Israel, who defeated him with great slaughter. ⁶For Pekah the son of Remaliah slew a hundred and twenty thousand in Judah in one day, all of them men of valour, because they had forsaken the Lord, the God of their fathers. ⁷And Zichri, a mighty man of Ephraim, slew Maaseiah the king's son and Azrikam the commander of the palace and Elkanah the next in authority to the king.

⁸The men of Israel took captive two hundred thousand of their kinsfolk, women, sons, and daughters; they also took much spoil from them and brought the spoil to Samaria. ⁹But a prophet of the Lord was there, whose name was Oded; and he went out to meet the army that came to Samaria, and said to them, "Behold, because the Lord, the God of your fathers, was angry with Judah, he gave them into your hand, but you have slain them in a rage which has reached up to heaven. ¹⁰And now you intend to subjugate the people of Judah and Jerusalem, male and female, as your slaves. Have you not sins of your own against the Lord your God? ¹¹Now hear me, and send back the captives from your kinsfolk whom you have taken, for the fierce wrath of the Lord is upon you." ¹²Certain chiefs also of the men of Ephraim, Azariah the son of Johanan, Berechiah the son of Meshillemoth, Jehizkiah the son of Shallum, and Amasa the son of Hadlai, stood up against those who were coming from the war, ¹³and said to them, "You shall not bring the captives in here, for you propose to bring upon us guilt against the Lord in addition to our present sins and guilt. For our guilt is already great, and there is fierce wrath against Israel." ¹⁴So the armed men left the captives and the spoil before the princes and all the assembly. ¹⁵And the men who have been mentioned by name rose and took the captives, and with the spoil they clothed all that were naked among them; they clothed them, gave them sandals, provided them with food and drink, and anointed them; and carrying all the feeble among them on asses, they brought them to their kinsfolk at Jericho, the city of palm trees. Then they returned to Samaria.

¹⁶At that time King Ahaz sent to the king of Assyria for help. ¹⁷For the Edomites had again invaded and defeated Judah, and carried away captives. ¹⁸And the Philistines had made raids on the cities in the Shephelah and the Negeb of Judah, and had taken Beth-shemesh, Aijalon, Gederoth, Soco with its villages, Timnah with its villages, and Gimzo with its villages; and they settled there. ¹⁹For the Lord brought

Judah low because of Ahaz king of Israel, for he had dealt wantonly in Judah and had been faithless to the Lord. [20]So Tilgath-pilneser king of Assyria came against him, and afflicted him instead of strengthening him. [21]For Ahaz took from the house of the Lord and the house of the king and of the princes, and gave tribute to the king of Assyria; but it did not help him.

[22]In the time of his distress he became yet more faithless to the Lord—this same King Ahaz. [23]For he sacrificed to the gods of Damascus which had defeated him, and said, "Because the gods of the kings of Syria helped them, I will sacrifice to them that they may help me." But they were the ruin of him, and of all Israel. [24]And Ahaz gathered together the vessels of the house of God and cut in pieces the vessels of the house of God, and he shut up the doors of the house of the Lord; and he made himself altars in every corner of Jerusalem. [25]In every city of Judah he made high places to burn incense to other gods, provoking to anger the Lord, the God of his fathers. [26]Now the rest of his acts and all his ways, from first to last, behold, they are written in the Book of the Kings of Judah and Israel. [27]And Ahaz slept with his fathers, and they buried him in the city, in Jerusalem, for they did not bring him into the tombs of the kings of Israel. And Hezekiah his son reigned in his stead.

After the brief high point reached by Jotham, Judah now plunges to an all-time low under the dreadful Ahaz, the first ruler since Saul (omitting the illegitimate Athaliah) whose failure is unmitigated. The first few verses (1–4) contain a formidable catalogue of offences, under the general comment that "he walked in the ways of the kings of Israel" (v. 2). His thorough and obdurate opposition to the Lord is reflected in his adoption of the gods and the practices of foreign religion (vv. 2–4; cf. Deut. 12:2f.), with its worship of images (in defiance of Exod. 20:4f.), and, most horrifically, its child-sacrifice (cf. 2 Kings 3:26f.). The dire consequences of so blatant a rejection of the Lord are hinted at in v. 3, where it is said that the practices which Ahaz now pursues were precisely those which had brought upon Israel's predecessors in the land their expulsion from it. And indeed the theme of loss of land, well-established in Chr. since the account of Saul, 1 Chr. 10, is prominent here, not only reminding of that king, but also foreshadowing the great Babylonian exile.

(a) *The Return of the North*

The central event of Ahaz's reign is what has come to be called the Syro-Ephraimite war. This war is well documented in the OT (2 Kings 16:5; Isa. 7; (Hos. 5:8–6:6)), and is so named because it involved a defence-alliance between Syria and the northern kingdom of Israel (Ephraim) against the great imperial power of the day, Assyria. It is probable that the alliance came against Judah in order to force it into the anti-Assyrian alignment. In fact, Ahaz appealed to Assyria for help, which was granted, and the alliance was defeated (2 Kings 16:7–9).

None of this comes across in Chr.'s account. While we read that both Syria and the northern kingdom attacked Judah (v. 5), there is no hint that they constituted an alliance. Furthermore, Judah suffers at their hands (contrast 2 Kings 16:5), and Ahaz's appeal to Assyria is prompted by a separate threat from the Edomites and Philistines (vv. 16ff.). These differences can be accounted for by Chr.'s own interests, though that does not mean they are unjustifiable historically. It is clear from 2 Kings 16:6 that the threat to Judah from the north was in fact accompanied by resurgence of Edom in the south. Chr. does not *deny* that there was an alliance; and its failure to *conquer* Judah (to use the terminology of 2 Kings 16:5) does not mean that there might not have been costly skirmishes. The more interesting question, however, is why the Chronicler has *chosen* to present matters in the way that he has.

The most important answer to this question lies in the fact that these events bring together once more the northern and southern parts of historic Israel. At the forefront of the Chronicler's concern in this chapter is the further tracing of their relationships. This explains why he treats the north as an entity in itself, rather than merely a member of an alliance. The succession of kings which he has treated since Rehoboam have, of course, all been southern. He has not supplied a history of the north because he does not recognize its separate status, and regards its people as being "in rebellion against the house of David" (2 Chr. 10:19). The victory of Abijah over Jeroboam (2 Chr. 13) was further attributed to the north's rejection of the true religion (vv. 4ff.). It has been well pointed out (Williamson) that the present account neatly turns the tables on the situation described in 2 Chr. 13. It is now the northerners who have the military ascendancy over Judah (vv. 5–7), who receive the ministry of a prophet (vv. 9ff.), who are susceptible to the appeal to repent and who, in measure, show reverence to the God of Israel (vv. 12ff.). Abijah's boast "we have not forsaken him" (13:10) finds a sad echo in 28:6. What emerges from the role-reversal is that the northerners, despite their long-standing and consistent apostasy, are not guilty, in principle, of any worse an offence than the southerners in their times of unfaithfulness. The way back for all of them (significantly, their relationship is described as that of "kinsfolk", or more accurately "brothers", vv. 8, 11) is the same, that of repentance. (The Chronicler falls short, however, of attributing any decisive repentance to Israel. He was well aware that the events recorded occurred not long before the final downfall of the north.)

The abiding relevance of all this lies in its exposure of the danger of believing that belonging to this or that brand of orthodoxy, subscribing to this or that set of doctrines, or standing in this or that tradition is a guarantee of being in a good relationship with God. This is by no means to diminish doctrine, without which faith is impossible. But the compassionate actions of the northerners (v. 15), so clearly approved in the narrative, belong centrally to the kind of appeal which the Bible consistently makes to the human heart (cf. Matt. 25:31–46; Luke 10:25–37; 1 Cor. 13; Jas. 2:14–26), an appeal which stands as an enduring corrective to the thought that doctrine and orthodoxy are all. The same approval should give pause to all who regard those of other ecclesiastical traditions as, by definition, "beyond the pale".

(b) *A Cry for Help*
If the first part of the story of Ahaz shows how he misdirected his worship, the second part (vv. 16–27) shows how he looked in the wrong place for help (v. 16). Ahaz's insistence on looking to Assyria rather than the Lord at the time of the Syro-Ephraimite crisis is also the theme of his confrontation with the prophet

Isaiah, who implores the king to trust for his deliverance in the Lord (Isa. 7:7–9), and shows that the only outcome of an appeal to Assyria will be suffering at that power's hands (vv. 17–20). The tragic irony of this misplaced trust is also exploited by Chr. Verse 20 is much too heavy-handed in RSV. It ought to read: "So Tilgath–pilneser came to him [there is something threatening here, but 'against' is too strong] and straitened him [i.e. made heavy financial demands]—but it was of no help!" Had Ahaz looked to the Lord there would have been deliverance and—in accordance with Chr.'s general emphases—enrichment. Instead—impoverishment, and to no avail. The following verses are even more pitiful, showing Ahaz turning frantically to the gods of Damascus—anywhere but to the God of his fathers. Again the cry for help has the opposite of the desired effect (v. 23). Obsessed by religion, he barricades himself and his people more and more effectively against God. There are many echoes of this in our day too.

ATONEMENT—I

2 Chronicles 29:1–36

¹Hezekiah began to reign when he was twenty-five years old, and he reigned twenty-nine years in Jerusalem. His mother's name was Abijah the daughter of Zechariah. ²And he did what was right in the eyes of the Lord, according to all that David his father had done.

³In the first year of his reign, in the first month, he opened the doors of the house of the Lord, and repaired them. ⁴He brought in the priests and the Levites, and assembled them in the square on the east, ⁵and said to them, "Hear me, Levites! Now sanctify yourselves, and sanctify the house of the Lord, the God of your fathers, and carry out the filth from the holy place. ⁶For our fathers have been unfaithful and have done what was evil in the sight of the Lord our God; they have forsaken him, and have turned away their faces from the habitation of the Lord, and turned their backs. ⁷They also shut the doors of the vestibule and put out the lamps, and have not burned incense or offered burnt offerings in the holy place to the God of Israel. ⁸Therefore the wrath of the Lord came on Judah and Jerusalem, and he has made them an

object of horror, of astonishment, and of hissing, as you see with your own eyes. ⁹For lo, our fathers have fallen by the sword and our sons and our daughters and our wives are in captivity for this. ¹⁰Now it is in my heart to make a covenant with the Lord, the God of Israel, that his fierce anger may turn away from us. ¹¹My sons, do not now be negligent, for the Lord has chosen you to stand in his presence, to minister to him, and to be his ministers and burn incense to him."

¹²Then the Levites arose, Mahath the son of Amasai, and Joel the son of Azariah, of the sons of the Kohathites; and of the sons of Merari, Kish the son of Abdi, and Azariah the son of Jehallelel; and of the Gershonites, Joah the son of Zimmah, and Eden the son of Joah; ¹³and of the sons of Elizaphan, Shimri and Jeuel; and of the sons of Asaph, Zechariah and Mattaniah; ¹⁴and of the sons of Heman, Jehuel and Shimei; and of the sons of Jeduthun, Shemaiah and Uzziel. ¹⁵They gathered their brethren, and sanctified themselves, and went in as the king had commanded, by the words of the Lord, to cleanse the house of the Lord. ¹⁶The priests went into the inner part of the house of the Lord to cleanse it, and they brought out all the uncleanness that they found in the temple of the Lord into the court of the house of the Lord; and the Levites took it and carried it out to the brook Kidron. ¹⁷They began to sanctify on the first day of the first month, and on the eighth day of the month they came to the vestibule of the Lord; then for eight days they sanctified the house of the Lord, and on the sixteenth day of the first month they finished. ¹⁸Then they went in to Hezekiah the king and said, "We have cleansed all the house of the Lord, the altar of burnt offering and all its utensils, and the table for the showbread and all its utensils. ¹⁹All the utensils which King Ahaz discarded in his reign when he was faithless, we have made ready and sanctified; and behold, they are before the altar of the Lord."

²⁰Then Hezekiah the king rose early and gathered the officials of the city, and went up to the house of the Lord. ²¹And they brought seven bulls, seven rams, seven lambs, and seven he-goats for a sin offering for the kingdom and for the sanctuary and for Judah. And he commanded the priests the sons of Aaron to offer them on the altar of the Lord. ²²So they killed the bulls, and the priests received the blood and threw it against the altar; and they killed the rams and their blood was thrown against the altar; and they killed the lambs and their blood was thrown against the altar. ²³Then the he-goats for the sin offering were brought to the king and the assembly, and they laid their hands upon them, ²⁴and the priests killed them and made a sin offering with their

blood on the altar, to make atonement for all Israel. For the king commanded that the burnt offering and the sin offering should be made for all Israel.

25 And he stationed the Levites in the house of the Lord with cymbals, harps, and lyres, according to the commandment of David and of Gad the king's seer and of Nathan the prophet; for the commandment was from the Lord through his prophets. 26 The Levites stood with the instruments of David, and the priests with the trumpets. 27 Then Hezekiah commanded that the burnt offering be offered on the altar. And when the burnt offering began, the song to the Lord began also, and the trumpets, accompanied by the instruments of David king of Israel. 28 The whole assembly worshipped, and the singers sang, and the trumpeters sounded; all this continued until the burnt offering was finished. 29 When the offering was finished, the king and all who were present with him bowed themselves and worshipped. 30 And Hezekiah the king and the princes commanded the Levites to sing praises to the Lord with the words of David and of Asaph the seer. And they sang praises with gladness, and they bowed down and worshipped.

31 Then Hezekiah said, "You have now consecrated yourselves to the Lord; come near, bring sacrifices and thank offerings to the house of the Lord." And the assembly brought sacrifices and thank offerings; and all who were of a willing heart brought burnt offerings. 32 The number of the burnt offerings which the assembly brought was seventy bulls, a hundred rams, and two hundred lambs; all these were for a burnt offering to the Lord. 33 And the consecrated offerings were six hundred bulls and three thousand sheep. 34 But the priests were too few and could not flay all the burnt offerings, so until other priests had sanctified themselves their brethren the Levites helped them, until the work was finished—for the Levites were more upright in heart than the priests in sanctifying themselves. 35 Besides the great number of burnt offerings there was the fat of the peace offerings, and there were the libations for the burnt offerings. Thus the service of the house of the Lord was restored. 36 And Hezekiah and all the people rejoiced because of what God had done for the people; for the thing came about suddenly.

(i)

With King Hezekiah we enter the home straight in our reading of Chr. From this point on we are more and more in the shadow of the Babylonian exile, which will be the subject of chapter 36.

With the kings who remain, there is an intensification in the judgments passed. These are either more or less completely favourable (Hezekiah, Josiah) or completely unfavourable (Amon and the kings of chapter 36), or repentance is specially dramatic (Manasseh). This intensification (which actually began with Ahaz) belongs to the fact that the Chronicler's work is reaching its climax. There is not only intensification in the judgments passed, however, but a tendency to evoke even more forcefully than usual the characteristics of the "typical" kings, Saul, David, and Solomon. We have seen strongly Saul-like features in Ahaz. Hezekiah now stands for the virtues of David and Solomon. We need only notice how much space (four chapters) is devoted to his reign to see that special significance is attached to it. Because of his attempt to effect a radical change of direction in Judah, he is arguably the most important figure in the book's final flourish.

It is worth remembering at this point that the end of Chr. is not so much an end as an arrival. It is the end of the long preamble to the treatment of Judah under Persia in Ezra-Nehemiah. Empire as represented by Assyria in the present chapters cannot but speak to the Chronicler's readers of empire in the form of Persia in their own day. It makes for an effective climax that two such exemplary kings as Hezekiah and Josiah should stand so close to the narrative which sets the scene for the Chronicler's time.

ATONEMENT—II

2 Chronicles 29:1–36 (*cont'd*)

(ii)

A comparison of Chr.'s treatment of Hezekiah with that of 2 Kings 18–20 reveals that, while the space given to him in each case is similar, the nature of the accounts is very different. While Kings spends only one verse (18:4) on his reform (dwelling more on that of Josiah), Chr. devotes three chapters to it (29–31). The story begins in chapter 29 with Hezekiah's appeal to the priests and Levites to sanctify themselves for the momentous task ahead of them (vv. 4–11), their cleansing of the Temple (vv. 12–19) and a service of rededication and atonement (vv. 20–36). It will be seen immediately how much this is a recapitulation of Solomon's initial dedication. The cleansing, indeed, corresponds to the work of building itself (2 Chr. 3–5) and therefore constitutes a kind of reconstruction after the abuses of Ahaz had effectively removed a temple from Judah. The ceremony of vv. 20–36 then corresponds to that in 2 Chr. 6–7. Solomon's work was, of course, undergirded by all the preparations of David, and his leading concerns—the establishment of right worship with priests and Levites functioning in the manner appointed by the law, and the importance of music in worship—are reflected here too (vv. 5f., 12ff., 28ff.).

(iii)

Two further observations may be made on this chapter:

First, there is Hezekiah's appeal to the Levites to "sanctify themselves" (v. 5). The whole chapter is, of course, suffused with the need for purity and meticulousness in the handling of the things of God. The word "filth" (v. 5) denotes ritual uncleanness in a general way, and refers here, no doubt, to the deposit and trappings of years of false worship. It is as if the whole Temple has to undergo again those initial acts of dedication which had set it apart once and for all from the sphere of the profane. (cf. Exod. 25–30, which legislates for the making and consecrating of the tabernacle. By virtue of this as well as its first consecration of Aaron and his sons as priests, 28–29, and its provision for a Day of Atonement, 30:10, the Exodus chapters underlie the present chapter in an important way. The parallel shows how much Hezekiah's actions are conceived as a new beginning.)

The specific implication of the command to the Levites to "sanctify themselves" is that they should change their garments, ritually, and abstain from sexual intercourse (for a period which is unspecified, cf. Exod. 19:10, 15; Gen. 35:2). It is clear, then, that it was one thing to *be* a priest or Levite, but quite another to be fit, at any given time, to *act* as such. It is probable that the clergy had become lax during the dark days of Ahaz. Many, indeed, defected to the worship of the Baals not only in Jerusalem but throughout the land (cf. 2 Kings 23: 5, 8f.). The appeal of Hezekiah may, therefore, have required an act of considerable repentance and renewal on the part of the clergy, and this may explain why they complied with varying degrees of alacrity (v. 34). There is certainly some implied criticism of the clergy for the fact that the Passover could not be held in the appointed "first month" but had to be held over to the second (30:2—Passover should have taken place on the fourteenth day of the first month, but 29:17 shows that cleansing of the Temple was still going on on the sixteenth).

The point which can be generalized here is that it is not enough in Christian service merely to be qualified or equipped, however impressive one's qualifications may be. Qualification only becomes meaningful when allied with discipline and determination.

Secondly, we should notice in Hezekiah, for the first time in Chr., a sense that the sins of a past generation can come home to roost in the present. He laments the unfaithfulness of "our fathers" (v. 6); he connects their downfall with the captivity of "our daughters and our wives" (note the three generations in v. 9); his exhortation to the Levites implies (v. 10) that God's anger at the aberrations of Judah under Ahaz—and perhaps her whole history of inconstancy—has yet to fall. Normally Chr. limits the effects of sin or obedience within each reign to that reign itself. Here we are made to feel that the oscillation between sin and repentance is not the only possible pattern in the life of God's people, but that there is also a radical kind of newness which is of a different sort. It is a newness which is prompted by a recognition that inherited patterns—so conventional as to be unquestioned—have been gravely wrong. It is a penitence which can go beyond the knowledge of personal sin to a burden for that of the whole Church. For Hezekiah it meant a special act of atonement for all of Israel. In our day it means that self-examination can never be a merely personal thing, but that Christians have a responsibility to scrutinize critically, on the broadest canvas, the life and work of the whole Church, and, while resisting the temptation to write off inherited structures—on the inadequate grounds that they are *structures* and that they are imperfect, since structure and imperfection are inevitably with us till eternity—recognize that the Church must always reform itself.

PASSOVER

2 Chronicles 30:1–27

¹Hezekiah sent to all Israel and Judah, and wrote letters also to Ephraim and Manasseh, that they should come to the house of the Lord at Jerusalem, to keep the passover to the Lord the God of Israel. ²For the king and his princes and all the assembly in Jerusalem had taken counsel to keep the passover in the second month—³for they could not keep it in its time because the priests had not sanctified themselves in sufficient number, nor had the people assembled in Jerusalem—⁴and the plan seemed right to the king and all the assembly. ⁵So they decreed to make a proclamation throughout all Israel, from Beer-sheba to Dan, that the people should come and keep the passover to the Lord the God of Israel, at Jerusalem; for they had not kept it in great numbers as prescribed. ⁶So couriers went throughout all Israel and Judah with letters from the king and his princes, as the king had commanded, saying, "O people of Israel, return to the Lord, the God of Abraham, Isaac, and Israel, that he may turn again to the remnant of you who have escaped from the hand of the kings of Assyria. ⁷Do not be like your fathers and your brethren, who were faithless to the Lord God of their fathers, so that he made them a desolation, as you see. ⁸Do not now be stiff-necked as your fathers were, but yield yourselves to the Lord, and come to his sanctuary, which he has sanctified for ever, and serve the Lord your God, that his fierce anger may turn away from you. ⁹For if you return to the Lord, your brethren and your children will find compassion with their captors, and return to this land. For the Lord your God is gracious and merciful, and will not turn away his face from you, if you return to him."

¹⁰So the couriers went from city to city through the country of Ephraim and Manasseh, and as far as Zebulun; but they laughed them to scorn, and mocked them. ¹¹Only a few men of Asher, of Manasseh, and of Zebulun humbled themselves and came to Jerusalem. ¹²The

hand of God was also upon Judah to give them one heart to do what the king and the princes commanded by the word of the Lord.

[13] And many people came together in Jerusalem to keep the feast of unleavened bread in the second month, a very great assembly. [14] They set to work and removed the altars that were in Jerusalem, and all the altars for burning incense they took away and threw into the Kidron valley. [15] And they killed the passover lamb on the fourteenth day of the second month. And the priests and the Levites were put to shame, so that they sanctified themselves, and brought burnt offerings into the house of the Lord. [16] They took their accustomed posts according to the law of Moses the man of God; the priests sprinkled the blood which they received from the hand of the Levites. [17] For there were many in the assembly who had not sanctified themselves; therefore the Levites had to kill the passover lamb for every one who was not clean, to make it holy to the Lord. [18] For a multitude of the people, many of them from Ephraim, Manasseh, Issachar, and Zebulun, had not cleansed themselves, yet they ate the passover otherwise than as prescribed. For Hezekiah had prayed for them, saying, "The good Lord pardon every one [19] who sets his heart to seek God, the Lord the God of his fathers, even though not according to the sanctuary's rules of cleanness." [20] And the Lord heard Hezekiah, and healed the people. [21] And the people of Israel that were present at Jerusalem kept the feast of unleavened bread seven days with great gladness; and the Levites and the priests praised the Lord day by day, singing with all their might to the Lord. [22] And Hezekiah spoke encouragingly to all the Levites who showed good skill in the service of the Lord. So the people ate the food of the festival for seven days, sacrificing peace offerings and giving thanks to the Lord the God of their fathers.

[23] Then the whole assembly agreed together to keep the feast for another seven days; so they kept it for another seven days with gladness. [24] For Hezekiah king of Judah gave the assembly a thousand bulls and seven thousand sheep for offerings, and the princes gave the assembly a thousand bulls and ten thousand sheep. And the priests sanctified themselves in great numbers. [25] The whole assembly of Judah, and the priests and the Levites, and the whole assembly that came out of Israel, and the sojourners who came out of the land of Israel, and the sojourners who dwelt in Judah, rejoiced. [26] So there was great joy in Jerusalem, for since the time of Solomon the son of David king of Israel there had been nothing like this in Jerusalem. [27] Then the priests and the Levites arose and blessed the people, and their voice was heard, and their prayer came to his holy habitation in heaven.

(i)

The second stage of Hezekiah's measures to put the worship of Judah on a proper footing again is a great celebration of the Passover. The Passover is significant from the Chronicler's point of view for two reasons. First, commemorating as it does Israel's escape from Egypt in her earliest days as a nation (Exod. 12f.), it comes to symbolize release from the bondage of an overlord in a more general way. As he moves towards the story of the fateful Babylonian captivity, he lays stress on the fact that this need not be the end of the nation. Rather, in the escape from Egypt there is at least one striking precedent for release from enslavement by a super-power. Hezekiah's Passover becomes an earnest of a similar release from Babylon. In the Chronicler's day the story would have sown the hope of a still future resurgence of Israel from under the yoke of Persia. If it sometimes seems in our day that the truth of the gospel has been eclipsed by myriad other philosophies, ancient and modern, the promise is also to us that there will be a day of triumph.

The second major point which the Chronicler makes out of Hezekiah's Passover concerns the nature of Israel. Notice that the king's appeal is not to Judah alone but to "all Israel and Judah"—the point is stressed by the reference to letters written to Ephraim and Manasseh. Here a further aspect of the conditions under David and Solomon is resuscitated, namely the unity of the people. Hezekiah's appeal to the north, and the response, albeit scant, from Asher, Manasseh and Zebulun (v. 11) is historically plausible because the northern kingdom had by this time ceased to exist. Many of its people had been taken as captives to other parts of the Assyrian Empire (vv. 6, 9; cf. 2 Kings 17:1-6). For the Israelites who remained, the only possible link with their historical traditions was via Jerusalem. How far the people of Israel had become like the surrounding nations, above all in religion, appears from the poor response to Hezekiah, despite his attempt to cut through the centuries of estrangement by appeal to the common ancestry and religious heritage of the two kingdoms (v. 6). His point survives the northern intransigence, however. It is in *principle* all Israel that gathers for the great Passover celebration. It is not by any deficiency in God's mercy that some are absent, but only by their refusal to take the proffered hand.

(ii)

It is worth pausing over the terms of the appeal (vv. 6–9), though some of it is by now familiar. The word "turn", or "return", in v. 6 is that which is often translated "repent". The biblical idea of repentance is more than simple remorse, but rather a turning from old ways into a new life-style. Verse 6 has a play on words. If the wayward in Israel will turn to God, he will turn to them. In the measure that they mend their ways towards him, he will alter his approach to them. Their exile is the result of his withdrawal of blessing. It is in his power to bestow it again, and he will do so when they respond aright.

There is a similar play on words in v. 9, where the "turning" as a moral act will have as its result a physical "return" from exile. Here again the close link between response and blessing is emphasized. The Lord's desire is for a dedicated people. The "yield yourselves" of v. 8 is literally "give your hand". The word "hand" often means "strength" in the OT. The sense then is that the people are not simply to make some intellectual assent to the demands of God, but to lay their capacities, their vigour, their talents before him. The service of God is not only for children, the infirm and the elderly. (It is said that when, in some places, the man of a house opens the door to a clergyman, he is likely to say, "Oh, I'll get the wife"!) The appeal of God is to "the seven ages of man" (male and female). It is a tragedy—and usually a delusion—to postpone thinking about religion till one is fit for nothing else.

(iii)

If most of the north was recalcitrant, the mood in Judah was different. The people were united under their leaders, we are told (v. 12), to obey God. Indeed their enthusiasm for the destruction of the vestiges of false worship and for the celebration of the Passover was such that the priests and Levites were ashamed (v. 15). Popular enthusiasm, indeed, has often outstripped—

even found itself in conflict with—the ecclesiastical authorities. That of a Francis of Assisi was contained and channelled. That of a Wesley was not. It is the mark of judicious and spiritual leaders that they can recognize and adapt to popular movements that arise from a real, if unconventional—even ignorant—love of God. The clergy here respond in a way that many Pharisees later could not. Hezekiah himself shows his wisdom by intuiting and invoking the Lord's readiness to overlook the eccentricities in worship of a people who had for long been unschooled in it (vv. 18–20, another "passover"!) Here is an answer to those who think that the religion of the OT is externalistic and unspiritual (though there are many others, e.g. Isa. 1:10–17). The reality of prayer did not depend, even for the fastidious Chronicler, upon external observance.

The mood of reform was evidently euphoric and invigorating, so much so that there was spontaneous and universal assent to a second week's observance (vv. 23ff.). Verse 25 catalogues the kinds of people who were there ("sojourners" is a technical term for those who were not Israelites by birth but who had settled in Israel and adopted her religion). There is a feeling that Israel is whole again, and the joy in Jerusalem is that which infects every large-scale turning to God.

PROVIDING FOR THE CLERGY

2 Chronicles 31:1–21

[1]Now when all this was finished, all Israel who were present went out to the cities of Judah and broke in pieces the pillars and hewed down the Asherim and broke down the high places and the altars throughout all Judah and Benjamin, and in Ephraim and Manasseh, until they had destroyed them all. Then all the people of Israel returned to their cities, every man to his possession.

[2]And Hezekiah appointed the divisions of the priests and of the Levites, division by division, each according to his service, the priests and the Levites, for burnt offerings and peace offerings, to minister in the gates of the camp of the Lord and to give thanks and praise. [3]The contribution of the king from his own possessions was for the burnt

offerings: the burnt offerings of morning and evening, and the burnt offerings for the sabbaths, the new moons, and the appointed feasts, as it is written in the law of the Lord. ⁴And he commanded the people who lived in Jerusalem to give the portion due to the priests and the Levites, that they might give themselves to the law of the Lord. ⁵As soon as the command was spread abroad, the people of Israel gave in abundance the first fruits of grain, wine, oil, honey, and of all the produce of the field; and they brought in abundantly the tithe of everything. ⁶And the people of Israel and Judah who lived in the cities of Judah also brought in the tithe of cattle and sheep, and the dedicated things which had been consecrated to the Lord their God, and laid them in heaps. ⁷In the third month they began to pile up the heaps, and finished them in the seventh month. ⁸When Hezekiah and the princes came and saw the heaps, they blessed the Lord and his people Israel. ⁹And Hezekiah questioned the priests and the Levites about the heaps. ¹⁰Azariah the chief priest, who was of the house of Zadok, answered him, "Since they began to bring the contributions into the house of the Lord we have eaten and had enough and have plenty left; for the Lord has blessed his people, so that we have this great store left."

¹¹Then Hezekiah commanded them to prepare chambers in the house of the Lord; and they prepared them. ¹²And they faithfully brought in the contributions, the tithes and the dedicated things. The chief officer in charge of them was Conaniah the Levite, with Shimei his brother as second; ¹³while Jehiel, Azaziah, Nahath, Asahel, Jerimoth, Jozabad, Eliel, Ismachiah, Mahath, and Benaiah were overseers assisting Conaniah and Shimei his brother, by the appointment of Hezekiah the king and Azariah the chief officer of the house of God. ¹⁴And Kore the son of Imnah the Levite, keeper of the east gate, was over the freewill offerings to God, to apportion the contribution reserved for the Lord and the most holy offerings. ¹⁵Eden, Miniamin, Jeshua, Shemaiah, Amariah, and Shecaniah were faithfully assisting him in the cities of the priests, to distribute the portions to their brethren, old and young alike, by divisions, ¹⁶except those enrolled by genealogy, males from three years old and upwards, all who entered the house of the Lord as the duty of each day required, for their service according to their offices, by their divisions. ¹⁷The enrolment of the priests was according to their fathers' houses; that of the Levites from twenty years old and upwards was according to their offices, by their divisions. ¹⁸The priests were enrolled with all their little children, their

wives, their sons, and their daughters, the whole multitude; for they were faithful in keeping themselves holy. [19]And for the sons of Aaron, the priests, who were in the fields of common land belonging to their cities, there were men in the several cities who were designated by name to distribute portions to every male among the priests and to every one among the Levites who was enrolled.

[20]Thus Hezekiah did throughout all Judah; and he did what was good and right and faithful before the Lord his God. [21]And every work that he undertook in the service of the house of God and in accordance with the law and the commandments, seeking his God, he did with all his heart, and prospered.

(i)

After the great Passover celebration (chapter 30) there is a further flurry of measures against the places of idolatrous worship (v. 1, following Deut. 12:2f.). Again it is made plain that the arena of the activity is "greater Israel" —i.e. not Judah alone— and the people are called "the people of Israel". The euphoria of the celebrations, therefore, continues after they have ended, in a determination to build upon the gains made.

When the dust has settled, Hezekiah turns his attention to re-establishing the regular worship on a proper footing, and to the provision for the regular income of the clergy. Verse 2 shows that he re-organized the clergy in divisions as David and Solomon had done (1 Chr. 23–24; 2 Chr. 8:14). The activities mentioned in the same verse cover their regular duties in a summarizing way. The phrase "burnt offerings and peace offerings" is often used as shorthand for the whole gamut of sacrifices, representing the distinction between those which were devoted in their entirety to the altar ("burnt offerings") and those of which part fell, by way of fee, to the officiating priest.

The OT speaks without reticence about the clergy's income. The present passage shares the concern with writings that pertain to other periods, e.g. Num. 18. There was no thought that it was "unspiritual" to talk about the clergy's income. Provision for them was seen as the means by which they might enjoy the fruits of the land which were their due as "brothers" in Israel (Deut. 18:2). Their resultant liberation to "give themselves to the law of

the Lord" (v. 4) shows that there was nothing incompatible between such enjoyment and the duty to give spiritual leadership.

(ii)

The reader cannot but be struck by the amount of offerings which
the people brought on behalf of the clergy. In doing so they were
doing no more than the law required (Deut. 14:22ff.; 26:2; Lev.
27:32). This is not to be disparaging, for there were times—
indeed it was probably typical—when offerings either were neglected or became a mockery (Mal. 3:8–12). On the other hand,
legalistic misinterpretations of the laws could result in a burden
upon the giver which must have been well-nigh intolerable. The
Book of Tobit (a Jewish Apocryphal writing) contains information which shows that the various tithe-laws (mainly Num. 18:20–
24; Deut. 14:22–29) were sometimes understood to require the
giving of *three* different tithes (Tobit 1:7–8)! The logical conclusion of this failure to grasp the spirit of the OT's legislation is
the absurd legalism condemned by Jesus in Matt. 23:23.

In a day when there is a resurgence of "tithing" in many
quarters—and when, perhaps, those who do not "tithe" are
troubled in conscience about it—it is important to understand
what are the implications of the OT legalism for modern
Christians.

The biblical tithe-laws belong to OT legislation. This means
that the attempt to apply them to our own age shares the problems which attend the application of all such legislation. Part of
the difficulty is simply in understanding precisely what was intended by a given law; part of it is the inappropriateness of much of
the material. (The reader who wishes to pursue the point should
ponder the laws of Deut. 22, or Lev. 19.) This is not to say that
biblical laws *cannot* be applied. It is often possible to identify
principles which are of universal validity—indeed it is imperative
to do so.

In the case of offerings, their "alien" character for twentieth-
century readers needs little demonstration. They were intended
for the upkeep of a *Temple*, an institution which not only spoke of
the presence of God in a way which is outmoded for the Christian

Church, but also was in some senses the centre of Israelite national life, since the capacity to participate in worship was essential to anyone's "Israelite" identity. The difference between these concepts and modern ideas is not simply a factor of distance in time, but of the transformation of the people of God, by Christ's atonement, from a national, political entity into an international, spiritual one. The approach to tithing, therefore, that looks to the laws as a *quantitative* measure is misguided. Rather, we must penetrate to the principle underlying them.

The principle is not far to seek in the present passage. The clue is in v. 4, the release of the priests to do their work of spiritual leadership. Translated into modern terms this means that the Church is obliged to facilitate its own mission. If the reader thought that the above remarks about the technical inapplicability of tithe-laws had the effect of reducing the obligation to give, it is not so simple. In reality, that obligation knows no bounds, because the real work of the Church is limited only by its ultimate goal, to bring every knee to bow before Jesus Christ. This means that Christian giving which is content with making its contribution to the building-fund is missing the mark. The issue is not for individuals alone. *Churches* cannot be content with a budget which simply secures the status quo for another year, but must seek to know how to expand their mission in the world.

We spoke above about troubled consciences. One upshot of the way in which the biblical laws function, for us, is that individual giving is *not* quantifiable by any external measure. Giving *is* a matter of conscience, and the burden must fall heaviest on those who have most. Some consciences are *rightly* troubled. Others are like the widow whose small gift Jesus praised (Luke 21:1–4), so that theirs might not be.

(iii)

The remainder of the chapter (vv. 11ff.) deals with the king's provision for the distribution of income to clergy dwelling outside Jerusalem, and not currently on duty in the Temple. The pattern was for the priests and Levites to have their own cities, with portions of land, scattered throughout the tribal territories. They came to Jerusalem for their tours of duty, when they were re-munerated directly from the offerings brought. It seems that all members of the family, from three years old (v. 16, i.e. after weaning) were counted in the total provision.

PRIDE AND A FALL—I

2 Chronicles 32:1–33

¹After these things and these acts of faithfulness Sennacherib king of Assyria came and invaded Judah and encamped against the fortified cities, thinking to win them for himself. ²And when Hezekiah saw that Sennacherib had come and intended to fight against Jerusalem, ³he planned with his officers and his mighty men to stop the water of the springs that were outside the city; and they helped him. ⁴A great many people were gathered, and they stopped all the springs and the brook that flowed through the land, saying, "Why should the kings of Assyria come and find much water?" ⁵He set to work resolutely and built up all the wall that was broken down, and raised towers upon it, and outside it he built another wall; and he strengthened the Millo in the city of David. He also made weapons and shields in abundance. ⁶And he set combat commanders over the people, and gathered them together to him in the square at the gate of the city and spoke encouragingly to them, saying, ⁷"Be strong and of good courage. Do not be afraid or dismayed before the king of Assyria and all the horde that is with him; for there is one greater with us than with him. ⁸With him is an arm of flesh; but with us is the Lord our God, to help us and to fight our battles." And the people took confidence from the words of Hezekiah king of Judah.

⁹After this Sennacherib king of Assyria, who was besieging Lachish with all his forces, sent his servants to Jerusalem to Hezekiah king of Judah and to all the people of Judah that were in Jerusalem, saying, ¹⁰"Thus says Sennacherib king of Assyria, 'On what are you relying, that you stand siege in Jerusalem? ¹¹Is not Hezekiah misleading you, that he may give you over to die by famine and by thirst, when he tells you, "The Lord our God will deliver us from the hand of the king of Assyria"? ¹²Has not this same Hezekiah taken away his high places and his altars and commanded Judah and Jerusalem, "Before one altar you shall worship, and upon it you shall burn your sacrifices"? ¹³Do

you not know what I and my fathers have done to all the peoples of other lands? Were the gods of the nations of those lands at all able to deliver their lands out of my hand? ¹⁴Who among all the gods of those nations which my fathers utterly destroyed was able to deliver his people from my hand, that your God should be able to deliver you from my hand? ¹⁵Now therefore do not let Hezekiah deceive you or mislead you in this fashion, and do not believe him, for no god of any nation or kingdom has been able to deliver his people from my hand or from the hand of my fathers. How much less will your God deliver you out of my hand!' "

¹⁶And his servants said still more against the Lord God and against his servant Hezekiah. ¹⁷And he wrote letters to cast contempt on the Lord the God of Israel and to speak against him, saying, "Like the gods of the nations of the lands who have not delivered their people from my hands, so the God of Hezekiah will not deliver his people from my hand." ¹⁸And they shouted it with a loud voice in the language of Judah to the people of Jerusalem who were upon the wall, to frighten and terrify them, in order that they might take the city. ¹⁹And they spoke of the God of Jerusalem as they spoke of the gods of the peoples of the earth, which are the work of men's hands.

²⁰Then Hezekiah the king and Isaiah the prophet, the son of Amoz, prayed because of this and cried to heaven. ²¹And the Lord sent an angel, who cut off all the mighty warriors and commanders and officers in the camp of the king of Assyria. So he returned with shame of face to his own land. And when he came into the house of his god, some of his own sons struck him down there with the sword. ²²So the Lord saved Hezekiah and the inhabitants of Jerusalem from the hand of Sennacherib king of Assyria and from the hand of all his enemies; and he gave them rest on every side. ²³And many brought gifts to the Lord to Jerusalem and precious things to Hezekiah king of Judah, so that he was exalted in the sight of all nations from that time onward.

²⁴In those days Hezekiah became sick and was at the point of death, and he prayed to the Lord; and he answered him and gave him a sign. ²⁵But Hezekiah did not make return according to the benefit done to him, for his heart was proud. Therefore wrath came upon him and Judah and Jerusalem. ²⁶But Hezekiah humbled himself for the pride of his heart, both he and the inhabitants of Jerusalem, so that the wrath of the Lord did not come upon them in the days of Hezekiah.

²⁷And Hezekiah had very great riches and honour; and he made for himself treasuries for silver, for gold, for precious stones, for

spices, for shields, and for all kinds of costly vessels; [28]storehouses also for the yield of grain, wine, and oil; and stalls for all kinds of cattle, and sheepfolds. [29]He likewise provided cities for himself, and flocks and herds in abundance; for God had given him very great possessions. [30]This same Hezekiah closed the upper outlet of the waters of Gihon and directed them down to the west side of the city of David. And Hezekiah prospered in all his works. [31]And so in the matter of the envoys of the princes of Babylon, who had been sent to him to inquire about the sign that had been done in the land, God left him to himself, in order to try him and to know all that was in his heart.

[32]Now the rest of the acts of Hezekiah, and his good deeds, behold, they are written in the vision of Isaiah the prophet the son of Amoz, in the Book of the Kings of Judah and Israel. [33]And Hezekiah slept with his fathers, and they buried him in the ascent of the tombs of the sons of David; and all Judah and the inhabitants of Jerusalem did him honour at his death. And Manasseh his son reigned in his stead.

(i)

Sennacherib's invasion of Judah was perhaps the greatest threat to the kingdom's existence before its fall at the hands of Babylon. To all appearances the might of Assyria far outstripped that of the remnant of the once great Davidic Empire. As Sennacherib closed in on Jerusalem, the northern kingdom was already destroyed for ever, its population scattered to various parts of his extensive territories. The Assyrian king, in his own official record of his Judean campaign, boasts that he proceeded to "shut up Hezekiah like a bird in a cage". This is confirmed by the account in 2 Kings 18, which tells that he not only advanced upon the fortified cities of Judah, but took them (v. 13), and that Hezekiah, fearing for Jerusalem itself, attempted to buy him off with treasures from the Temple (vv. 14–16).

The substance of the Assyrian boast (2 Chr. 32:13f.) must have seemed all too justified to the people of Jerusalem, and thoroughly intimidating (v. 18. The "language of Judah" is Hebrew. 2 Kings 18:26 records an appeal by the Jerusalem officials that the Assyrian envoy, there known as the Rabshakeh, speak in Aramaic, so that the people might not understand. Aramaic was the diplomatic language of the day, while Hebrew was the Judean vernacular. The passage of time made Aramaic the vernacular in Israel—as it was in Jesus' day—while Hebrew became the language of the learned.) It was, of course, Assyrian policy to direct their demands to the people themselves, as part of the time-honoured psychological ploy of making the enemy *believe* that he cannot win. All the biblical accounts of Assyria's advances stress her boasting about past victories, with its implication of the impotence of the local gods (cf. 2 Kings 18:33f.; Isa. 10:8–11). It was clearly a calculated strategy.

PRIDE AND A FALL—II

2 Chronicles 32:1–33 (*cont'd*)

(ii)

There are, as ever, important differences between the presentations of Sennacherib's invasion in Kings and Chr. In Kings the events stand out as being of overwhelming importance. The demise of the north is taken as an opportunity for a major theological excursus (2 Kings 17), and the deliverance of Jerusalem is an event of unsurpassed moment. The Chronicler does not record the final collapse of the north, perhaps because he never regarded it as a legitimate kingdom in any case, and because his overriding interest in its decline has been the consequent opportunity for a return to the Jerusalem fold, which has already, in some measure, happened (30:11). Furthermore, the invasion of Sennacherib is not accorded any special status among attacks on Judah which he has recorded. Indeed the Assyrian army is on the paltry side when compared with that of Zerah the Ethiopian (14:9ff.). These differences can be accounted for by his accustomed concerns—to show that faithfulness to God is rewarded with victory, wealth and international prestige (vv. 22f.). While the Kings narrative makes Assyria's approach dramatic and frightening—which it undoubtedly was, the Assyrians being renowned for their cruelty to the vanquished—Chr. draws its tooth in the very first verse. The opening words, literally, "After these things and this truth'', refer to Hezekiah's outstanding services to true religion, thereby effectively announcing his invincibility and Sennacherib's doom. Let us look more closely at the roles of Assyria and Hezekiah.

(iii)

Two things distinguish Assyria from other nations that have come against Judah. First, she comes *in spite of* the righteousness of Hezekiah. In this, however, she is not quite unique, since she resembles Zerah, who advanced upon the righteous Asa. The Chronicler has neatly dealt with any feeling of anomaly in this by means of his opening verse. The second distinguishing factor is Assyria's defiance of Yahweh. These two factors together enable him to turn the event into an object lesson—no human might can measure itself against the Lord.

On one level Assyria's challenge could be viewed merely as good military tactics. We have already referred to its psychological effectiveness. Notice the tightening of the screw, v. 12, when the Assyrian plays on popular fears about the abolition of the by now ingrained Baal-religion. On the other hand it might be said that the attack on Yahweh was "nothing personal". All ancient peoples regarded their own fortunes as bound up with the relative capacities of their gods. Assyria had every reason to be scornful about the gods they had so far encountered, and none to think that Yahweh would be different—yet. However, the gauntlet thrown down in vv. 14f. can rightly be regarded as *hubris*, that ultimate human defiance of the divine, if only because the Assyrian ascribes his successes to, and locates his confidence in, himself alone (i.e. "my hand . . . the hand of my fathers"), not his gods. There is a further insult to Yahweh in the implication that he will bring his people into famine and thirst (v. 11), when so much of the OT insists that he is the real author of plenty (e.g. Hos. 2:8). Assyria's fate, and that of Sennacherib himself (vv. 21ff.), is just. It is unusual for Chr. to dwell on the *personal* fate of the antagonist, and there is a special irony in his falling "in the house of his god". The OT is relentlessly scathing about the impotence of other gods, especially when they are made to challenge Yahweh directly (cf. 1 Sam. 5:1–5).

(iv)

Hezekiah plays his part *almost* without blemish. Verse 7 finds him confidently exhorting the people, sure that God will act. There is an instructive word-play between vv. 5 and 7, hidden by the English. The word translated "he set to work resolutely" means literally "he strengthened himself". It is a word that Chr. often uses to denote the strength which is available for those who seek God. The same word then occurs in Hezekiah's exhortation, v. 7: "Be strong..." Hezekiah is therefore able to communicate his own confidence in God to the people. Verse 8b finds them, literally, "leaning upon" the words of Hezekiah—a typical OT picture of faith.

The Chronicler, however, has reservations about Hezekiah's faithfulness, although he is unusually enigmatic about them (vv. 25f.). 2 Kings 20:12ff. suggests that his reception of the Babylonian envoys, here mentioned in v. 31, was culpable. The Chronicler, clearly presupposing a knowledge of that account on the part of his readers, probably accepts that judgment also, but it seems to be a different matter from the one recorded in v. 25. It is only possible to refer to his insistence elsewhere that punishment for a lapse from obedience is mitigated by repentance (cf. 19:2f.). Verse 26 points forward to a greater visitation, presumably referring, though not as explicitly as 2 Kings 20:16ff. (= Isa. 39:5ff.), to the Babylonian exile.

By way of a final footnote, a word is in place about Hezekiah's diversion of the waters of the spring Gihon to the west side of the City of David (v. 30). This was achieved by means of a tunnel through over five hundred metres of rock, a remarkable feat of engineering, still known as "Hezekiah's Tunnel", and negotiable by the more intrepid visitor to Jerusalem. There is a cool reference to this project in Isa. 22:9–11, which seems to agree ill with the record here, where it is one of the tokens that Hezekiah "prospered in all his works" (v. 30). Had the Chronicler taken a dim view of the matter he could easily have referred to it as part of Hezekiah's failure (v. 25). We can perhaps minimize the difference between Chr. and Isaiah, however, by saying that Chr. makes no *specific* assessment of the tunnel project, merely citing it as part of the strength which is his reward for more general obedience, and by noting that Isaiah does not direct *his* remarks at Hezekiah in particular.

THE PITS—AND A WAY OUT

2 Chronicles 33:1–25

[1]Manasseh was twelve years old when he began to reign, and he reigned fifty-five years in Jerusalem. [2]He did what was evil in the sight of the Lord, according to the abominable practices of the nations whom the Lord drove out before the people of Israel. [3]For he rebuilt the high places which his father Hezekiah had broken down, and erected altars to the Baals, and made Asherahs, and worshipped all the host of heaven, and served them. [4]And he built altars in the house of the Lord, of which the Lord had said, "In Jerusalem shall my name be for ever." [5]And he built altars for all the host of heaven in the two courts of the house of the Lord. [6]And he burned his sons as an offering in the valley of the son of Hinnom, and practised soothsaying and augury and sorcery, and dealt with mediums and with wizards. He did much evil in the sight of the Lord, provoking him to anger. [7]And the image of the idol which he had made he set in the house of God, of which God said to David and to Solomon his son, "In this house, and in Jerusalem, which I have chosen out of all the tribes of Israel, I will put my name for ever; [8]and I will no more remove the foot of Israel from the land which I appointed for your fathers, if only they will be careful to do all that I have commanded them, all the law, the statutes, and the ordinances given through Moses." [9]Manasseh seduced Judah and the inhabitants of Jerusalem, so that they did more evil than the nations whom the Lord destroyed before the people of Israel.

[10]The Lord spoke to Manasseh and to his people, but they gave no heed. [11]Therefore the Lord brought upon them the commanders of the army of the king of Assyria, who took Manasseh with hooks and bound him with fetters of bronze and brought him to Babylon. [12]And when he was in distress he entreated the favour of the Lord his God and humbled himself greatly before the God of his fathers. [13]He prayed to him, and God received his entreaty and heard his supplication and brought him again to Jerusalem into his kingdom. Then Manasseh knew that the Lord was God.

¹⁴Afterwards he búilt an outer wall for the city of David west of Gihon, in the valley, and for the entrance into the Fish Gate, and carried it round Ophel, and raised it to a very great height; he also put commanders of the army in all the fortified cities in Judah. ¹⁵And he took away the foreign gods and the idol from the house of the Lord, and all the altars that he had built on the mountain of the house of the Lord and in Jerusalem, and he threw them outside of the city. ¹⁶He also restored the altar of the Lord and offered upon it sacrifices of peace offerings and of thanksgiving; and he commanded Judah to serve the Lord the God of Israel. ¹⁷Nevertheless the people still sacrificed at the high places, but only to the Lord their God.

¹⁸Now the rest of the acts of Manasseh, and his prayer to his God, and the words of the seers who spoke to him in the name of the Lord the God of Israel, behold, they are in the Chronicles of the Kings of Israel. ¹⁹And his prayer, and how God received his entreaty, and all his sin and his faithlessness, and the sites on which he built high places and set up the Asherim and the images, before he humbled himself, behold, they are written in the Chronicles of the Seers. ²⁰So Manasseh slept with his fathers, and they buried him in his house; and Amon his son reigned in his stead.

²¹Amon was twenty-two years old when he began to reign, and he reigned two years in Jerusalem. ²²He did what was evil in the sight of the Lord, as Manasseh his father had done. Amon sacrificed to all the images that Manasseh his father had made, and served them. ²³And he did not humble himself before the Lord, as Manasseh his father had humbled himself, but this Amon incurred guilt more and more. ²⁴And his servants conspired against him and killed him in his house. ²⁵But the people of the land slew all those who had conspired against King Amon; and the people of the land made Josiah his son king in his stead.

(i)

Manasseh furnishes the most outstanding example of the possibilities of both wickedness and conversion. For evil doing, Manasseh is more or less a byword in the OT. (cf. 2 Kings 23:26, which traces the final fall of Judah to him.) Even that of Ahaz pales beside the sheer determination of Manasseh to steep himself in everything that was forbidden by the Lord. The list of his crimes in v. 6 is designed to show the flagrancy of his defiance, reflecting as it does the prohibitions of Deut. 18:10–12. (These were various forms of black magic, designed to put the power of God at man's disposal.) In Deut. those who commit such things are described as "an abomination to the Lord", the strongest expression of divine indignation in the OT.

The intensity of Manasseh's sin is stressed by the double reference (vv. 4, 7f.) to the Lord's promise, again in Deuteronomy (12:5 etc.), that he would "put his name" in Jerusalem for ever. His putting his name there implied a claim to sole rights over the place, at the expense of other gods (Deut. 12:3). Manasseh's acts are, therefore, a calculated attempt to throw off the lordship of Yahweh, to claim independence from the Covenant, to drive him from the land which he had given Israel. The effect of this presentation is to show the extreme danger in which Manasseh himself stands of being driven from the land. As well as a double reference to the Lord's name, there is a double reference to his expulsion of Israel's predecessors in the land because of *their* attachment to the kinds of practices now indulged in by Manasseh (vv. 2, 9). This again reflects the context of Deut. 18, where we read (v. 12) that it is precisely because of soothsaying, augury, sorcery etc. that the nations were driven out. Verse 9, then, prepares the reader for *Manasseh's* expulsion, as the natural and just consequence of his crimes.

Yet the opening verses (1–9) point forward in a different way also. They are not simply a catalogue of his sins or a pointer to his fate. Rather they present the full range of possibilities. The double reference to the putting of the Lord's name in Jerusalem *for ever* (vv. 4, 7) serves not only to accuse Manasseh, but to reiterate the promise and stress its eternal validity. Both possibilities—expulsion because of wickedness, enjoyment of the land because of righteousness—are played out in what follows.

(ii)

Manasseh's repentance (v. 13) is even more remarkable than his wickedness. On one level this is so because the account of his reign in 2 Kings 21:1–18 gives no inkling of such a repentance (nor indeed of a "carpeting" in Babylon). The omission by the author of Kings does not mean that Chr.'s version of events cannot stand. His selection of material may just as much as the Chronicler's have been governed by his theological purpose; or he may simply not have known of the event. Nothing can be proved. It can be said, however, that an encounter with Assyria such as Chr. reports does not lack historical plausibility, and might have had as its context the imposition of vassal-treaties by the emperor, Esarhaddon, in 672 B.C. (Myers). Babylon, incidentally, is not yet a power in its own right. It appears here as part of the Assyrian Empire. Its mention does have the effect, however, of adumbrating the true Babylonian exile.

The repentance of Manasseh is remarkable on a deeper level, both because of the degree of infamy which preceded it and because it follows the rejection of an appeal from the Lord (v. 10—corresponding to the prophetic appeals which are a regular feature), and the consequent punishment. It is worth pointing out that all previous rejections of the prophetic appeal have resulted in unmitigated disaster (e.g. 16:17ff.). The case of Manasseh, then, shows that no depth of moral turpitude precludes a return to the Lord by way of repentance. The repentance is described in vv. 12f. in terms which, as on previous occasions, are strongly reminiscent of those of 7:14 (see on that verse). Manasseh's reaction to "distress" (v. 12) makes an instructive contrast with that of Ahaz, who simply increased his resistance to God (28:22). These two opposite reactions to suffering are true to experience. Some add the pain of bitterness to that which they endure already. Others, more sure of the love of God, seem to manifest the best qualities of character more and more as their suffering increases (cf. Rom. 5:3–5; 1 Peter 1:3–9).

Manasseh's return to the Lord results in his resumption of the kingship in Jerusalem (v. 13), some restitution for his previous desecrations (vv. 15f., which, however, can hardly have been complete in the light of v. 22 below), and an increase in his military capability (v. 14), a sign that in the Lord's eyes he is secure in the land.

It is well to remember once more that, at this stage of Chr., we are in the shadow of the story of the exile. Its readers encounter in Manasseh possibilities which speak strongly to them. Having grown accustomed, perhaps, to a certain mediocrity in their life after exile they may have been tempted to think that past sins had blighted future hopes. Chr. shows here that the Lord is always ready to restore his people's fellowship with him and bless them in new and unexpected ways. He has put his name in Jerusalem "for ever".

(iii)

The story of Amon (vv. 21–25) is hardly more than a footnote to that of Manasseh, perhaps reflecting the brevity of his reign. Since, however, Amon reverted to the evil of the early Manasseh, undoing his father's reforms, his reign explains why Josiah subsequently had to undertake further reforms.

JOSIAH'S REFORM—I

2 Chronicles 34:1–33

¹Josiah was eight years old when he began to reign, and he reigned thirty-one years in Jerusalem. ²He did what was right in the eyes of the Lord, and walked in the ways of David his father; and he did not turn aside to the right or to the left. ³For in the eighth year of his reign, while he was yet a boy, he began to seek the God of David his father; and in the twelfth year he began to purge Judah and Jerusalem of the high places, the Asherim, and the graven and the molten images. ⁴And they broke down the altars of the Baals in his presence; and he hewed down the incense altars which stood above them; and he broke in pieces the Asherim and the graven and the molten images, and he made dust of them and strewed it over the graves of those who had sacrificed to them. ⁵He also burned the bones of the priests on their altars, and purged Judah and Jerusalem. ⁶And in the cities of Manasseh, Ephraim, and Simeon, and as far as Naphtali, in their ruins round about, ⁷he broke down the altars, and beat the Asherim and the images into powder, and hewed down all the incense altars throughout all the land of Israel. Then he returned to Jerusalem.

⁸Now in the eighteenth year of his reign, when he had purged the land and the house, he sent Shaphan the son of Azaliah, and Maaseiah the governor of the city, and Joah the son of Joahaz, the recorder, to

repair the house of the Lord his God. ⁹They came to Hilkiah the high priest and delivered the money that had been brought into the house of God, which the Levites, the keepers of the threshold, had collected from Manasseh and Ephraim and from all the remnant of Israel and from all Judah and Benjamin and from the inhabitants of Jerusalem. ¹⁰They delivered it to the workmen who had the oversight of the house of the Lord; and the workmen who were working in the house of the Lord gave it for repairing and restoring the house. ¹¹They gave it to the carpenters and the builders to buy quarried stone, and timber for binders and beams for the buildings which the kings of Judah had let go to ruin. ¹²And the men did the work faithfully. Over them were set Jahath and Obadiah the Levites, of the sons of Merari, and Zechariah and Meshullam, of the sons of the Kohathites, to have oversight. The Levites, all who were skilful with instruments of music, ¹³were over the burden bearers and directed all who did work in every kind of service; and some of the Levites were scribes, and officials, and gatekeepers.

¹⁴While they were bringing out the money that had been brought into the house of the Lord, Hilkiah the priest found the book of the law of the Lord given through Moses. ¹⁵Then Hilkiah said to Shaphan the secretary, "I have found the book of the law in the house of the Lord"; and Hilkiah gave the book to Shaphan. ¹⁶Shaphan brought the book to the king, and further reported to the king, "All that was committed to your servants they are doing. ¹⁷They have emptied out the money that was found in the house of the Lord and have delivered it into the hand of the overseers and the workmen." ¹⁸Then Shaphan the secretary told the king, "Hilkiah the priest has given me a book." And Shaphan read it before the king.

¹⁹When the king heard the words of the law he rent his clothes. ²⁰And the king commanded Hilkiah, Ahikam the son of Shaphan, Abdon the son of Micah, Shaphan the secretary, and Asaiah the king's servant, saying, ²¹"Go, inquire of the Lord for me and for those who are left in Israel and in Judah, concerning the words of the book that has been found; for great is the wrath of the Lord that is poured out on us, because our fathers have not kept the word of the Lord, to do according to all that is written in this book."

²²So Hilkiah and those whom the king had sent went to Huldah the prophetess, the wife of Shallum the son of Tokhath, son of Hasrah, keeper of the wardrobe (now she dwelt in Jerusalem in the Second Quarter) and spoke to her to that effect. ²³And she said to them, "Thus says the Lord, the God of Israel: 'Tell the man who sent you to

me, ²⁴Thus says the Lord, Behold, I will bring evil upon this place and upon its inhabitants, all the curses that are written in the book which was read before the king of Judah. ²⁵Because they have forsaken me and have burned incense to other gods, that they might provoke me to anger with all the works of their hands, therefore my wrath will be poured out upon this place and will not be quenched. ²⁶But to the king of Judah, who sent you to inquire of the Lord, thus shall you say to him, Thus says the Lord, the God of Israel: Regarding the words which you have heard, ²⁷because your heart was penitent and you humbled yourself before God when you heard his words against this place and its inhabitants, and you have humbled yourself before me, and have rent your clothes and wept before me, I also have heard you, says the Lord. ²⁸Behold, I will gather you to your fathers, and you shall be gathered to your grave in peace, and your eyes shall not see all the evil which I will bring upon this place and its inhabitants.'" And they brought back word to the king.

²⁹Then the king sent and gathered together all the elders of Judah and Jerusalem. ³⁰And the king went up to the house of the Lord, with all the men of Judah and the inhabitants of Jerusalem and the priests and the Levites, all the people both great and small; and he read in their hearing all the words of the book of the covenant which had been found in the house of the Lord. ³¹And the king stood in his place and made a covenant before the Lord, to walk after the Lord and to keep his commandments and his testimonies and his statutes, with all his heart and all his soul, to perform the words of the covenant that were written in this book. ³²Then he made all who were present in Jerusalem and in Benjamin stand to it. And the inhabitants of Jerusalem did according to the covenant of God, the God of their fathers. ³³And Josiah took away all the abominations from all the territory that belonged to the people of Israel, and made all who were in Israel serve the Lord their God. All his days they did not turn away from following the Lord the God of their fathers.

Josiah was by all accounts one of the successes of the Judean monarchy. The author of Kings regarded him as unsurpassed in piety (2 Kings 23:25). To the prophet Jeremiah, whose early ministry coincided with his reign, he was a paragon whose faithfulness condemned his unworthy successors in Jerusalem (Jer. 22:15f.). In Chr., he has all the qualities of Hezekiah, without (apart from the strange circumstances of his death) the enigmatic reservations; he shows the early promise of a Joash, without disappointing it later on.

JOSIAH'S REFORM—II

2 Chronicles 34:1–33 (*cont'd*)

(i)

Considering his reputation, it is perhaps not surprising that Josiah should have perpetrated the reformation of religion which has come to be widely regarded by historians as the most significant in the whole period of the monarchy.

This view derives largely from 2 Kings 22–23, in which Josiah clearly occupies a climactic position, his reforms distinguished from any that were undertaken by his predecessors. The distinctiveness of his reform is somewhat diminished in Chr., partly because the Chronicler records a larger number of attempts at reformation throughout the monarchy period, and partly because he lays so much stress on the importance of Hezekiah's in particular. In some ways, Josiah's work can be seen as a reclamation of the gains of his illustrious forefather. In others, however, it surpasses them. Josiah appears to have been more thorough in his destruction of the places of false worship (vv. 4, 6f.), even executing those who worshipped and officiated there (vv. 4–5). He also extended his measures, it seems, to a larger portion of "greater Israel" than Hezekiah had done, the territory of Naphtali and Simeon being mentioned along with Ephraim and Manasseh as areas of his activity (contrast 31:1). This implies access to parts that were well to the north, i.e. well into Assyria's dominions. Such activity on Josiah's part is remarkable, but has been thought to be not inconsistent with the incipient decline of Assyria. It has even been suggested that, in her decline, Assyria had given Josiah vassal-status in regard to the former Israelite territory (Myers). For the Chronicler, with his ideal of a twelve-tribe Israel, true reform must extend to the whole of the historic territory, even if only a small remnant of the Israelite people now dwells there.

(ii)

Josiah is remarkable for his youthfulness at the time of his first zeal to re-establish the worship of the Lord. It is at the age of sixteen (v. 3) that he begins to "seek the God of David his father". (The link with David is established not only by the mention of his name but by the use of the verb "seek", designating proper worship and obedience.) He is twenty—and the year is 628 B.C.—when the reforms begin.

This detail is in contrast with the account in Kings. A natural reading of 2 Kings 22 suggests that it was the discovery, in 621 B.C., of the "book of the law" (2 Kings 22:8; cf. v. 14 of our chapter) that precipitated the reform. In Chr. the reform is at least well under way, perhaps complete (v. 7), by the time of the discovery. There are reasons to think that Chr. has preserved an account of the matter that conveys more precisely what actually happened. The author of Kings has evidently telescoped and schematized his material because he wants to stress the penitence of Josiah following the reading of the book, and the consequences for his reign. Chr. has wanted to insist that the circumstances of the discovery—or loss—of the book did not materially affect the opportunity for Josiah to act righteously, and has therefore made known the actual chronology of events.

This raises questions concerning the identity of the book of the law and the circumstances of its loss and rediscovery. Scholars are more or less unanimous that the book was what we now know as Deuteronomy.

This is sometimes urged on the grounds that Josiah's measures correspond to central requirements of Deuteronomy, especially Deut. 12, i.e. his destruction of the places of Baal-worship. Such a view, however, depends on attaching little credence to Chr.'s chronology of events, since the measures were taken before the discovery. More important, perhaps, is the Lord's statement, in Huldah's prophecy (v. 24 of our chapter), that he will bring upon Jerusalem "all the curses that are written in the book". This is strongly reminiscent of Deut. 27:15ff.; 28, passages which carry warnings of dire punishments which will result from disobedience to God's Covenant (along with promises of blessing for obedience). Josiah's celebration of Passover (2 Chr. 35) could also arise from Deut. 16. These sorts of points make it likely that Deuteronomy—or parts of it—belonged to what was found. It is by no means impossible, however, that longer parts of the Torah or Pentateuch were discovered also. (How much of it then existed is a matter of contention among scholars, which need not be entered here.)

There is no record of the circumstances in which the book went missing. According to Deut. 31:24ff., the "law" (again the reference could be either to Deuteronomy alone or to the whole Pentateuch) had its rightful place beside the ark of the covenant from Israel's days in the desert, and could therefore have entered the Temple *with* the ark in the days of Solomon. Its loss could have occurred at any time thereafter, probably in a period when the Temple was neglected or desecrated. This could have been close to the time of Josiah, e.g. under Manasseh, which would explain Chr.'s picture of kings throughout the period knowing the standards laid down in the Torah, and occasionally effecting reforms similar to Josiah's. The memory of its broad demands would also have survived the relatively short interval, especially among faithful priests and among prophets. Zephaniah, for example, probably ministered in the early part of Josiah's reign, and may have influenced him.

This is significant in itself. Prophets often address kings in Chr. It may be that this was the typical way in which the latter were exposed to God's words. (It was not the exclusive means—the Temple liturgy, represented in our Bibles by the Psalms, was another.) Josiah, however, is *un*typical in that he actually *seeks out* a prophetic interpretation of events. Among spiritual people, there is a difference between a general consciousness of the standards and demands of God and an urgent quest for his word here and now, for today. It is this urgency which is usually attended by strength of faith, a firmness of purpose and a clarity of vision in the Christian life.

The tenor of Huldah's words (vv. 23ff.) is that a judgment will fall on Judah because of her chronic sinfulness. Because of Josiah's eager submission to God, however, it will not come during his reign (vv. 27f.). Josiah's response to this word is far from complacent. (Contrast Hezekiah's reaction to a similar prophecy recorded in 2 Kings 20:16–19.) On the contrary, he gathers Judah for a great act of covenant renewal, determined that the people shall be worthy of the mercy received. Such a spirit is precisely that which the New Testament also regards as genuinely spiritual (cf. Rom. 5:18–6:4).

JOSIAH'S PASSOVER—I

2 Chronicles 35:1–27

¹Josiah kept a passover to the Lord in Jerusalem; and they killed the passover lamb on the fourteenth day of the first month. ²He appointed the priests to their offices and encouraged them in the service of the house of the Lord. ³And he said to the Levites who taught all Israel and who were holy to the Lord, "Put the holy ark in the house which Solomon the son of David, king of Israel, built; you need no longer carry it upon your shoulders. Now serve the Lord your God and his people Israel. ⁴Prepare yourselves according to your fathers' houses by your divisions, following the directions of David king of Israel and the directions of Solomon his son. ⁵And stand in the holy place according to the groupings of the fathers' houses of your brethren the lay people, and let there be for each a part of a father's house of the Levites. ⁶And kill the passover lamb, and sanctify yourselves, and prepare for your brethren, to do according to the word of the Lord by Moses."

⁷Then Josiah contributed to the lay people, as passover offerings for all that were present, lambs and kids from the flock to the number of thirty thousand, and three thousand bulls; these were from the king's possessions. ⁸And his princes contributed willingly to the people, to the priests, and to the Levites. Hilkiah, Zechariah, and Jehiel, the chief officers of the house of God, gave to the priests for the passover offerings two thousand six hundred lambs and kids and three hundred bulls. ⁹Conaniah also, and Shemaiah and Nethanel his brothers, and Hashabiah and Je-iel and Jozabad, the chiefs of the Levites, gave to the Levites for the passover offerings five thousand lambs and kids and five hundred bulls.

¹⁰When the service had been prepared for, the priests stood in their place, and the Levites in their divisions according to the king's command. ¹¹And they killed the passover lamb, and the priests sprinkled the blood which they received from them while the Levites flayed the victims. ¹²And they set aside the burnt offerings that they might distribute them according to the groupings of the fathers' houses of the lay people, to offer to the Lord, as it is written in the book of Moses. And so they did with the bulls. ¹³And they roasted the passover lamb with fire according to the ordinance; and they boiled the holy offerings in pots, in cauldrons, and in pans, and carried them quickly to all the lay people. ¹⁴And afterward they prepared for themselves and for the priests, because the priests the sons of Aaron were busied in offering the burnt offerings and the fat parts until night; so the Levites prepared for themselves and for the priests the sons of Aaron. ¹⁵The singers, the sons of Asaph, were in their place according to the command of David, and Asaph, and Heman, and Jeduthun the king's seer; and the gatekeepers were at each gate; they did not need to depart from their service, for their brethren the Levites prepared for them.

¹⁶So all the service of the Lord was prepared that day, to keep the passover and to offer burnt offerings on the altar of the Lord, according to the command of King Josiah. ¹⁷And the people of Israel who were present kept the passover at that time, and the feast of unleavened bread seven days. ¹⁸No passover like it had been kept in Israel since the days of Samuel the prophet; none of the kings of Israel had kept such a passover as was kept by Josiah, and the priests and the Levites, and all Judah and Israel who were present, and the inhabitants of Jerusalem. ¹⁹In the eighteenth year of the reign of Josiah this passover was kept.

²⁰After all this, when Josiah had prepared the temple, Neco king of Egypt went up to fight at Carchemish on the Euphrates and Josiah went out against him. ²¹But he sent envoys to him, saying, "What have we to do with each other, king of Judah? I am not coming against you this day, but against the house with which I am at war; and God has commanded me to make haste. Cease opposing God, who is with me, lest he destroy you." ²²Nevertheless Josiah would not turn away from him, but disguised himself in order to fight with him. He did not listen to the words of Neco from the mouth of God, but joined battle in the plain of Megiddo. ²³And the archers shot King Josiah; and the king said to his servants, "Take me away, for I am badly wounded." ²⁴So his servants took him out of the chariot and carried him in his second

chariot and brought him to Jerusalem. And he died, and was buried in the tombs of his fathers. All Judah and Jerusalem mourned for Josiah. 25 Jeremiah also uttered a lament for Josiah; and all the singing men and singing women have spoken of Josiah in their laments to this day. They made these an ordinance in Israel; behold, they are written in the Laments. 26 Now the rest of the acts of Josiah, and his good deeds according to what is written in the law of the Lord, 27 and his acts, first and last, behold, they are written in the Book of the Kings of Israel and Judah.

(i)

Despite the magnificence of Hezekiah's Passover it seems (from v. 18) that Josiah's surpassed it. Here, as there, there is a huge gathering of the population in Jerusalem. It requires an effort of the imagination for us in the modern western world to picture such a scene, though if we have seen, even on film or television, an Islamic *haj*, we shall be on the right lines. Jerusalem in Josiah's day was not a large city. The convergence upon it of the entire population of Judah, for the purposes of worship centred on the Temple, must have taken possession of it. Local people braced themselves for the influx, and perhaps prepared to cater for it. Then they began to arrive, family after extended family, tired from journeys of which some at least had been long especially in view of the conditions under which people travelled, even if it was, mercifully, not yet the hottest time of year. The mass of human needs in such a situation needs no elaboration, though it is clear that food was going to be no problem in view of the rich provision by king, princes and priests (vv. 7f.) for the feast itself. People no doubt provided for themselves, picnic fashion, until the main event got under way.

The problems posed in such a situation, however, paled into insignificance beside the grandeur and evocative power of it all. Here the *Israelite* began to see, or saw again, what it was to be *Israel*. The peasant who worked his own piece of land for most of the year to keep his little family alive knew that he was of the greater family of God, a son of Abraham, belonging to the chosen people that now pressed upon the House that marked the presence among them of the One who had given them their land and underwrote their whole existence. The thought and conversation of each were dominated by Passover.

This was the experience which had for so long been shunned (v. 18), and which Josiah now commanded. Such an experience had been written into the Mosaic law by the Lord himself, not for the occasion of Passover only, but three times in the year, the other two feasts being the feasts of Weeks and Booths (cf. Deut. 16:9–15). The reason is not far to seek. Israel must be drawn constantly back to its roots, to know again and again its true identity, to be delivered from the delusion that comes from the normal preoccupation with the routine, the menial and the material, that the sum of life is no more than this. To the same end Jesus' parents would one day make the journey from Nazareth and discover that, while still a child, he knew more about the meaning of Passover than they (Luke 2:41–51).

That which characterizes the people of God essentially is their knowledge of his past faithfulness to them, and their hope that that knowledge is a guarantee of future security, understood by the Christian in terms of eternity. The worship and open acknowledgment of him *as a people together* functions today as it did in ancient Israel—though the outer form of both people and worship is necessarily different—to create and sustain that self-understanding.

JOSIAH'S PASSOVER—II

2 Chronicles 35:1–27 (*cont'd*)

(ii)

The spirit that inspires Josiah is a new resolve to obey God's commandments. The very holding of the feast constitutes his major contribution to this, for reasons which we have seen. He is careful also about details, such as the correct date (v. 1; cf. Exod. 12:6), and the proper functioning of the priests and Levites (vv. 3–6). There is a striking feature of Josiah's instructions to the

Levites, namely in the command to "Put the holy ark in the house which Solomon the son of David, king of Israel, built" (v. 3). The ark, as we recall, did in fact take its place in the Temple back in the days of Solomon (2 Chr. 5). Furthermore, David had actually anticipated that the building of the Temple would release the Levites from duties such as carrying the ark, and had consequently redefined their duties (1 Chr. 23:26ff.). Those instructions too, are echoed here, if faintly, in the final sentence of v. 3.

The command relating to the ark has been considered a problem by commentators in view of the absence of any record of the ark's having been *removed* from the Temple at any time following its first placement there. It *could* have happened in the process either of desecration or of repair, though such a circumstance would almost certainly have been recorded. Attempts at avoiding the plain meaning of the phrase are not successful either. The likeliest interpretation, therefore, is that Josiah deliberately re-enacted the placing of the ark in the Temple as a symbolic gesture. His purpose in doing so is not obscure. The history of Israel and Judah, with glorious exceptions, had witnessed a profound neglect of Temple-worship as it had been prescribed in the law. In particular the Passover had not been celebrated on the scale or with the attention to propriety of this one (this with *one* exception, namely Hezekiah's). The prophecy of Huldah announcing Judah's fall (34:23ff.) was still fresh in Josiah's mind. The celebration of Passover was part of his covenant renewal (34:31). In the course of it, Josiah re-enacted the bringing of the ark as a declaration that Judah was ready to start again. Such symbolic acts of rededication still have their value today, whether in the lives of individuals or of churches.

(iii)

Verses 10–15 describe the sacrificial preparations for the feast. The task of the clergy was immense, as the Temple became a huge butchery and the people came endlessly to carry off the beasts, duly slaughtered, to the places where they would celebrate in families. There was always this double aspect to the keeping of Passover, on the one hand the attendance at the Temple—or, in early Israel, some other sanctuary—for the ritual slaughter, and on the other the actual celebration in homes. (It seems from Deut. 16:7 that many people would have brought tents and camped around Jerusalem for the seven-day duration of the feast. The same text implies, however, that they would not actually have eaten there, but close to the Temple. In Jesus' day the meal was eaten in houses in the city, cf. Luke 22:7–13.) The slaughter of the Passover lamb was accompanied by burnt offerings (v. 12), for which the other animals (kids and bulls, v. 9) were used. The "fat parts", v. 14, refers, in general sacrificial parlance, to those parts of animals which are not *wholly* consumed sacrificially on the altar. In this case the reference is probably to the Passover lamb.

(iv)

There is considerable irony in the fact that the splendid efforts of Josiah in relation to Judah's worship were followed by his rather ignominious demise. The wider political scene in the ancient Near East at the time of Josiah's reform was witnessing the rise of the coming power in the region, Babylon. This was ominous for Judah, and had Josiah but known it he might have acted differently. As it was, he became embroiled in a battle of the superpowers. Pharaoh Neco of Egypt marched to the assistance of the declining Assyria in the vain attempt of the latter—finally brought to nought at the decisive battle of Carchemish—to withstand Babylon. Josiah's move against Neco was presumably bound up with his policy of renouncing Assyrian influence within his borders, and he may even have felt that the rise of Babylon was a thing to be encouraged. Politically and militarily it was a miscalculation. The Chronicler gives us a deeper cause, however, namely Josiah's refusal to hear the word of God on the matter.

The circumstances of this refusal are strange, because of the fact that the word comes through Neco himself (v. 21). It is not quite unprecedented in the OT histories for an antagonist of Israel to claim direct authority from Israel's God. Assyria's Rabshakeh claimed precisely this (2 Kings 18:25—a detail omitted from the account of that siege in 2 Chr. 32). The difference here is that the enemy's claim is presented as fact by the Chronicler himself, who makes Josiah's refusal the reason for his death (v. 22). It is hard not to feel a certain bewildered sympathy for Josiah here. How *should* he believe the word of an invader of the promised land, intent on his own bellicose interests, when he said that he had been sent by God, especially in view of Huldah's prophecy that Judah would be delivered in his day, and of his own efforts to be faithful?

It is possible to meet the difficulty in one of two ways. Either we might take the line that the word of God is always recognizable as such and that Josiah's conscience must have informed him that it was right to cede to Neco. Or again, we might suppose that Neco's claim—presumably originally in terms of Egyptian deities—was supported by an interpretation from within Israel's prophetic circles, which made it plain that this was in fact Yahweh's will. This explanation is offered by an apocryphal book (1 Esdras 1:28) which attributes the interpretation to Jeremiah. As historical evidence 1 Esdras does not count. Yet the suggestion is not without plausibility in view of the fact that Jeremiah typically *did* counsel a policy of non-resistance to the imperial power (Babylon), urging that it was acting under God (cf. Jer. 37–38).

In any case Josiah's fatal failure on this occasion accounts for his downfall, and explains the non-fulfilment of Huldah's prophecy that he would die "in peace" (34:28). The rest of Huldah's prophecy remained in force since, despite Josiah's death, Judah did not fall at this time.

All Judah mourned the passing of one of Judah's greatest kings. The most significant accolade is supplied by Jeremiah (v. 25), and is remarkable in view of the fact that, as is generally held, Jeremiah cannot have believed that Josiah's efforts had the efficacy actually to convert people's hearts. This is a reasonable deduction from the fact that his prophetic ministry begins right in the middle of the reforms, in 626 B.C. Here is an ironic demonstration that, however well-intentioned, no amount of external reforms can effect real change in people.

THE LAST KINGS

2 Chronicles 36:1–16

¹The people of the land took Jehoahaz the son of Josiah and made him king in his father's stead in Jerusalem. ²Jehoahaz was twenty-three years old when he began to reign; and he reigned three months in Jerusalem. ³Then the king of Egypt deposed him in Jerusalem and laid upon the land a tribute of a hundred talents of silver and a talent of gold. ⁴And the king of Egypt made Eliakim his brother king over Judah and Jerusalem, and changed his name to Jehoiakim; but Neco took Jehoahaz his brother and carried him to Egypt.

⁵Jehoiakim was twenty-five years old when he began to reign, and he reigned eleven years in Jerusalem. He did what was evil in the sight of the Lord his God. ⁶Against him came up Nebuchadnezzar king of Babylon, and bound him in fetters to take him to Babylon. ⁷Nebuchadnezzar also carried part of the vessels of the house of the Lord to Babylon and put them in his palace in Babylon. ⁸Now the rest of the acts of Jehoiakim, and the abominations which he did, and what was found against him, behold, they are written in the Book of the Kings of Israel and Judah; and Jehoiachin his son reigned in his stead.

⁹Jehoiachin was eight years old when he began to reign, and he reigned three months and ten days in Jerusalem. He did what was evil in the sight of the Lord. ¹⁰In the spring of the year King Nebuchadnezzar sent and brought him to Babylon, with the precious vessels of the house of the Lord, and made his brother Zedekiah king over Judah and Jerusalem.

¹¹Zedekiah was twenty-one years old when he began to reign, and he reigned eleven years in Jerusalem. ¹²He did what was evil in the sight of the Lord his God. He did not humble himself before Jeremiah the prophet, who spoke from the mouth of the Lord. ¹³He also rebelled against King Nebuchadnezzar, who had made him swear by God; he stiffened his neck and hardened his heart against turning to the Lord, the God of Israel. ¹⁴All the leading priests and the people likewise were exceedingly unfaithful, following all the abominations of the nations; and they polluted the house of the Lord which he had hallowed in Jerusalem.

¹⁵The Lord, the God of their fathers, sent persistently to them by his messengers, because he had compassion on his people and on his dwelling place; ¹⁶but they kept mocking the messengers of God,

despising his words, and scoffing at his prophets, till the wrath of the Lord rose against his people, till there was no remedy.

The final chapter of Chr. rounds off the pre-exilic history almost in summary fashion, abandoning the normal method of treating each king at length and grouping the last four together. The reason for this is partly a matter of presentation. The brief treatment of the end of Judah allows the outstanding reign of Josiah to retain a more obviously climactic position, thus leaving a fresher memory in the reader's mind of the possibility of faithfulness and blessing. There is also a historical factor in the grouping, since these four kings had in common the fact that, in their reigns, Judah was now effectively under, first Egyptian, then Babylonian control. They also have in common their rebellion against the Lord.

Fuller details about the four kings are known from elsewhere and Chr. assumes knowledge of them. The reign of Jehoahaz, otherwise known as Shallum (Jer. 22:11), is the least fully documented, perhaps because of its brevity. 2 Kings 23:32 records that "he did what was evil in the sight of the Lord", a fact which Chr. leaves us to infer. Jeremiah also records his exile to Egypt (22:11f.). In the immediate aftermath of Josiah's fall at Megiddo, Judah was under Egyptian control until the decisive battle of Carchemish (605 B.C.). It was thus that Pharaoh Neco could determine who reigned there. His alteration of Eliakim's name to Jehoiakim effects no real change of meaning except to substitute part of the Lord's personal name Yahweh (= Jeho-) for the more general name for God. This amounts to an acknowledgment by Neco that Yahweh ruled in Israel.

With Jehoiakim, the imperial power in Israel has passed to Babylon, Egypt having now renounced its claims in Palestine. The Chronicler is now more explicit in his adverse judgment (v. 5). One main source of information about Jehoiakim is the Book of Jeremiah, which deals in much more detail with the period which Chr. here passes over quickly. Jehoiakim appears there as one who showed flagrant and haughty disregard for the word of God as spoken by the prophet (see especially Jer. 36:9–

26). It is only in Chr., however, that we are told that Nebuchadnezzar "bound him in fetters to take him to Babylon" (v. 6).
Whether he was actually taken there is not obvious from this
phrase. The action of binding him as a prisoner may have been no
more than a symbolic demonstration of his status, which may or
may not have required an actual trip to the new seat of empire.
(See on Manasseh and Assyria, 2 Chr. 33.) What *is* clear is that
Nebuchadnezzar began to despoil the Temple in Jehoiakim's
reign. This aspect of the Babylonian devastation is stressed by the
Chronicler, because the cessation of worship there has at least as
much theological significance for him as the removal of the
people. He returns to the theme in the case of Jehoiachin
(v. 10) and of Zedekiah (vv. 18f.).

It was under the next king, Jehoiachin, also known as Jeconiah
(1 Chr. 3:16; Coniah, Jer. 22:24), that the first major deporta-
tions to Babylon took place, in the year 597 B.C. (2 Kings 24:8–
17). His reign, like that of Jehoahaz, was brief and wicked.

This first deportation, however, was not designed to put an end
to the kingdom. Nebuchadnezzar, following the example of the
Egyptian Pharaoh before him, set up his own puppet king in
Jerusalem, Zedekiah, a son of Josiah and therefore Jehoiachin's
uncle (cf. 2 Kings 24:17; the term "brother", v. 10 of our chapter,
is probably used loosely in the sense of "relative"). Zedekiah
maintained his vassal-status for eleven years before rebelling
against Nebuchadnezzar. The Book of Jeremiah depicts Zedekiah as an insecure, weak, hunted man, under pressure from his
"hawks" to resist Babylon, yet not unwilling to appeal to
Jeremiah and hear his message of non-resistance. (See e.g. Jer.
38:19–26; cf. 37:3.) Finally bending, however, to the pressure to
declare independence, he pays a heavy price, himself deported,
with the loss of his sons and his eyes (2 Kings 25:7). Chr. condemns his rebellion because it constituted the breach of an oath to
the Lord, v. 13 (cf. Ezek. 17:12–21, which elaborates this aspect
of Zedekiah's disobedience).

The Chronicler's treatment of the four kings comes to something of a climax with Zedekiah. Here we begin to see some of his
characteristic vocabulary being used (e.g. "he did not humble

himself", v. 12). Here too he widens his horizons to implicate the leaders, and indeed the people at large, in the guilt which was to usher in disaster (v. 14). Notice how their unfaithfulness is depicted in the strongest possible terms, and that it is particularly condemned in relation to the desecration of the Temple which had been a consequence of their worship of other gods. The theme of intensity and of persistence in sin is further emphasized by the statement that the people had refused to be dissuaded from their evil ways even by God's prophets. What constitutes the greatest evil for the Chronicler—and it is a theme that is taken up elsewhere in the Bible—is not wrongdoing in and of itself, but wrongdoing in defiance of the clear knowledge of what is right (Mark 12:1–12; Luke 16:31; Isa. 1:2f.).

EXILE AND BEYOND

2 Chronicles 36:17–23

17Therefore he brought up against them the king of the Chaldeans, who slew their young men with the sword in the house of their sanctuary, and had no compassion on young man or virgin, old man or aged; he gave them all into his hand. 18And all the vessels of the house of God, great and small, and the treasures of the house of the Lord, and the treasures of the king and of his princes, all these he brought to Babylon. 19And they burned the house of God, and broke down the wall of Jerusalem, and burned all its palaces with fire, and destroyed all its precious vessels. 20He took into exile in Babylon those who had escaped from the sword, and they became servants to him and to his sons until the establishment of the kingdom of Persia, 21to fulfil the word of the Lord by the mouth of Jeremiah, until the land had enjoyed its sabbaths. All the days that it lay desolate it kept sabbath, to fulfil seventy years.

22Now in the first year of Cyrus king of Persia, that the word of the Lord by the mouth of Jeremiah might be accomplished, the Lord stirred up the spirit of Cyrus king of Persia so that he made a proclamation throughout all his kingdom and also put it in writing: 23"Thus says Cyrus king of Persia, 'The Lord, the God of heaven, has given me all the kingdoms of the earth, and he has charged me to build him a house at Jerusalem, which is in Judah. Whoever is among you of all his people, may the Lord his God be with him. Let him go up.'"

The axe falls (v. 17)! The final devastation of Judah by Babylon is one of the decisive events in the whole history of Israel, surpassing any of the other "exiles" which Chr. has reported in the course of its account. It was, indeed, one of the stimuli which resulted ultimately in modern Judaism, because it taught the Jews to live without Temple or political status. Independence would not be theirs again (with the exception of the remarkable Maccabean renaissance between the decline of Greece and the rise of Rome), even though Temple and religious liberty would be regained after the return from Babylon.

The Chronicler is well aware of all this. He has allowed as much by virtue of the place given to Huldah's prophecy (34:23ff.) and of the telescoping of this final chapter, which gives to the Babylonian captivity the intensity of a climax. Yet the particular gravity of that crisis is stressed purely to show that, while it may differ from previous "exiles" in *degree*, it does not do so in *kind*. For his readers in the small post-exilic community, all his previous demonstrations of the possibility of restoration from the utmost ignominy and distress are now brought to bear upon their own experience. The exile and restoration had not been of their generation. Yet those events were stamped upon their consciousness. It may be that they felt that some of the prophetic promises of restoration (e.g. Ezek. 34; 37–39) had been but meagrely fulfilled in their somewhat handicapped situation. The Chronicler's desire for his people is that they rise above defeatism and see that the securing of a glorious future is within their grasp if they will only take the road of obedience. The requisite patterns of behaviour have been his theme thoughout the book. He now turns his attention to showing that the exile was not decisive.

He does so in two ways.

(i) Taking up the language of Lev. 26:34f., he shows that the seventy years of exile had functioned so that the land might "enjoy its sabbaths". The reference is to sabbath *years*, not days, according to the law which provided that every seventh year the land should remain uncultivated, so that the Lord might demonstrate that his bounty was independent of the people's labour (Lev. 25:1–7. The same thinking underlay the sabbath day.) The exile is thus interpreted as a "catching-up" period, in which the land is left fallow for a number of years equal to the number of *sabbath* years neglected in the whole period of the monarchy. (That period is thus reckoned as 490 years, which may be a round figure, or may correspond exactly to the time from Saul's accession—whose precise date is unknown—to the restoration.) The exile is presented, therefore, as the repayment of a debt which is now satisfied. (For "the word of the Lord by Jeremiah" see Jer. 25:11, 29:10. The seventy years can be reckoned either from the date of Babylonian ascendancy in Palestine, c. 605 B.C., to the release from exile, 537 B.C.—which is approximate, or from the final sack of Jerusalem, 586 B.C., to the dedication of the new Temple, 516 B.C., which is exact.)

(ii) The second way in which the Chronicler shows that the exile was not final is by borrowing the first three verses or so from the beginning of the Book of Ezra, and thereby relating the decree of Cyrus permitting the Jews held in Babylon to return to their homeland. The book ends, therefore, on a high note. On one level it points the reader forward to the Books of Ezra and Nehemiah, which tell the story of the re-establishment of the returning community in the land. On another, it points forward to the endless possibilities for a people that walks with its God. There has been discussion of the question whether Chr. has a messianic message. Some have said that it is intended to preserve a Temple-centred status quo. It can be no accident, however, that the Chronicler has made his chief models of obedience and open-ended possibility the greatest kings of Israel, David and Solomon. He leaves us no hint that he had "inside information" about a coming greater son of David. Yet it is clear, with hindsight, that all he promised of blessing, wealth, wisdom and the presence of God—not in a Temple but in the human heart—has been finally and dramatically realized in Jesus Christ (see 2 Cor. 6:16; Col. 2:2f.; John 14:23).

FURTHER READING

P. R. Ackroyd, *I and II Chronicles, Ezra, Nehemiah* (Torch Bible Commentaries) (SCM Press, 1973)

J. M. Myers, *I and II Chronicles* (Anchor Bible) (Doubleday, 1965)

D. F. Payne, *Kingdoms of the Lord* (Paternoster Press, 1981)

H. G. M. Williamson, *1 and 2 Chronicles* (Marshall, Morgan and Scott, 1982)

H. G. M. Williamson, *Israel in the Books of Chronicles* (Cambridge University Press, 1977)